STOCKWELL-MUDD LIBRARIES
DA585.C7E74
Stafford Cripps: master statesman

3 5044 00303 3757

Stafford Cripps:

MASTER STATESMAN

Stafford Cripps:

MASTER STATESMAN

Eric Estorick

The John Day Company   NEW YORK

COPYRIGHT, 1949, BY ERIC ESTORICK

This book, or parts thereof, must not be reproduced in
any form without permission.

This book is published by the John Day Company, 62
West 45th Street, New York 19, N.Y., and on the same day
in Canada by Longmans, Green & Company, Toronto

DA
585
.C7E74

Manufactured in the United States of America

74535

FOR

RICHARD J. WALSH

IN FRIENDSHIP

Acknowledgments

I HAVE had the benefit of the criticism and the advice of a number of persons during the gathering of the material and the writing of this book. I gratefully acknowledge my indebtedness and express my thanks for material concerning Sir Stafford's family background to Sir Alfred and Lady Egerton, the Hon. Leonard Cripps, Mrs. Barbara Drake, Miss Elizabeth Lawrence, the Misses Millie and Ethel Slocock, Frank Yeo, Fred Kirby, N. R. Udal, Lord Terrington, Peggy Cripps, and the late J. B. Furley; for material concerning his legal career I must thank Lionel Heald, K.C., D. N. Pritt, K.C., Gregory Krikorian, and Geoffrey Wilson; for data and interpretive material referring to Sir Stafford's public career my thanks go to those persons already acknowledged in the Prologue and to J. T. Murphy, Graham Spry, George Blaker, Herbert E. Rogers, Major Robert Kitson, Sir Wilfred Freeman, Sir Edwin Plowden, Miss Honor Balfour, Sir Charles Bruce-Gardner, Gilbert Watkinson, James Mash, Claud Simmonds, Norman Luker, Sir Frederick Bain, Barbara Forbes Adam, Allan Jarvis, Carol Johnson, the Rev. Mervyn Stockwood, the Rev. John Collins, Victor Mishcon, Eric Wolff, Woodrow Wyatt, R. H. S. Crossman, Mrs. Barbara Castle, Maurice Webb, Konni Zilliacus. I must also thank Mr. B. F. St. J. Trend, and Miss C. L. Bruce of the Chancellor of the Exchequer's staff for making many arrangements on my behalf.

I wish to express my gratitude for documentary material made available to me and for permission granted for publication. I must add that since this is a biography of a man and not a book of fiction, all the characters are real and not imaginary. They can, therefore, be held responsible for only what is directly attributable to them by direct quotation. All other observations and opinions are those of the author.

To Richard J. Walsh and Henry Dessau, for their great personal interest and assistance, I add my grateful thanks and to Lady Cripps, whose wisdom and help have brought this work to fruition, a profound and affectionate acknowledgment.

Contents

A section of illustrations from photographs appears following page 54.

Stafford Cripps:

MASTER STATESMAN

Prologue

WHEN the author decided to embark on this biography he approached Sir Stafford and Lady Cripps for their assistance and met with a most generous response. They allowed him to use private correspondence, manuscripts, diaries, and family records, but of course without accepting any responsibility for what appears in the book. The author is equally indebted for conversations and correspondence to Winston Churchill, Anthony Eden, the Earl Halifax, Sir John Anderson, the Countess Mountbatten of Burma, and to Sir Stafford's Labour colleagues, especially Herbert Morrison, Arthur Greenwood, Hugh Dalton, Aneurin Bevan, John Strachey, Harold Wilson, Hugh Gaitskill, and to many others.

In 1941 the author introduced to the American public his subject *Stafford Cripps: Prophetic Rebel* (less than a dozen pages of that book reappear in this one) with the words: "He is a man about whom we Americans want to know and about whom we shall want to know much more." He was then British Ambassador to Moscow and had signed the pact of alliance between the United Kingdom and the Soviet Union which contributed so greatly to the triumph of the allies in World War II. Today he is Britain's Chancellor of the Exchequer, controller and co-ordinator of her economy, and recognized as a world statesman of the highest order.

This is not the story of a man who rose from humble origin to power. It is that of a son of the English gentry, steeped in the traditions of "the enlightened upper middle class," trained to serve in church and state "with cultivated refinement and sense of social obligation," who became a scientist, lawyer, churchman, politician, and a leader of the Labour Government. Such a career is not peculiar in British politics, although Sir Stafford's is probably the most striking in modern times. In England more than in any country in the world scions of the ruling class place themselves at the head of resurgent movements of the working class.

I

It is true that the Cripps-Potter family were not aristocrats; they had no hereditary titles and were not assimilated into the aristocracy like the Woods' (Halifax) and Guinesses (Iveagh), both nineteenth-century titles. They were kin to what Beatrice (Potter) Webb, an aunt of Cripps, has called the "country gentlemen and public service families," and which included the Hobhouses, Farrers, Aclands, and Stracheys. All these families contributed to what may be described as the liberal conscience of England.

Unlike the French Revolution, which was largely anticlerical, the liberal conscience of England evolved as part of a peculiar religious history. The great English revolutionaries of the seventeenth century, from Cromwell to Winstanley, to say nothing of the "turbulent priests" of earlier ages, St. Thomas á Becket, Wycliffe, John Ball, Jack Straw, More, Latimer, clothed their campaigns from beginning to end in scriptural texts and formulae. Many of the Chartist leaders were clergymen, like Ernest Jones, who claimed to preach "the democracy of Christ." Labor today is still largely Nonconformist. As Clement Attlee, Britain's Prime Minister, has written,

England in the Nineteenth Century was still a nation of Bible readers. To put the Bible into the hands of an Englishman is to do a very dangerous thing. He will find there material which may send him out as a preacher of some religious, social or economic doctrine. I think that the majority of those who have built up the Socialist movement in this country have been adherents of the Christian religion—and not merely adherents but enthusiastic members of some religious body. There are probably more texts from the Bible enunciated from Socialist platforms than from those of all other parties.

Stafford Cripps is in the direct line of this great tradition. First and foremost he is an Englishman. No matter what his activity, he stamps it with English nationalism. His Christianity is English Christianity. His Socialism is British Socialism. But he is more than a nationalist. He is a Christian nationalist who is intensely religious. Organized religion is to him the moral power house for rousing the Christian conscience, and his politics are his practical application of the Christian ethic. He is preacher and prophet as well as statesman, ever proclaiming "what ye sow that shall ye also reap," and "by their deeds ye shall know them."

At the same time he is a man of immense intellectual capacity and achievement, a trained scientist, a great lawyer, an organizer of huge industry, a man of tireless and yet controlled energy. He is often referred to as the apostle of austerity and an ascetic. The first has nothing to do with the latter. It is a political label put upon him as a result of war economy. For in February, 1942, in his first speech to the House of Commons, as spokesman of the wartime coalition government, Cripps said:

> The circumstances are very grave, and the Government are convinced that it is the wish of the people in this country to treat this grave situation with all the seriousness and austerity that it undoubtedly demands.

He is neither austere nor an ascetic. On the contrary, he and his family abound in good nature; they laugh more than most people and see humor in many small things. He is a vegetarian and a teetotaller. He became a teetotaller on moral grounds. Today he is, no doubt, a vegetarian from choice, but he became such in the search for a diet that he could digest after an illness contracted while serving in World War I. His struggle against this illness led him to habits of self-control which have given rise to the charge of asceticism. It might well be said that he became convinced when young that

> "Self-knowledge, self-reverence, self-control,
> These alone lead life to sovereign power,"

for out of the struggle against illness he gained a knowledge of himself and brought his whole way of life under the conscious control of his mind. He learned from F. Mathias Alexander about conscious control of the psychophysical organism, and cultivated habits that would enable him to get the maximum of health and the maximum of life out of every twenty-four hours. Above all, he has been inspired with the purpose of translating into economic, political, and social life the ethical teaching of Christ. His religion is neither that of one day in seven nor a zealous fanaticism; it is an every-day practice. It was this that drove him into the British Labour movement, inspired his ambitions, and brought him into the front rank of statesmanship. This biography is, therefore, more than a formal record of a man's rise to power. It is also an attempt to interpret the most outstanding English representative of the liberal Christian conscience, of the "country gentlemen and public service families" who made so great an impression upon nineteenth century England and played so great a part in shaping the British Labour and Socialist movement.

While the tradition is the same, the setting has vastly changed. The pedestrianism of the last century has been superseded by the storms and upheavals of this one, wherein Britain and her Empire have been shaken to their foundations by war and revolution. Set against the background of these stirring times, Sir Stafford's story is at one and the same time his personal history and that of his impact on the world of men and things as it rushes into the "age of the common man."

I. Family Background

RICHARD STAFFORD CRIPPS, born in London on April 24, 1889, was the fifth child and fourth son of Charles Alfred and Theresa Cripps. Before her marriage his mother was Theresa Potter. The Cripps and the Potters represent two streams of English life, the origins of which reach far back into English history, and from which derived England's parliamentary system of government. To this very day there stands in the Thames Valley, not far west from the house in which Richard Stafford Cripps was brought up, the ruins of Copcott where, in the reign of King John, lived one Willmus Cripps, then known too as Sire Crispe de Stanlake.

The Potter family streams back to the tenant farmers of Yorkshire who left farming behind on the tide of the industrial revolution. When Charles Alfred Cripps married Theresa Potter in 1881, a son of the ancient English squirearchy joined with a daughter of the manufacturing and merchant class which rose to power and affluence in the age of Queen Victoria.

Thus two remarkable families came together, each steeped in its own tradition, each characteristic of the class differentiations in the ruling forces of England, rich and conscious of power, issuing orders as if by nature and taking for granted that those not in their confraternity should execute the orders. Beatrice Potter, sister of Theresa, and later the lifetime partner of Sidney Webb, wrote of her father:

By temperament the least autocratic and most accommodating of men, he spent his whole life giving orders. He ordered his stockbroker to buy and sell shares, his solicitor to prepare contracts and undertake legal proceedings. In the running of the timber yards, his intervention took the form of final decisions with regard to the new developments in buying and selling, the new agreements with railway companies as to rates and transport facilities. When those

maps of continents were unrolled before him, I listened with fascinated interest to eager discussions, whether a line of railway should
run through this section or that; at what exact point the station
or junction should be placed; what land should be purchased
for the contingent town; whether this patch or that, of forest, coal-
field or mineral ore, should be opened up or left for future generations to exploit. . . . And when, one after another, my sisters'
husbands joined the family group, they also were giving orders; the
country gentleman on his estate and at Sessions; the manufacturer in
his mill; the ship-owner to his fleet of ships on the high seas; the
city financier in the money market floating or refusing to float
foreign government loans; the Member of Parliament as Financial
Secretary to the Treasurer; the surgeon and the barrister well on
their way to leadership in their respective professions.

Thus confidently were the men of the Potter family playing
their parts in the key positions of commercial and industrial
England. At the same time, Charles Alfred Cripps was a successful young barrister, a country gentleman, an accomplished
debater, a Conservative remote from industrialism, practicing
law before the Parliamentary Committee in the House of Commons, and living at his country house and on his farm in Buckinghamshire.

Charles Alfred Cripps was the third son and sixth child of
Henry William and Julia Cripps. Henry Cripps had been a
scholar and Fellow at New College, Oxford, a contemporary of
Gladstone. At thirty he had become famous as a Queen's Counsel and an authority on ecclesiastical law. His standard work,
The Law Relating to Church and Clergy, was later edited by
his son and again revised and brought up to date by his grand-
son, Stafford. Although he was pressed to stand for Parliament,
Henry William Cripps refused. He preferred county and local
affairs, in which he "took pride and satisfaction." He was a
classical scholar and saw to it that his son Charles received his
first lesson in Latin grammar on his sixth birthday. A good
weekday for him would include hunting and partridge shooting until lunch, and afterward the reading of Greek plays with
the children.

His wife, Julia, was the daughter of Charles Lawrence, also
of Cirencester, and niece of Sir William Lawrence, the great
surgeon. She was well educated, spoke several languages,

studied music, art, and literature, and was deeply religious—a classic example of the most cultured of the Victorian middle class. An entry in her diary, made when she was twenty years old, reads:

I am daily more convinced of the utility of reading the Psalms and Lessons appointed by the Church for each day. Nothing is got through without regularity and a uniform plan. Up at five, read the Psalms and Lessons. Worked. Took geranium cuttings and put fresh glasses on the bees. After breakfast wrote letters and studied as usual. Writing German, reading French history, etc., then reading Tasso again that I may not forget my Italian. Reading Wheatley on Common Prayer until bedtime. Very interesting to find how ancient and carefully selected our beautiful liturgy is.

One Sabbath day in 1841 the spread of industrialism created a sensation. She wrote in her diary:

A steam engine came up to the station from London for the first time about 9 o'clock. It occasioned such confusion and bustle that papa ordered it back again to Kemble. The men were all at work as on a weekday, and Mr. Powell (the Rector) came up to speak to papa about it before church, in consequence of which it was stopped. It was very extraordinary and wrong to send it upon Sunday. Mr. Powell, in a short and interesting address before his sermon, mentioned the efforts which had been successfully made to stop such a profanation of the Sabbath, and entreated all his hearers to remember the Sabbath day and to keep it holy.

Henry Cripps and his family came to live at Parmoor, a property of nearly four hundred acres in the lovely Chiltern Hills. In 1884 Charles Alfred became its owner. Henry Cripps then leased a house close to Parmoor and retired from his profession at the age of sixty-nine.

Henry was the eldest son of the Reverend Henry Cripps, vicar of Preston and Cirencester, in the County of Gloucester. And the Reverend Henry was the son of Joseph Cripps who was born in 1765 and grew up during the American War of Independence and the beginning of the industrial revolution. He represented Cirencester in ten Parliaments and became the "father" of the House of Commons. He was a banker, deputy governor of Van Dieman's Land Company, a justice of the peace, and chairman of the Gloucester Quarter Sessions.

It was in this tradition, enfolded in well-to-do Christian paternalism, that the father of Stafford Cripps was reared. With Christian love, deeply entrenched in the family, went Christian duties. One of the boy's duties was to take food to the cottages when there was sickness among the farm workers. He said in later years that what he learned on these visits of the poverty in the lives of the farm workers convinced him that drastic changes were necessary in the economic life of England before it could honestly claim to be a Christian country.

When he went to Henley Grammar School at the age of eight, he was already learning the first elements of Greek and Latin under his father's tuition. Later he was placed under a famous coach who prepared pupils for the very private "public school," Winchester College. Founded in 1387, Winchester College was in 1865 a conservatively run institution where Charles Alfred, as junior fag in Sixth Chambers, had "to rise at five o'clock in the morning, to light the fires and make the preparations for the toilet of the prefects, when later they left their beds, so as to be in time for morning chapel."

At New College, Oxford, Charles Alfred had a brilliant academic career. He took first class honors in mathematics, history, law, and civil law. He was also no mean sportsman—an amateur boxer and a good footballer who won his way to the Oxford University team. He played in the cup-tie final the only time Oxford won it.

He had long ago made his choice of a career. Before he left Winchester College he wrote to his father,

If you think there would ever be any chance of my getting on, I should much rather be a barrister than in any other profession but it is impossible for me to know how far there would be any such prospect, and so you must tell me. I should not expect to get on nearly so well as you have done, but then there are several lower grades which would content me, since

"Non omnia possumus omnes."

There would in any case be the same opportunities for me as for most of the other young barristers when they first begin.

He had little to fear. He became a lawyer, a Queen's Counsel, a politician and statesman, and finally lifted his family from the ranks of the squirearchy to the aristocracy by becoming a baron, Lord Parmoor. He was created a peer in 1914 to sit in the Privy Council Appeal Court. The Canadians were at that time complaining of the weakness of the court, which was strengthened by his appointment.

Parmoor ultimately became a minister in two Labor Governments. But when Stafford was born in 1889 Charles Alfred Cripps was the head of a Conservative household with a long Conservative tradition, situated in a Conservative constituency, sure that God was in his heaven, serene, comfortable, self-confident, with the Christian ethic his inspiration. To the Cripps tradition, however, he had brought by marriage another which, though similar in important respects, was also different. Theresa Potter too was deeply religious, but interwoven with her nonsectarian Christianity was the personal and social idealism of the reformer and missionary. For the Potter family were essentially liberals, breaking through the conservatism of the countryside with the radicalism of town life.

The "Potters of Tadcaster" are a well-known family. Cobbet's famous *Register* once referred slightingly to the social origin of Stafford Cripps' great-grandfather, Richard Potter, M.P. He retorted:

I never at any time denied that my Father [John Potter, 1728-1802] was a draper at Tadcaster. He had a large family and they in succession managed his shop, his entire attention being devoted to a farm in the neighbourhood of the town. These facts are known to several merchants in Manchester who did business with my Father's family. As a farmer my Father was excelled by few. When he took his farm the land was in a most wretched state; a great part of it being a rabbit warren. He introduced a new system in that part of the country which was very successful. But there was another trait in my Father's character, which Mr. Cobbett's attack has brought to my mind which I never think of but with honest pride; he was a steadfast and consistent friend of Freedom, abhorring Tyranny in all its acts, from the Despot on the throne, to the petty tyrant in the village. During the American War of Independence, when a deluded multitude illuminated for a victory over our American brethren, he would not allow his windows to glow with a light for the triumph of power over justice. The Populace broke them, and I am sure they might have pulled the house down before his independent spirit would have stooped to a compromise with his principles. At the commencement of the

French war of 1793 against the Liberties of France and during its
continuance, my Father never flinched from raising his voice in
the humble and limited sphere in which he lived against this crusade against Liberty. . . .

John Potter's great-granddaughter Georgina Potter Meinertzhagen, wrote in her family memoir, *From Ploughshare To
Parliament*, that in 1789 he

took the farm of Wingate Hill near Tadcaster, and employed his
large family of four boys and four girls at the farm and shop, both
succeeding so well, that at his death he left a fortune of £12,000
to his family. The sons, as they grew up, went out into the world
bent on making money in trade. The eldest son John got into debt
and had to hide from his creditors for some years. He was eventually shipped off to America, and died there of yellow fever. . . .
William, the second son, the Quaker, is to me one of the most
interesting personages. . . . This sage and energetic elder brother,
"Citizen Potter" must have been a remarkable man in his way.
Sometimes he quite surpasses himself in his worldly wisdom, and
one turns for relief to the simpler and more contented disposition
of Richard. "Always *appear* to be busy, even if you are *not*."
"Practice *economy*, with an appearance of *generosity*," do not
recommend themselves to us as very high-minded axioms. But then
I can fancy William saying "It is difficult for a poor man to be
generous unless he *is* economical: the thriftless can seldom do you
a good turn," and William, with all his eye to the main chance
was ever ready to help brothers and sisters. "It is the opinion of
some people that the shopkeeping trade cannot be carried on without some little deviation from truth, but I am of a contrary sentiment . . . for my part I have the sacred idea of the obligation
between man and man. I should shudder as much at being detected
in a lie as being detected in a depredation of property."

And then he adds somewhat hastily,

"I do not mean for a moment to inculcate a disregard for getting
money."

Mrs. Meinertzhagen continues,

As for honest, good Richard, with his soft heart, and keen enthusiasm for philanthropy and reform, his love of the land and out-
door life, he must have been a lovable creature. He was *of* the
people and *for* the people; a thorough-going Radical, working

hard all his life in the cause of reform; and who will now say that reform was not needed in those days? Reform in our Prisons and Penal Laws, in our Representation and Taxation. . . .

As for Tom, he was quite as keen, but not so hot as Richard— a practical man of few words and less writing—and not so apt to be run away by his feelings.

Thomas Potter became well known for his championship of the abolition of slavery. He became the mayor of Manchester in 1838 and was knighted on the occasion of the Queen's visit to that city in 1840. His son John also became the mayor of Manchester and was knighted in 1851. While he was mayor he founded the first Free Lending Library in the world. A younger son, Thomas Bailey Potter, became a member of Parliament in 1865 and for thirty years was known as "Principles" Potter. Until his death in 1897 he was president of the Cobden Club.

Richard Potter, who became a prosperous Manchester manufacturer, was, like his father, a "consistent friend of freedom, abhorring tyranny in all its acts." He spoke out against the French war, advocated justice for Ireland, went to considerable exertion to reduce the disgracefully heavy sentences which the courts meted out for trifling offences, and was an enthusiastic adherent of the Anti-Slave Trade Campaign. During the Luddite Riots of 1812 he sympathized openly with the workers and went to London to oppose Lord Wharncliffe, "who was supposed to be rude and bullying, but we plucked up and let him know we did not care for him."

In 1832, on hearing of the Lords' rejection of the Reform Bill for the third time, Richard, with two others, posted up to London with a petition signed by 24,000 people asking the House of Commons to "stop supplies" until the Lords gave way. The envoys received enough publicity for the inhabitants of the towns on the way to turn out and cheer them vigorously. When the bill was passed, Richard Potter was elected in the first reformed Parliament and was a close friend of Cobden, Bright, and Daniel O'Connell.

His namesake son, Richard, married the daughter of Lawrence Heyworth, M. P. They had nine daughters and a son. The son died in infancy. One of the daughters was Beatrice, who later married Sidney Webb, and another was Theresa, the mother of Stafford Cripps.

Margaret, one of the famous nine daughters, who married a well-known Liberal lawyer and politician, Henry Hobhouse, left the following sketch of Richard Potter, Junior,

Handsome, determined looking. Very strong; can travel night and day and spend whole days walking, driving and riding with slight fatigue at sixty-six years.

A man taking a large grasp of any subject and able to master details well. Great power of organising and governing men. Devoted to business. Fond of poetry. Affectionate, open-hearted, simple-minded to a peculiarity, and yet, when necessary, a most adroit diplomatist. Very unconventional, like his mother and children. Very sanguine, restless. Favourite pursuits: affairs, especially if requiring ingenuity and diplomacy. Very considerable originating powers for schemes of all sorts requiring patience and skill. Devoted to family life and his children. No art or music. A wonderfully versatile man, which adaptability to circumstances his children all inherit.

Richard Junior was graduated from the New London University, of which his father, a leading Unitarian, was one of the founders. He was called to the bar but did not practice long. He nursed his father through his last illness with much devotion, and, after his death, took to a life of leisure. It was on a tour of Italy that he met Lawrencina Heyworth. She was a highly educated woman, unusually competent in languages, including Greek and Latin. After their marriage it was their intention to settle in Hertfordshire and live as *rentiers*. But in the financial panic of 1848 he lost a considerable part of his fortune and was forced to go back to work. He became a big businessman and lost all his interest in his father's and his own early associations with radicalism.

Herbert Spencer, after his first meeting with Richard Potter, wrote of him,

Mr. Potter commanded my highest admiration. He is, I think, the most lovable being I have yet seen. He is evidently genuine. His amiability is not that of manner but of reality. He has a noble head—a democratic one of course, but one so beautifully balanced in other respects, that one can delight in contemplating it. The perfect agreement between his head and his face is remarkable: the features are Grecian and their expression is exactly what a phrenologist would anticipate.

He is, I believe, very poetical—admires Shelley enthusiastically, and conceives him by far the finest poet of his age, in which I quite coincide with him. In fact we sympathized in our sentiments on all subjects on which we conversed, and although I might feel somewhat flattered by this, I must say I felt so strongly the beauty of his disposition as contrasted with my own, that I felt more dissatisfied with myself than I have done for a long time past.

Richard Potter and Herbert Spencer remained life-long friends. But not a sentence of Spencer's "Synthetic Philosophy" did Richard Potter ever read. He was completely indifferent to it, whether spoken or written. Beatrice Potter Webb, who was refused permission by Spencer to write his biography when she married Sidney Webb, the Socialist, writes of her father's attitude:

Always cheerfully beneficent, my father had a genuine if somewhat pitying affection for the philosopher on the hearth; he would walk with him, he would fish with him, he would give him sound advice and tell him tales from business life which illustrated this or that economic "law" in which they both believed; but argue with him or read his books he would not. "Won't work, my dear Spencer, won't work," my father would say good-humouredly, when the professional doubter defiantly proclaimed his practice on a Sunday morning of deliberately walking against the tide of church-goers. . . .

My father enjoyed intellectual society, he delighted in talks with Huxley, Tyndall, and James Martineau, and when his friend, James Anthony Froude asked him on one or two occasions to join the afternoon walk with Thomas Carlyle, he did so in a spirit of reverential awe. . . . When I tried to interest him in the "law of increasing heterogeneity and definiteness in structure and function at work"—so the philosophers demonstrated—throughout the universe, my father answered in this wise; "Words, my dear, words. Experience tells me that some businesses grow diverse and complicated, others get simple and more uniform, others again go into the Bankruptcy Court. In the long run and over the whole field there is no more reason for expecting one process rather than another. Spencer's intellect is like a machine racing along without any raw material; it is wearing out his body. Poor Spencer, he lacks instinct, my dear, he lacks instinct—you will discover that instinct is as important as intellect." And then taking out his engagement book, he added in a more sympathetic tone, "I must see whether I can't arrange another day's fishing with him—poor man."

Richard Potter's wife, Lawrencina Heyworth, was an exceptional woman. She was, John Bright said, "one of the two or three women a man remembers to the end of life as beautiful in expression and form." Her daughter Beatrice describes her:

Soft hazel brown eyes, large and deeply set, veiled by overhanging lids and long eyelashes set off by delicately curved and pencilled eye-brows; eyes uniting in their light and shade the caress of sympathy with the quest of knowledge. To this outstanding beauty were added fine flossy hair, an easily flushed fair skin, small flashing teeth, a low musical voice, pretty gestures and long delicate hands; clearly a woman to charm, perhaps to inspire.

Beatrice also says, "She had inherited from her father an iconoclastic intellect." She was ever questioning man's relation to the universe and the right conduct of life. She studied the Greek Testament assiduously as she did also the fathers of the church, and was exemplary in her practice of religious rites.

Michael Chevalier wrote after a visit to the Potters that he

discovered that the mistress of the house knew much more Greek than himself, apologised, and retired from the field. . . . Note that this female Hellenist is a woman of the world and even stylish. Moreover, she has nine daughters, two nurses, two governesses, servants in proportion, a large well-appointed house, frequent and numerous visitors; throughout all this, perfect order; never noise or fuss, the machine appears to move of its own accord.

She never visited the servants' quarters and seldom spoke to any servant other than her own maid. She acted by deputy, training each daughter to carry out "a carefully thought-out plan of the most economical supply of the best regulated demand."

She could meet Herbert Spencer on his own ground and enter the realm of "words, words." Herbert Spencer recalls in his autobiography:

Mrs. Potter was scarcely less argumentative than I was and occasionally our evening debates were carried on so long that Mr. Potter, often playing chiefly the role of listener, gave up in despair and went to bed; leaving us to continue our unsettleable controversies.

"Herbert Spencer," says Beatrice, "was far and away the most intimate of the family friends, was always arguing with my mother on the origin of religion, deriding and denouncing ecclesiasticism and all its works; and I think it was he who brought into our circle of acquaintances Francis Galton and Sir Joseph Hocker, Huxley and Tyndall, whilst to Spencer's annual picnic George Henry Lewes and occasionally George Eliot."

In later years, when all nine daughters were married, their mother became absorbed in lonely studies, especially of foreign languages and their grammars. Unable to find an answer which her intellect could grasp to the contradiction between her mystical longings and her rationalized knowledge of the world, she "left the wise to wrangle and the riddle of the universe let be." She once smilingly assured her daughter, "I shall know twelve languages before I die."

In such a Victorian home of culture, business, and religion, surrounded by all the virtues of prosperity and hard work, grew Theresa, the sixth of the nine daughters, who became the mother of Stafford Cripps.

Beatrice, with whom Theresa spent the winter of 1880 and the spring of 1881 in Italy, wrote of her,

Theresa was a born artist. That is, of course, apparent in her wonderful gift of expression, her power of seizing the really significant facts about a person or an event—a power which I imagine to be the essence of the artist's faculty. But it was also apparent in the intense pleasure that great works of art gave her. In Italy she was almost intoxicated with delight. . . . For tenderness—tenderness of an exquisite character—was one of Theresa's most beautiful gifts. I remember in Rome when I was ill for five weeks, how she threw over all her sight-seeing to remain day after day in that dark room. I can see her now, moving about the room in the night, preparing poultices and drinks for me; always with the same gracious, loving cheering smile, absolutely forgetful of herself, and thinking only how she could give me rest and confidence.

Her sister Kate once wrote:

Theresa, our ox-eyed Juno, imperial butterfly, tall as Georgina and Blanche are . . . is still sentimental and full of interest, and . . . of skill at embroidering with gold what she's interested in;

her geese are still swans and her spirit, despite much illness, buoyant.

Soon after her return from Italy, Theresa married Charles Alfred Cripps. In a memoir written after his wife's death, Cripps gave a delightful description of the earnest, almost prayerful, approach of the parents and the lovers to what they regarded as a sacred act, the dedication of two lives to each other and the union of two families. Here is the characteristic paternal approval and religious sanctification of marriage by the Christian Victorians. Cripps wrote:

On Friday, September 2nd, I went again to Standish. Your father and mother were there and also Uncle Willy and Aunt Blanche. On Sunday Uncle Arthur, Aunt Mary and Cousin Bill came over from Longfords. I shall never forget a walk with your mother in the splendid autumn evening, or how we sat talking on Monday morning under the old oak tree in the Standish garden. I left Standish on Monday, returning to Parmoor. On Thursday morning a short pencil note called me back to Standish, and in the afternoon the greatest blessing which the world can give, the devotion of a pure, noble-minded woman, had been promised to me.

Mother appreciated to the full the solemn responsibilities involved in marriage. She did not decide without earnest and anxious consideration. Her father was our Galleotto, and wrote her the following letter on the Monday on which we had talked together under the old oak trees:

"Though I have divers weighty and anxious matters on my mind, there is nothing that more occupies my imagination and heart than the momentous question you have to decide. None of my children are nearer or dearer to me than you now, and ever since your infancy, and I often pray God that he may guide you right. My own judgment is clear that in Alfred Cripps you have [a man] quite acceptable to me, and your mother, and all your sisters. But having disburthened myself of this, the one vital essential point remains for you, and you only, to decide. Marriage is the nearest of earthly ties, and is the type and symbol of the union above and beyond the considerations which weigh with me, demands a thorough personal preference and affinity, without which there is danger. You may trust Alfred Cripps honour and sensibility in inviting him to come to Standish, on the clear understanding that the visit is designed to enable you without committing yourself in the smallest degree, to test your heart. Whatever you ultimately do, you may rely until death separates us, that you shall have the full affection and respect of your father and mother, and we shall be perfectly satisfied with your choice either way."

After Thursday mother could write to her father: "I feel sure that his companionship through life will be one of the greatest blessings which could come to me."

And to her mother, "It is impossible to write much on a subject on which one feels so much and I know, dear mother, you will be content at present with my full assurance that I expect to be happy."

When Cripps and Theresa Potter were married in October, 1881, he was at the beginning of his great professional career. They bought a house in London at Elm Park Gardens where Stafford was born seven and a half years later. They lived there during the week while Parliament was sitting, at other times at Parmoor, the permanent family residence.

It was the happiest of marriages. Theresa Cripps shared her husband's life to the full. When he became a candidate for Parliament in 1893, she addressed political meetings. Children came quickly; Stafford was the fifth child and the fourth son of the marriage.

Stafford was only four years old when his mother died suddenly. Of this catastrophe his father wrote:

On a Sunday morning we were walking together in the woods and gardens at Parmoor, on Sunday midday we were having luncheon together with the children, on Sunday afternoon we were told that there was no reason for the slightest anxiety, on Monday morning, the 22nd May, 1893, just before ten o'clock the end came, and my wife rested from illness and pain.

It would appear that Theresa Cripps had thought that death was on its way, for she left behind two papers, which reveal the woman in her entirety. To her husband she wrote,

This paper, my darling husband, contains my will and wishes in case of death. Everything of every description (money, jewelry and possessions) I leave to my truest husband wishing for his sake, it were a thousand times more in value than it is. He will give some little memorial of me to those friends or relations who will really value it, and will give my likeness to all who ask for it. And it makes no difference to me, my own husband, where you bury my body because I will always be with you when you are near it or far away from it, in my own living spirit, if God will allow me, and surely he cannot separate such love as ours, even if he wills to separate our bodies and lives for a time. And I shall love to watch you working out all that is highest and noblest in your nature, that the world may be made better through it, and each night my spirit will unite with yours in prayer as it has done on earth, and we will seek God and truth together. You will teach my children to love only what is true, and ever to seek further truth, and make it known to others, whatever career they choose. And your brave spirit, which has always helped me and loved me through dangers and difficulties will not grieve too much because we are parted, and if you can find another companionship where there can be the truest help and love between you, it is better you should marry; whom you can love, I shall love too. I write this not in fear of death, but knowing how near death may be; we all live in the midst and presence of it, and we should not fear it; it only means fuller life and temporary separation of our lives here, but not, I believe of our love or of our spirits. Your ever loving, ever grateful wife.

But the message is incomplete without the letter concerning her children. Of them she said,

I should like the children brought up as much as possible in the country, and to be educated much in the same style as their father was. I should like their living to be of the simplest, without reference to show or other follies. I should like them trained to be undogmatic and unsectarian Christians, charitable to all churches and sects studying the precepts and actions of Christ as their example, taking their religious inspiration directly from the spirit of the New Testament. I look upon Christ's words and the record of His life as we have it in the four Gospels, and the spirit of His faith as St. Paul preached it, as the great hope and light to guide mankind to the entrance of a vast spiritual existence. . . . No quarrelling in money matters; I trust my children's sense of what is fair and right. I implore my children to stand by one another through thick and thin, in joy, sorrow, success or failure, or even disgrace, and to choose Christ as their sole Hero and Master.

So beautiful Theresa Cripps left her beloved family closely knit by deep affection and dedicated to a vision of personal life belonging to the culture of a period already beginning to disintegrate. Of that disintegration, none within the family and few within the nation were yet wholly conscious. Stafford's father shared the dream of his wife as completely as if it were his own; indeed, it was his own in all its fantasy, its ethics, and its insulation against the world at large. Its material foundations were in the county family, with roots running deep and far through many generations of successful lawyers and bankers, enjoying rich incomes and the commercial success of men of property.

That skillful, though frequently mistaken delineator, Beatrice, describes a visit to Parmoor the Christmas after the death of her sister:

Alfred's home is strangely attractive—with a dash of sadness in it—especially to Theresa's sisters. A charming house, designed largely by Theresa. The soft luxurious covering, the quaintness of the furniture, the walls covered with her portraits, all bring back to me the memory of her gracious personality, so full of sympathy, with a vivid imagination. Alfred himself has regained all the lightheartedness of his charming disposition. Possibly it is the rebound from the sadness of his most intimate thoughts, but to the mere spectator he seems more lighthearted than of old. He is again the young man—unattached—absolute master of his own life. And he is in the full tide of prosperity. An enormous professional income (he told Arthur that he made £1,000 a week during the Session) has enabled him to buy the family estate and sit down in front of a promising constituency. Doubtless he sees before him a brilliant career. Dear old Father used to call him "the little jewel of an advocate"—a term which just fits him. . . . With this disposition he could hardly be a reformer. He has become of late years more and more Conservative opportunist—bent on keeping the soft places of the world for his own class—but ready to compromise and deal whenever his class would lose more by fighting. He has almost a constitutional dislike of economic or social principles. I doubt whether Alfred ever thinks out an economic or political problem. Why should he? He knows on which side he is retained, and there will be time enough to get up the advocate's fact when the question turns up.

Charles Alfred's aged father did not subscribe to this view of his son's Conservatism. The elder Cripps claimed that "his son Alfred had been an exceedingly good Liberal all his life, and had only been stirred up by the great crisis of Home Rule." Alfred himself says that while he was at Oxford he accepted the economic teachings of Ricardo and Mill:

I found it a serious handicap to question this teaching and not to regard it as practically of a sacrosanct character. When I went to London I was elected a member of the Reform Club, and classed as a left-wing Liberal. A free trader in principle, I was never convinced that there were quasi-mechanical rules which could generally be relied upon to regulate demand and supply, and as incidental thereto the question of employment and unemployment.

It would appear that Beatrice Webb was not quite so objective in her estimate of Alfred's political outlook as she might have been, and on this she did subsequently revise her views. His Conservatism was not so deeply entrenched as she estimated. Certainly, in 1892, he was a long way from becoming a Socialist. Indeed, when he heard of Beatrice Potter's engagement to Sidney Webb, he wrote in his diary,

On Friday, January 8th, I just heard Beatrice has become engaged to Mr. Sidney Webb. I do not know him or what is his character. I hope it may be for the best but can at present form no opinion of any kind. Mr. Webb is known as a writer on Socialism and in this respect his opinions are totally opposed to mine.

It is true to say that he was oblivious of the social process which was cracking the foundations of the Cripps tradition of enlightened patronage toward the lower orders, with its heavenly immortalism and its sanctification by love and earthly economic success. The England of Sire Crispe de Stanlake ushered in the age of Magna Charta, and the England of Joseph Cripps of Cirencester saw the industrial revolution reshape the entire economic and social life of the country. Charles Alfred Cripps had grown to manhood in the first years of the eclipse of the "workshop of the world" and the rise of a new social power that would never be content with the benevolence of the county gentleman. Such a way of life had been good, while it lasted, for all who had been born to give orders. Cripps continued to live its practice and dream its dreams, but occasionally the evidence of the changing times came into his home—people with ideas heralding the new age which was so near.

There came Henry Hobhouse, Ecclesiastical Commissioner for England and Member of Parliament for Somerset, who had married Theresa's sister, Margaret; Leonard Courtney, a lawyer and professor of political economy, who had married another sister; and Beatrice and Sidney Webb. They were all discussing the "condition of the people" and striving to "bridge the gulf between the classes" at a time when the Christian conscience was shocked by what had been revealed of the lives of millions in the industrial towns and cities of England.

Before her marriage, Theresa had spent some months in the East End of London, performing for a time the social work carried on by her elder sister Kate, afterward Lady Courtney. This brought her, and later, her husband, into close connection with Charles Booth, the author of the monumental study, *Life and Labour of the People in London,* who had married a cousin, Mary Macauley.

"Very interesting people," Alfred thought. But what impact could they make on him? His life was regular, comfortable and rich, unaffected by the booms and slumps of industry.

Industrial England, however, had changed almost beyond recognition. A distant voice on the Potter side of the family had testified of the coming change. Richard Potter senior, prosperous manufacturer like his father before him, had been a "consistent friend of Freedom, abhorring tyranny in all its acts." This man had championed the new rising class of industrial workers at the dawn of the century. During the Luddite Riots of 1812, he openly sympathized with them and went to London to oppose the Manchester Police Bill. From that same class came Robert Owen, Frances Plaice, and Joseph Hume, all of whom did much to foster the development of trade-unionism. The first great political awakening of the new industrial working class, shown in the rise of Chartism, had died away. But the new class differentiation remained and the gulf between the middle class and the working class became deeper and wider, so that the millions were known as "the people of the abyss."

The social conscience of men and women of the middle class was stirred. They cried aloud to heaven of their discoveries. Friedrich Engels, a mill owner in Manchester, published what he knew in *Conditions of the Working Class of England* in 1845. Oastler, Shaftesbury, and Chadwick, philanthropists, campaigned for reforms. Dickens, Carlyle, Ruskin, and William Morris, artists and writers, indignantly protested

and conjured up visions of a new society. John Stuart Mill and
Karl Marx analyzed the economics of the time, and their works
began a new understanding of social history. Charles Kingsley,
F. D. Maurice, General Booth, and Cardinal Manning, each
in his own way, blazed a trail of Christian indignation that
such "regions of inequity" could exist in great districts of
industrial England. There abounded, too, a class consciousness
of sin, as the social cesspools were revealed. Arnold Toynbee,
in the years of Alfred Cripps' young manhood, expressed this
most pathetically in the following appeal:

We—the middle classes, I mean, not merely the very rich—we
have neglected you, instead of justice we have offered you charity,
and instead of sympathy we have offered you hard and unreal advice; but I think we are changing. If you would only believe it
and trust us, I think that many of us would spend our lives in your
service. You have—I say it clearly and advisedly—you have to forgive us, for we have wronged you; we have sinned against you
grievously—not knowingly always, but still we have sinned, and
let us confess it; but if you will forgive us—nay, whether you will
forgive us or not—we will serve you, we will devote our lives to
your service, and we cannot do more. We will do this and only
ask you to remember one thing in return. If, that is, you get your
material civilisation, remember that it is not an end in itself.
Remember that man, like trees and plants, has his roots in the
earth, but like the trees and plants, he must grow upwards towards
the heavens. If you will only keep to the love of your fellowmen
and to great ideas, then we shall find happiness in helping you;
but if you do not, then our reparation will be in vain.

At the turn of the century, university graduates like Clement
Attlee went to live in settlements among "the masses," to
investigate and to reform. The Potters, and like-minded members of the same class, swept to one side the charitable overflow of sentiment and cash into dark places; they wanted to
know why these conditions should prevail and how a fundamental change in the nature and character of all society could
be brought about. Beatrice Potter found her partner, Sidney
Webb, and together they began their tremendous studies of
the institutions which handled the problems produced by
poverty, and of the social welfare of the working population
—"English Local Government" and "English Poor Law His-

tory." The Webbs went on to examine the organizations which the new social class, produced by the industrial revolution, had itself created to fight poverty and the forces which created poverty, in such works as the *History of Trade Unionism* and *The Co-operative Movement in Great Britain*.

A new political awakening had begun which would soon sweep through the land. In the very year that Stafford Cripps was born, 1889, the Second International of the Workingmen's Association was formed. Recently organized Socialist organizations like the Social Democratic Federation led by the middle-class disciple of Karl Marx, H. M. Hyndman, the Fabian Society led by Sidney Webb and George Bernard Shaw, and the Trades Union Congress, were all represented. The year saw the beginning of the organization of general labor, as distinct from the organization of skilled workers which had characterized trade-unionism hitherto. Tom Man, John Burns, Will Thorne, all skilled workers and members of the skilled unions, joined with Ben Tillet of the dockers to lead the famous Dock strike and the strike of the gas workers. This meant that the "people of the abyss" were on the move out of the demoralized and poverty-stricken regions of social darkness. They were forming big battalions of the working-class movement to strive toward a new society.

In that year, too, the *Fabian Essays* were published. These revealed that the Fabian Society, the organization of the British intelligentsia, had begun its work armed with a theory which damned the existing order of society as morally indefensible and technically inefficient. The Fabians aimed to transform society by the rational conversion of the efficient middle-class administrators, and to awaken the political consciousness of the workers and bring them under the tutelage and leadership of the Fabians. These adumbrations of class organization and movement had broken through the franchise limitations set by the Reform Act of 1832. They called forth compulsory free education, shortened the working day, and invoked much factory legislation. There was indeed an assemblage of forces for a great march against the domains of power and privilege.

These events claimed no thought in the mind of Charles Alfred Cripps at the time when Stafford was born. Nor was he conscious of the fact that Britain's place in world affairs

was no longer that of undisputed master. Although the year
1889 saw England in the midst of her imperial expansion in
Africa, her power relations with other nations were no longer
as of yore. Up to 1860 Britain had been the leading industrial
country, with France a poor second. She was still the leader in
1870, with the United States a good second. By 1880 the United
States was ahead, and by 1889 far ahead. In less than another
decade Germany took second place, with Britain third. True,
Britain's navy continued to sail the seven seas, supreme, enjoying twice the strength of any other two powers. But her potential of armed power had been surpassed and the arena was
becoming congested.

Nor were the changes in the power structure of society
peculiar to England. Wherever the industrial revolution got
into its stride, by its very nature it produced two classes. The
first of these, the industrial capitalists, superseded the power
of the landed gentry. The other, composed of industrial
workers, roused itself to organize with an eye on some great
tomorrow. In 1861 the landed aristocracy of Russia was forced
to abolish serfdom. In 1875 the first Russian Workers' Union
was formed. And when Bismarck's Germany battered the
French army in 1870, the Paris Commune of Workers hung
for a few short weeks like a red star on the horizon of Europe,
as if heralding a new age.

The shape of things to come between the powers dominating
the world became discernible, too, as England's industrial su-
premacy passed into eclipse. In 1884 the Triple Alliance of
Germany, Austria, and Italy was signed and Germany participated in the carve-up of Africa. In 1885 the German East
Africa Company was formed. Almost simultaneously the British East Africa Company was established. In 1889 the Franco-
Russian Entente came into being.

So Stafford Cripps was born in a home that was well-to-do,
in a regime which to all within the home seemed as stable as
the hills around them. He was born to parents steeped in the
Christian ideal of personal salvation through service to the
neighbor who was close at hand. Their earthly horizons were
extremely limited while their heavenly horizons ranged into
life eternal. The death of his mother in his fifth year was a
sad loss to Stafford. But so great was the impress of her per-

sonality upon her family and so deeply was it integrated with the religious, patriarchal tradition of generations of Crippses and Potters, that she would live on in the lives of her children as a powerful influence through all their days. In none would this be more manifest than in her youngest child, Stafford. Her husband, yet to break through his political insularity and feel the impact of the social and historical forces which were passing him by, was for a long time to live intimately with the memory of his lost wife. He was the missionary of her messages to their children.

Such was the background and such the environment into which Richard Stafford Cripps was born in 1889 and left motherless in 1893.

II. Formative Years

PROBABLY no man ever held more firmly to the Christian doctrine of personal immortality than did Charles Alfred Cripps. Death, he believed, was the entrance to a larger life. When his wife died, so vivid was his memory of her and so completely had her personality pervaded their home, that her continued presence and communion became very real to him. He was a good father who loved all his children dearly. He was intimate with all of them and would be an abiding influence in their lives.

To none did this apply more than to Stafford, who, by the time he was three years of age, everyone recognized "would be the cleverest of the family." There is a prophetic paragraph in Charles Alfred Cripps' diary of June 4, 1890, when Stafford was not yet fifteen months old. He wrote "Baby does not sleep well, but his mother thinks he has too great a brain development, and looks on him as the rising genius among her boys."

When Stafford was born, there came to Parmoor as governess to the only daughter, Ruth, a gentle little lady fifty years of age, Miss Mary Marshall, whom everyone called "Mazelle." She had spent most of her life in France and brought back with her to England such a vivacious spirit, combined with a generous unselfishness, that she was more of a companion of the children in self-government and direction than a representative of parental authority. This was a wise and fortunate appointment, for no woman was better qualified to help the father keep the memory of his wife fresh and bright in the minds of his children and to inculcate by example his religious and ethical code.

Cripps' legal and political activities held him in London during the week and he returned to Parmoor only at the week ends. But this did not mean that he forgot his family for five

days a week and remembered them for two. It simply meant
more work for the postman and very frequent letter-writing
between him and the children, from the youngest up. However
short the letters, they breathed the deep affection and loyalty
of the family. There are still extant some little letters from
Stafford written in these early years. The very first, written
at the age of four to his mother, reads:

Dear Mother,
I love you about two hundred pounds. I send you a cowslip
bell. Franky and Dora came to play with us yesterday.
Ta-ra-aboom-de-hay!
Love Kisses
Stafford.

His first letter to his father, written shortly after his mother's
death, follows:

Dear Father,
I love you very much. Best kisses to dear loving Father I like
and love dear Mother very much
Lots of love from Staffie.

The elder Cripps replies to his child on June 12, 1893:

My dear dear Little Stafford,
I am writing to you in the evening just when I think you are
saying your prayers and thinking of dear dear Mother. You will
never forget her if you ask her spirit to help you and to come quite
near to you whenever you want love and help. Mother's one wish
was to give love and help to all who wanted help and love, and she
often told me that she wanted her boys to think how much sorrow
they could save to others, by being always kind and thoughtful.
. . . I have often told Mother that her boys would grow up to love
her more, and that if they loved her, they would be good and
great. Now Mother cannot talk to you every day, but the more
you think of her, the nearer will she be to all of us. Only Pater
can be with you and you must always help Pater to teach you just
as Mother wished to teach you. . . . I can only tell you a little at
a time how Mother loved you. She would have gone through any
grief or sorrow if only to help you to be good and kind. She wished
you to grow up loving Jesus and you must come to Pater whenever
he can help his dear little Stafford.
Your very loving Father.

An instant reply:

Dear Pater,
   I love you very very very very very much all the rest is kisses
to pater

                                             Stafford.

An artist was commissioned to paint a remembrance portrait
of Theresa Potter with Stafford seated on her lap. Anticipating
the tedium of posing, Cripps wrote to his son:

I hope Staff is a very good boy. It is such a treat for him to be
in Mother's picture—Pater remembers how often he saw you sitting
in Mother's lap, just as you will be sitting in the picture. Mother
always said that she could quite trust Staffie and laughed at Pater
when he said that Staffie wanted someone to look after him. I wish
I could be more with you all; but we shall have a beautiful holiday
together, and we can try and do each day just what we know Mother
would like.

Three months after his mother's death, Stafford was taken
to the home of his aunt, Mary Playne, at Longfords, Minchin-
hampton, where he spent many happy days. Remembering his
aunt, Stafford Cripps relates that

Mrs. Playne played a tremendous part in my life. She more or
less adopted me directly my mother died. She was a most brilliant
woman and most like my Mother in character. I spent a great deal
of my holidays there—every summer. After Isobel and I were married we went there too. I regarded Longfords as my second home.
My Aunt Mary had one boy very much older than myself. I was
page at his wedding. I was about four or five at the time. I remember afterwards going to Harrods to choose my present. It was a
knife. I still have it.

Longfords was a big estate with large lawns and a sloping
park. On that slope, flower shows and giant teas were held.
The annual festivities included such features as merry-go-
rounds and swing boats, which brought joy to Stafford and
other youngsters. The garden parties also brought the entire
family together. Among the guests were Stafford's aunt and
uncle, Beatrice and Sidney Webb. Stafford says of Beatrice:

Although she was my godmother, I never came close to her as a
child. She was rather a terrifying person, so obviously interested in

the intellectual development of the grown boys of the family that she did not attract young children. It was not until I really grew up that I came into close contact with her.

Writing of this period, Leonard Cripps, the third of the four sons, says that Stafford

was the darling of the gods—that is, of our nurse and governesses. Others of us may have felt neglected while our little infant brother absorbed the spotlight and began to create a sort of controlling interest in our nursery. . . . Stafford's wisecracks and judgement in his very early childhood were achieved with great care and solemnity and obtained for him the nickname of Dad, which has stuck to him ever since. I can remember aunts and uncles who were vastly amused at our small Solomon, and who all agreed that he would at least finish up as Lord Chancellor. He often admitted to me that that was his real intention in life.

Stafford says that he always knew he was going to be a lawyer, for he was trained in the technique of advocacy at a very early age. When his father came home for week ends, he would give his sons legal briefs, tied in red string, for which he would pay them the sum of one shilling and a penny. Thus they were inspired to write briefs on such subjects as pantry filchings, insubordination, games and rules. While this technique served to inform the elder Cripps of his four sons' and daughter's activities of the week, its purpose was also to promote character development. Leonard Cripps reveals that

Stafford recognised the necessity of getting to work at an early age to earn a living. With us, he started, when very young, three independent businesses.

In the first instance, a small cafe was established in the little room next to the bathroom, where tea and light refreshments were served on Saturdays and Sundays to enable my father's guests to purchase their tea instead of enjoying it in the drawing-room free.

The second business was market gardening. We had, some mile or so from the house, a small allotment which was not in use, and so was given to us to produce vegetables, which were purchased from us by the house.

The third business was only going in summer holidays. It consisted of collecting rakings and gleanings from the cornfields and dumping them into an old barn by means of our donkey and cart, which Stafford, being the baby, invariably drove. At the end of

Albion
College
Library

the harvest our bailiff took the contents of the barn over at an agreed price.

It was a bad week when the profits fell below a shilling or two on the combined businesses.

The truth of the matter was that Stafford's moral education was so strong in him that he could never tolerate doing nothing.

His sister Ruth, now Lady Egerton, telling about life at Parmoor, says:

At Parmoor, the children lived a life all their own. After the death of my mother, my father did not want aunts to come to Parmoor; he wanted the children to grow freely and was in a sense, a radical in this matter, as he did not want a chaperone in the house. My father did not believe in intensive education. He himself believed that he was overworked at school. He wanted his children to take responsibility. Stafford in those days was very independent and sure of himself. This may be ascribed to my father's tendency to treat children as adults. As a result Stafford never shirks taking responsibilities.

For a short time Stafford was sent to St. David's School at Reigate. He found it an ordeal at first but very soon he wrote to his father:

Dear Pater,

This week I am one from the top and there are four in the form. Next week there will be five in the form and I expect I shall be third. This week I have beaten the boy below me by 11 marks. Next holidays I must go and stay with Mr. Sutton's boy in London because I promised to. I got my Kodak and am sending two films to Eastmans. Please can you send me some films for it if you can, from any photographers. Mr. Marsh if you can. I liked the knife very much the one you asked Fred to give me. Best love from,

Dad. [The family nickname.]

Another letter indicates that he does not remain for long in the second position:

This week I am top by 50 marks. I get full for everything except neatness, and in that I got 15 out of 20. It is awful I can say I got full for everything *except* neatness. Last written lesson I got V.G. for the first time—that means very good.

Boarding schools run three terms a year with fairly long holidays between. These holidays the children usually spent at Parmoor, where they had a daily "lesson hour" with their tutor, a Mr. Elwell, and for the rest of the day were free to follow their own inclinations. Stafford's favorite exercise was riding. Fishing, shooting, and hunting were tame sports for him compared to galloping across the open country.

There was nothing he liked better than to be making things. He liked using tools and learned to build boats and to construct all sorts of objects. Here is a letter he wrote to his father, at the age of eight years:

Dear Father,

I hope you are none the worse for your journey. . . . We are awfully jolly here. Len, Tomy and I have a carpenter's shop and we also make fretwork brackets. Yesterday I had a race with Mr. Elwell it was awful fun we fair galloped for all we could go and Nipper (whom you must thank Uncle for) beat Eighteen by about 2½ lengths and I could hardly pull him up for about 150 yards. We raced across the moor and common to the first lot of firs. Poor old Nipper runs up and down all the ditches he never attempts to jump. It is awfully dull without you and Ruth. . . . I am now reading Short History of the English People. It is much nicer than that dry tripe of Sir Henry Havelock. Sir H. H. is all the names of the musses and Pa's tutors etc.—and their addresses why he was at one school and not at another and how he liked them, oh gracious all rot and bunkum you might call it. I am a subscriber to a home now at ten shillings a year but they think that I am Mrs. Cripps and not Master Cripps. . . .

We are all going to make a boat today, a good one too, one that will hold you sitting down and in ordinary clothes not change I hope it acts if it does not we shall be angry. Well that is all I know so I say goodbye. With best wishes,

Dadialissimus.

Before his father could come home to see the results of the boat-building, Stafford wrote him again. And this time we can see the lawyer mind emerging as he analyzes a little incident of the day. He says:

Dear Pater,

I suppose you have heard all about the boat. I went in it yesterday it is awful fun. They have built another wall and are going to run the bottom with clay very soon. The deepest side is about 1 ft. 6 ins. in the shallowest part, in the deepest about 2 ft. Yesterday I decided to go for a ride with Edmund. But just as he was starting there was an accident with one of his carts and he had to wait and see what damage had been done and then he forgot what time he arranged to meet me at the bottom of Chisbirch Hill (it was ¼ past two really) and at about 20 past two he started from the moor to meet me at Chisbirch now for my side of the question. I started from here at 10 to two, trotted to the bottom of the hill, at least I biked and the men rode nipper down there as I was passing keenes at the top I heard the two o'clock bell going and when I reached the bottom they said it was half past two which of course was rather silly as it could not be true. It must have been just about 5 minutes past two I waited there a very long time and again asked the time they said 3 o'clock and said they knew he had passed some time before we came which must have been an untruth on their part as he did not start until twenty minutes past two so I am going to see the truth today. That is all to say best love from,

Dad.

A story has got around that Stafford built bridges in his holidays at this time. He will not have it. He says:

We never built a bridge anywhere. There was a big concrete tank built at the bottom of the garden filled with water for fire prevention, as there were only deep wells. In this tank there was a split in the concrete across the middle, and that was where the bridge was formed. We kept two alligators there—they were about six or eight feet long. My brother, Fred, was responsible for things like that. He obtained them by answering an advertisement in the newspaper. The alligators lasted out through the summer. In the winter they were put into the Grape House where there was a little tank and hot water pipes. Then they sat on the pipes and died.

Stafford fell ill between school terms; he caught measles and shortly thereafter had pneumonia. He was a very sick boy for a time and he recalls with humor that "there was a death-bed scene but no death."

His precocity now prompted his father to send him to a different school. To avoid family embarrassment, which no doubt would have occurred had he forged ahead of his brothers at the same school, he was sent at eight years of age to a boarding school at Rottingdean on the Sussex coast.

At twelve he was sent to Winchester College, whose rooms

and grounds had felt the impact of many Cripps footsteps. His first year was full of hard work in Chernocke House. He looked after the clothes of the Captain of the House and rose early every morning, as had his father before him, to make tea for the prefects. One of his first letters to his father from Winchester complained of his difficulties; it also brought Stafford's wishes that his father emerge victorious in a Parliamentary election:

Dear Pater,

I have not much to say except 1st I hope you will easily get in without much trouble. 2nd to tell you that my work is very hard to me and I am trying to do it my best yet I get sworn at like anything for being lazy etc. I cannot do more than a certain Standard but I am expected to do work as well as chaps who are above me.

He advanced quickly from the "Junior Juniors" and at sixteen he was the youngest member of the top form. He was house prefect and Captain of the Houses VI Winchester football team. Fellow house- and team-mates were A. P. Herbert, to become famous in later years as a writer; Horace Woodhouse, who became Lord Terrington and was for a brief period in 1911 a lawyer in Chambers with Stafford; and Richard Coit, a cousin. Lord Terrington relates that Stafford, at Winchester, regarded him "as a 'dangerous radical' because my father was a Liberal M.P. while Stafford's father was a Conservative!"

While Stafford was in these days a conservative young gentleman, and a *bon vivant* according to some reports, Terrington relates that the sight of a poor begging woman, just as Stafford and he were about to enter a restaurant, caused Stafford to remark that his dinner was spoiled by the sight. In conversation with the author, Terrington added, with obvious relish at the memory, that the first alcoholic drink he ever tasted was as Stafford's guest at the "Green Man," a popular pub in Winchester. All the Cripps boys were regarded with awe because their father permitted them to entertain at the Royal Hotel. The elder Cripps loved and trusted his sons and always took the view that they should "choose their own way."

At Winchester, sports occupied Stafford considerably. He preferred racquets to cricket, but above all he retained his love for riding. Since there was no opportunity for riding during term time, he bought a bicycle at a most convenient moment —just as he was sixteen years of age. He wrote to his father:

You know that you never gave me a birthday present. Well, I thought that as I have just bought a bike which cost £8. 10. od. you would like to give it me. If you would you can send a cheque for £8. 10. o. I invested in the Derby, but came out 3s. 6d. to the bad, as I had an investment on Flotsam.

Even in those days his energy and his interests were extraordinary. While at Winchester, he also gave some time to modern languages and English literature. After he was fourteen he spent many of his holidays on the Continent, wandering either alone or with friends.

From the age of sixteen he specialized in science. During one holiday at Parmoor he produced what his brothers called "Stafford's Folly." Inspired by the example of the Wright brothers, he determined to build a biplane glider and fly it. In due course he completed its construction; an old carriage pulled the glider to the top of the neighboring hill on a day perfect for the experiment. Stafford was to be pilot as well as engineer, but the project came rapidly to grief. There is a note in his father's diary of October 20, 1909, which says, "Stafford has been busy constructing an air plane. It took much time. It was broken to a certain extent on the first trial and he is now mending it." That ended the experiment but not his interest in aeronautics and engineering.

Stafford had a business mind, too, and what could he do better than become at sixteen a director of his father's local newspaper, known as the *South Bucks Standard*. For the next five years he was in complete charge of the financial side of the paper. Its politics did not interest him in the least; but the technical and business tasks appealed to his active mind. He always wanted to know how things were done and then to do them. His curiosity was unbounded.

At eighteen, specializing in chemistry, he won the first chemistry scholarship ever offered for New College, Oxford. The examiners were so impressed by his answers to their questions that they sent the papers to Sir William Ramsey, at University College, London, who in turn was so impressed that he suggested that Stafford should go to University College and work under him.

Stafford's science master at Winchester, W. B. Croft, was very proud of him. Writing to Charles Alfred Cripps, he says that Stafford

has been working in the right way; his eye fixed not always on the prize but usually a little beyond that, entering into the love and enthusiasm for the subject which belongs to it. Without this feeling school exercises are often an injury to the mind. . . . I should like also to commend his habits of readiness and punctuality which quietly add to the power of good abilities.

Dr. H. M. Burge, principal of Winchester, had become very fond of Stafford during the final year at Winchester. He wrote to Stafford's father:

I write at once to rejoice with you in your son's success, which he thoroughly deserves, and also his promise. I can only say that I told the Warden of New College, he is a fellow of *quite* first rate ability. But better than all that, he is a fellow of real high purpose and genuine appreciation—I respect and like him very much.

Mr. Furley, Cripps' headmaster, has remarked that

critics of Stafford have often complained about his lack of training in the humanities. Stafford was a good student of history and there he earned some of his best grades. He studied Latin and Greek until he was fifteen and had to take examinations in those subjects when he took his scholarship examination at New College. Stafford at Winchester was lovable and disarmed all hostility. He was liked and respected by all the boys.

Stafford gave up his scholarship to New College and went instead to University College. That brought him to live in London. Here he had to look around for some new means of keeping fit, for he was a firm believer in physical fitness. Instead of horseback riding he became fascinated with roller skating and often, after his day in the laboratory, would make his way to the Olympia skating rink. Soon he was taking part in many University activities and in organizing the social life of his college. In a short time, he was elected president of the Student Union. His first public appearance was as chairman for A. E. Housman, the famous poet, in the Foundation Oration at

University College. Later he was chairman when his father opened the new University College playing fields at Perivale. In one of Sir William Ramsey's laboratories, he met another young scientist, Alfred Egerton, who was a few years later to become his brother-in-law.

1910 was an eventful year for Stafford. He was twenty-one years of age. During his holiday abroad he stayed with a German family at Hamburg. It was in this year that a Dr. Crippen killed his wife, cleared out of England, and caused a search for him in all countries, including Germany. A facetious friend addressed a letter to Stafford in Hamburg "Dr. Crippen" and Stafford had to bear the brunt of resulting inquiries.

This was also an election year. His father had lost his seat in the general election of 1908 and was now the Conservative candidate in a by-election at Wycombe. Filial loyalty and the directorship of what was known locally as the "Cripps Chronicle" demanded that Stafford should lend all the aid at his command. Although he had not the slightest idea about the issues, it was exciting while it lasted. And this time a new light shone into his life.

A fair young woman with blonde hair came to the office one day and volunteered to help fold election circulars. Stafford looked down from an opening above, and seeing her, inquired and found out who she was—Isobel Swithinbank. That day, with a group of other persons, they lunched at the same inn but did not speak to each other.

During the summer Stafford's sister asked Isobel to Parmoor. There was a large and very gay house party of young people, and they all went to Henley together. A week or two later, Isobel went up to London to stay at the Cripps' town house. During her visit, plans were laid for a skiing party in Switzerland, directly after Christmas. In the late summer Isobel went off to Scotland with her parents. Stafford, journeying in Europe, began a correspondence with her and from Nuremberg sent her a little Teddy bear in Bavarian dress. Then came the year's-end visit to Switzerland. The party consisted of Ruth, Leonard and Stafford Cripps, Isobel, Alfred Egerton, later to become Ruth's husband, and Ethel Slocock, a niece of Charles Alfred Cripps, who acted as chaperon.

After a few days of mutual assistance on the skiing trails,

Stafford and Isobel became engaged. They "were summoned home to report" and left their skis. (The next time they skiied together was in the forests outside Moscow, in 1941!) Miss Slocock chaperoned the ebullient young couple to Dover. Enid Allhusen, Isobel's sister, met the group at Dover and accompanied them home while Miss Slocock, who had suffered an unfortunate channel crossing, ruefully made her way back to Klosters. It was suggested at first that, owing to Stafford's youth and the fact that he had as yet not even passed his Bar examinations, he and Isobel should not marry for at least five years. They rejected this proposal and made such nuisances of themselves that in the following July they were allowed to be married. Stafford was twenty-two years old, his wife two years his junior.

But true to family tradition on both sides, the fathers, though forced by the enthusiasm of the young people to agree to an early marriage, registered their votes and discussed the future. The following letter from Isobel's father to Charles Alfred Cripps on January 19, 1911, reveals that Stafford has decided definitely to follow in the steps of his father and grandfather and devote himself to the law and politics. Harold Swithinbank, head of the new family to unite with the Cripps, in one of the most lucid and prophetic family documents extant, wrote to Stafford's father:

Your son has probably ere this had a talk with you as to his plans for the future, as Isobel has had with me. I fully recognise that this is a matter rather for him and for you to decide, and that I can have little voice in the matter so far as regards what I may consider as tending towards the ultimate happiness of my daughter when she becomes his wife. But at the same time I would ask you that before any decision is made, the matter should be very carefully considered from every point of view.

From the conversation I had with you and a subsequent talk with Stafford himself, I gather that at the present moment two alternatives are being considered:

a. That your son should take advantage of the scientific training he has had and a natural aptitude he possesses for the application of science to practical purposes, to engage in business life with a view not only to eventually becoming a successful business man, but of being able the sooner to make a comfortable home for his future wife.

b. That he should, following his father's footsteps adopt a career at the bar, for which he is already entered, with a view to turning his scientific training and knowledge to account in that profession, and eventually entering political life.

These I take it are the two alternatives at issue for the moment, and had it been absolutely essential for the young couple seriously to consider whether after a certain period of waiting, they had or had not jointly a sufficient income to justify them in commencing married life, and to enable them to tide over that period of waiting which might naturally be expected to ensue before a substantial addition to that income could be expected from the exercise by Stafford of his profession, I should have been inclined to favour the idea of his at once immersing himself in business.

But after our conversation of last week I take it that the young couple will start life with a united income sufficient to free them from anxiety as to the immediate present.

We have to look further ahead than they at their time of life are likely to do, and the day will probably come when the necessity for amassing money in business will no longer exist, and when it does I cannot help thinking that both Stafford and Isobel will be happier in political life, with the opportunity for the former to engage in science for science's sake, than they could be were he immersed in business life, with all its ties and cares. Isobel has been brought up in the country and knows little of town life. That she would adapt herself to other conditions I have no doubt, but I question whether the absorption of her husband in business life would be so conducive to her happiness as the exercise of a profession which, although strenuous at times, would for a certain portion of the year at all events, not prove so great a tie.

I should be very glad to have a further talk with you over the matter when opportunity arises, but in the meantime I hope no definite decision will be made in the matter.

I am sorry to say that Isobel has been suffering from a severe cold, but she seems determined to be well enough to come to you this afternoon.

There was no doubt as to Stafford's course. His elder brother Seddon was already launched on a legal career. But he did not drop his scientific studies, nor did his interest in science lessen. Indeed, in the early days of married life he still pursued his studies of science as well as law. He invented a pyknometer, a device for measuring the density of liquids and gases. At twenty-two he was part author of a paper read before the Royal

Society, "The Critical Constants and Orthoberic Densities of Xenon,"—the youngest student ever to read a paper before that learned body.

He passed his final examinations for the Bar in the summer of 1912. He was twenty-four when he was called to the Bar of the Middle Temple. Here he spent his first year as a barrister studying cases, revising and editing the family textbooks: his grandfather's volume on the "Church and Clergy" and his father's on "Compensation."

His political opinions had hardly taken shape. He had grown up in the shadows of his father's politics which had arisen from his career as a lawyer richly exploiting the law-making institution of Parliament. Stafford himself writes of these early years and particularly of his young manhood:

In the days before the last war I was almost entirely politically unconscious. Brought up in a traditionally Conservative middle-class family, seldom meeting anyone other than Conservatives, I accepted that environment quite naturally, and from time to time participated in some election or other political activity in the same way that I engaged in any other sport or social event. I was neither aware of democracy nor of politics in any real sense of the word. The course of events, so far as I was concerned, seemed to run smoothly and there appeared to me no reason why I or any other young man of my acquaintance should trouble himself with political controversies or electoral disputes. Educated as a chemist and with the prospect of a professional career at the Bar before me, I concentrated upon my studies, varying them with visits abroad whenever the opportunity and money were available.

He was tall, dark-haired, upright, of happy temperament, intensively active, athletic, quick in thinking and in acquiring knowledge, essentially practical, combining manual and intellectual activity with the readiness of a born experimentalist. The Crippsian feelings of family loyalty and love for one another were strongly developed in him. His father, his governess, Mazelle, and his aunt, Mrs. Mary Playne, had succeeded in keeping him ever-conscious of his mother and, with equal success had woven into the very texture of his mind all the implications and spirit of Theresa Cripps' faith and personal hope.

In his development, as in that of his forebears, there was no sense of history or of being part of a society in transition. All seemed as it were yesterday, stable and permanent. His religion was a personal religion. His ethics were personal ethics, governing his attitude toward other individuals without regard to the nature of society. The great tidal forces of social history had passed him by as they had passed by his father. The drama of the struggle for world power, the growing rivalry of the modern imperial giants, about to plunge them into an Armageddon, could not be seen from his corner of the world's theater.

Nor did his marriage to Isobel Swithinbank, the granddaughter of J. C. Eno, inventor of the famous "Fruit Salt," bring him any greater awareness of the great social trends of the time. She brought him love and an outlook similar to his own, which blended into his aims, ambitions and ideals and gave strength to all that he had derived from his mother. Here was no challenger to shake him out of beliefs that had become instinctive, into new ways of thought. She would be lover, wife, mother to his children, nurse in sickness, comrade in strength, his faith her faith, his ambitions her ambitions.

It is necessary to add, however, that at University College he came into contact with a completely different order of people from his friends and family. While the young couple were engaged and Isobel was taken by her family on a motor tour to France, Stafford wrote a long letter to her expressing his perplexities about "poverty and riches." Isobel, though she had lived in an environment of riches, had often had sincere but unexpressed questionings on this subject herself. These feelings were to have a certain portent for the future, but at this time the experience was not acute enough for articulation.

In the summer of 1914, Stafford Cripps, father of two infant children, John and Diane, studied cases in the Temple Chambers, sat upon the window sill and played games with his colleagues, and lightheartedly discussed the titbits of the day. Their future was assured and the world seemed a jolly good place in which to live. This summer, too, saw Stafford's father promoted to the House of Lords as Baron Parmoor of Frieth.

Parmoor was the name of his house, Frieth the name of the nearest village.

Suddenly the revolver shot of Sarajevo echoed round the world. The epoch of war and revolution had begun. Without a moment's hesitation Stafford and his brothers volunteered for service in the armed forces. His elder brother, Seddon, became an officer in the Lincolnshire Yeomanry. Freddie joined the Royal Buckinghamshire Hussars, fought at Gallipoli and in Palestine and France, was wounded and decorated; a heroic soldier indeed. Leonard rejoined the Fourth Hussars.

In October of 1914 Stafford, now a soldier, went to France as the driver of a lorry presented to the Red Cross by his wife's grandfather. He was engaged for a year at the Boulogne base in a shuttle service supplying heavy goods. Here he qualified for the Mons Medal. While at this work he was instrumental in providing a new and special type of slipper for men suffering from frostbite. He was waiting under orders at Boulogne in 1915 to proceed to Ypres for gas work when he was recalled for work in the Explosives Department of the Ministry of Munitions, because of his ability as a chemist.

Now a new kind of life began. For a time he worked at Waltham Abbey to learn the practical scientific work of his department. He rented a little red brick villa at Cheshurst, near Waltham Cross, and, as a surprise for Isobel, arranged for her old "Nana" who had cared for her since babyhood to come and help. To Isobel's joy she was there to greet her on the doorstep. Stafford was alternately on day and night shift and did a very thorough and intensive short course, working through every process. Isobel and Nana were up at five thirty to get his midday dinner ready, tied up in a red cotton handkerchief, before he took off on his bicycle.

After a time he was sent to the Government factory at Queensferry, the largest explosive factory in the British Empire, which specialized in high explosives.

Again, with his wife and children, he took a house near the factory. His job was an important one. Besides working as a practical chemist he was responsible for the organization of thousands of working people. As usual, Cripps tackled the job thoroughly and studied carefully, yet rapidly, every detail of the workings of the plant and the production processes. His capacity was so quickly revealed in the lowering of production costs that he was made assistant superintendent. His energy seemed inexhaustible. He worked sixteen to twenty hours a day.

✓ Here he made his first real contact with the working class, although the experience rang no political bells in his mind. He conducted himself as the most efficient of managers, a Christian gentleman, patriarchal in his willingness to meet the lowliest working men and women in the factory, to listen with unfailing courtesy to every grievance, and to consider every suggestion from whatever quarter it might come.

It was an experience he was not likely to forget, although his complete absorption in it obscured at the time its social and political significance. There came a day, however, some twenty years later, when Britain was again at war, that, standing on the opposition side of the House of Commons, he joined in the challenge to the Government to take profiteering out of the industrial prosecution of the war. He told the story of his experience at the Queensferry Munition plant. He said,

I was for a considerable period of time in a position of management in what was, I think, the largest Government factory in this country. It was a factory which was erected at a cost of £7,750,000. It was a factory which was destroyed at the end of the war at the request of the people who have put this Amendment on the Paper. Among other units in this factory at Queensferry were the two finest sulphuric-acid plants in the world at the time, and part of my job was to deal with the cost accounts of the factory. In order to deal with them efficiently I had access to the cost accounts of every other sulphuric-acid manufacturing plant in England, France, Italy, Canada and the United States of America, to compare the standard which we were manufacturing and to see what economies could be made. We had to start with an entirely unskilled staff. Not a single person either of the management or the operatives had ever worked in a chemical or explosive factory before that factory was started in wartime. It was started up on war prices. We have to pay very heavy prices for our sulphur (which comes from Sicily) owing to war insurance and freight and for other war materials as well. Our cost figures were lower than those of any pre-war sulphuric acid manufacturer in this country. In fact they were so much lower that a year or two after we had started up, a deputation of the sulphuric acid manufacturers of England came to see the Minister of Munitions and said, "we ask you to give an undertaking that you will destroy this factory at the end of the war, as otherwise every sulphuric acid manufacturer goes out of business." . . . And as a result, immediately after the war these two plants, the most efficient in the country, became derelict, and I presume that the remains of them are probably to be seen today on the site of Queensferry where they were put. That was a tremendous loss to the industry of this country. For the first time, oleum manufacture had been started; that is to say, a high concentration of sulphuric acid was available for sending in railway trucks to any manufacturer at a price that was very much lower than anything that could be quoted by other manufacturers. In normal times, where there was no acute crisis or a war, would they have contemplated putting such a factory up if they knew that at the end of two and a half years there was a danger of having to close down as a result of pressure from these very people?

After some months he became exceedingly ill. Overwork, fumes from the chemical plant, and intestinal disease, which he had contracted in France in the first year of the war, laid him prostrate. The doctors thought that he had little chance of recovery. He was taken to a nursing home in Chester and later came to London. After some months he recovered sufficiently for himself and his wife to live in a tiny flat in Half Moon Street while he found a desk job in the Ministry of Agriculture. A few more months of work and illness dragged him down again. For the next two years he was an invalid.

III. The Youngest K.C.

NOT until 1919 was Stafford Cripps able to resume his profession. He began where he had left off, under H. A. Colfax, K.C., preparing patent cases in which his scientific knowledge was of great value. But he was far from being physically fit, and he had before him a long struggle against ill health. It would be difficult to assess how much his search for health has played in the molding of the person he is today. It certainly encouraged him to make a decision in keeping with the Cripps tradition. He had come from the countryside. He returned to it. A few miles from Cirencester, where the Cripps had lived for centuries, he bought an old manor farm, with deeds going back to 1615. The name of the house was "Goodfellows" and it was situated on the edge of the village named Filkins. Here the Cripps brought their three children, John, Diana, and Theresa; at "Goodfellows," too, Peggy, their fourth child, was born in 1921.

Filkins was a backward place, of Saxon origin, that could trace its history to the early twelfth century. Once it had been part of a little manor estate, surrounded by open fields until the days of the enclosures. It had no church until 1850 when it became a separate parish. All the houses and barns were built of the famous golden stone of Filkins and great slabs of it were used for fencing the gardens.

Goodfellows once consisted of two blocks of buildings set at a right angle. As Cripps' practice grew and he made more money, he enlarged and altered the house into a T shape. The stone and the slates for the additions were dug from the neighboring fields and the craftsmanship was that of the best mason of Filkins, George Swinford, to make certain that the new blended with the old. With garden, trees, ground and fields in keeping with the wider landscape, far away from the tur-

moil that was London, Goodfellows became home indeed, a
model of contemporary village planning, untouched by the
storms of the world.

Cripps divided his time between the law courts and Goodfellows and with a bailiff managed the farm. He studied sheep-
breeding and had great success with his pedigree Ryeland
sheep. He planted hedges around a beautiful lawn, chopped
trees, and equipped a carpenter's shop where he pursued
his hobby of furniture making. This became a rendezvous for
a friend he had made during his short time at the Ministry of
Agriculture: Sir Lawrence Weaver, author, architect, and
critic. Although he was twelve years Cripps' senior, they became firm friends and until ten years later, when he died, they
spent many evenings together. Between them, in 1923, they
founded the Ashtead Potteries Ltd., a nonprofit friendly society
for the training and employment of seriously disabled ex-
servicemen. The society was started with the idea of incorpo-
rating into pottery manufacturing the most up-to-date technical
methods, based upon a study of the industry in all European
countries and the idea of raising the standard of craftsmanship. The Ashtead plan was the result of a question which
Stafford asked one morning—whether it were not possible to
make a jam container more attractive for the breakfast table
than the ordinary pot.

As another result of this friendship the Cripps one day added
two boys to their family. The Weavers had two sons, Toby
and Purcell. In January, 1927, Lady Weaver was stricken with
pneumonia and died at Goodfellows. From that time Isobel
Cripps became a second mother to the boys, and three years
later, when Sir Lawrence also died, the Cripps took both of
them into the family as their own.

"The man who is a good citizen is not necessarily a bad
husband and father," said Cripps in one of his early church
speeches; "in fact he is probably a good one." Of this there
can be few better examples than Cripps himself. Goodfellows
could be held up as a model of the English county family.

A maternal forebear, William "Citizen" Potter, had been
fond of regaling his family with maxims about the salient
characteristics of the English. On one occasion he said, "Always
appear to be busy, even if you are not." A highly respected

Quaker and Radical, his high principles and worthy sentiments did not prove sufficient to preserve him from the clutches of drink. There is nothing in Stafford Cripps' life to indicate that he has ever suffered any anxiety over the fate of William "Citizen" Potter, or that he has deliberately patterned his life in antithesis to this ancestor. He has never had to *appear* to be busy. He has, in fact, been so busily occupied throughout his life that a by-product of this habit has been the development of an outer calm and ease, as if to contravert William Potter by appearing "always to be free, ready, available, even if you are not."

His legal work grew rapidly. His first important case to arrest the attention of the public, as well as that of the legal profession, dealt with the invention of a black dye. The case lasted ten days. He so lucidly explained to the Court of Appeal the chemical process involved in the making of the dye, showing his mastery of every detail, that his reputation as an exponent of patent cases was quickly and definitely established.

Apart from his intellectual ability and remarkable memory, his capacity for sustained hard work was the main factor in his success. From the very beginning he always knew more about his case than anyone else on either side. He was often able to correct his opponent's prepared speech, with the latter's full approval, and to refer the judge to documents which no one else could find. He frequently worked over his documents until the early hours of the morning to make sure that his case was thoroughly prepared. Consequently, he was never taken by surprise nor at a loss to counter any move of his opponents, however astute. It is perhaps not realized by the layman how much of the apparent superiority of some counsel is due to sheer energy and concentration. The "infinite capacity for taking pains" was always one of the attributes of Stafford Cripps. A solicitor who had once briefed him never thought of employing anyone else, if he was available, and thus he had an ever widening circle of clients.

English barristers do not take instructions from clients, but only through the medium of a solicitor, the two branches of the legal profession being quite separate. A young barrister, therefore, cannot originate, still less purchase, a practice for himself; he works as an individual, not as a member of a firm, and anything in the nature of advertising is absolutely forbidden. The young man begins his career as a pupil to one of the barristers already in a set of chambers. If he is fortunate and there is room for him, he may be able to become a regular member of the group, gradually building up a practice of his own, until finally he may even take over the chambers himself, when the previous head retires from the bar or is appointed to judicial office. By this means there grows up an almost hereditary system, with the highest traditions of unselfishness and mutual help.

An informal system of "devilling" is common, whereby the beginner looks up cases and assists in their preparation. But apart from this, every member of a well-regulated set of chambers can and does take advantage of the help of every other, however senior, in dealing with his legal problems. Thus, when an opinion is given, it has often been tested by prolonged debate between able and experienced lawyers who have no ax to grind and get no fees of any kind, but whose criticism strengthens the confidence of the actual giver of the opinion. Members of the chambers will often be found having tea together in the senior members' room after the courts rise at four o'clock. There is an active impression of companionship and freedom, more reminiscent of a university common room than of a lawyer's office.

Such was the atmosphere of Cripps' chambers after the 1914-1918 war when he shared them with, among others, the late Aubrey Lawrence, a distinguished ecclesiastical lawyer and a very charming person. On one occasion this eminent chancellor of several dioceses suddenly found the copy of the *Times,* which he stood reading, a mass of flames. Cripps had lit it with a match. Lawrence, though startled, was not in the least upset. For in those days Cripps was always fond of a joke, and there was usually a "leg-pull" of some kind to be expected. Mock trials on trifling subjects were a specialty.

But there is about the work of the bar itself at times an almost monastic air, and the severe self-discipline which it involves is combined with intense individualism and strong competition. These may have had a marked effect on Stafford Cripps. A busy barrister has little or no personal contact even with his lay client, and still less with the outside world in

general. Certainly Cripps' moral standards seemed to be so
high as to make almost impossible demands on human nature.
His colleagues were far below his level in this, but their education and upbringing were generally such as to respond to
his example. This perhaps tended to give him an unduly high
estimate of the extent to which the man in the street could be
expected to appreciate his exalted morals.

His rise to success at the bar was unusually rapid. Starting
his career after the war on the Oxford Circuit, he was briefed
in a number of small cases, in county courts, and at quarter
sessions, which he conducted with ease and mastery. He was
soon noticed by the solicitor to the Great Western Railway,
who began to employ him regularly in minor cases of a technical nature, such as arbitration to settle the value of property acquired for the extension of the railway, where his gift
for cross-examination of experts such as surveyors or engineers
appeared at once. He was also briefed by other solicitors, for
the same reason, in connection with the valuation of property
for the purpose of local taxes.

Meanwhile, at his chambers in London, there was a substantial good will in patent work and he soon got his chance
in the simpler aspects of this work. He made no mistake about
taking it, and the patent agents who consulted him in connection with applications and oppositions in the Patent Office
soon realized that they had to deal with a man of unusual
stature. Apart from his scientific qualifications, which were
quite out of the ordinary, he handled difficult cases with a
certainty and authority seldom shown by a junior member
of the bar.

Within five years of his return to the bar, he had a sound
practice of the highest class. He was then retained in a case
which was to prove a landmark in his career. His client was
the Duff Development Company, which since 1916 had been
in litigation with the government of Kelantan, one of the un-
federated Malay States. The dispute concerned a concession
which the company had for the development of a large tract
of country containing mining, timber, and rubber-growing
areas. It involved two hearings before the House of Lords, besides an arbitration which lasted seventy-nine days.

Cripps was responsible for the strategy of the case. Many

important questions of arbitration were raised. There were highly complicated issues of constitutional law to be examined. The Colonial Office had with the utmost cynicism claimed on Kelantan's behalf that the Sultan was an independent foreign sovereign. As such, it was argued, he was not subject to the jurisdiction of the British courts unless he voluntarily submitted to be bound. Cripps handled the matter so skillfully that in the end the Colonial Office felt compelled to sanction the payment of no less than £387,000 to the company.

This important case brought Cripps into close contact with several of the leading K.C.'s of the day, including Sir Douglas Hogg, and Mr. F. J. Maugham (both afterward Lord Chancellors), Lord Justice Scott, and Mr. W. H. Upjohn, probably the most formidable legal figure of his generation. Cripps showed that he was quite at home in this company, and one and all of them recognized his outstanding ability. They were particularly impressed by his cross-examination of a distinguished professor whom he reduced to speechlessness by reference to his own published works. They admired also the masterly way in which he had indexed and digested the voluminous evidence, thus giving his own leaders an immense advantage over their opponents. The Colonial Office solicitor began almost at once to brief Cripps in the Privy Council, where he appeared more than once as a junior in cases raising questions of colonial administration.

He also became known in matters directly affecting the public. The Middlesex County Council, the City of London Corporation, and finally the London County Council, employed him as their junior counsel in compensation cases. When the four main-line railways came to be amalgamated and their charges for passengers and freight were reviewed for the purpose of providing a standard revenue (the first step toward nationalization, taken by the Coalition Government in 1921), the London County Council was interested in the charges for workmen's fares and season tickets. Cripps gained a great success for them, working in close touch with an equally little-known representative of the London Labour Party named Herbert Morrison. Each recognized the other's capacity at once, and this association had important consequences in later years.

Legally, the railway inquiry was to mark Cripps out in yet another field. For apart from putting him in the front rank of experts in railway law, it led naturally to his employment at the Parliamentary Bar, that is, in private bills before committees of the Lords and Commons and in government and local inquiries. But for his many other fields and for his coming into Parliament itself, which must automatically exclude him from such practice, Cripps could have easily become leader of the Parliamentary Bar, had he so chosen.

He was rapidly coming to the top of the tree in the conduct of patent actions, an extremely difficult and arduous task for any man who specializes in that field and no other, but a phenomenal one for Cripps, who had as varied a practice as anyone at the Bar. He gained valuable experience from working under well-known patent lawyers. They in turn found that they had sitting behind them not a mere beginner but a man who knew more about their cases than they did themselves and who was prepared to intervene in the argument, when required, with telling and often decisive effect.

It was not long before he was being spoken of as the most brilliant man at the Bar. His father knew the toll which this success must be exacting. Stafford's health and work in the law had always been Parmoor's concern. Father and son visited each other as frequently as was possible. Hurriedly penned notes, comments of special events of the day, Easter, Christmas, and birthday letters that were longer and more personal, and often throughout the years long messages on historical, political, and religious problems, passed between father and son until Parmoor's death in 1941.

Writing to Stafford at Christmastime in 1923, when his son was ill, Parmoor said:

The law is a great strain even for the robust and there is no room for much outside work—above all things, avoid evening meetings and night journeys after hard work at the courts. I know more than one of my friends who tried this, and had to suffer from the evil effects. It is more than the average strength of man can do, and it should not be attempted. I know this may mean disappointment but this must be faced. A time will come to you when the call for religious and public work will be stronger and then possibly the conditions of your professional life may be such, that you could do such work either as a judge or in some other sphere. There is no need to be in any way cast down about the future. . . .

The following year, in a New Year's letter, Parmoor developed another theme:

May your next year be as progressive as 1924. I should ask you to think carefully over the question of taking silk and not delay too long. My own father was always advising me in a contrary direction and did not much like the risks and chances if they could be avoided. I am all for going ahead. . . .

It is a great delight to me to hear so much of you from my own profession, although I have rather parted from the Bar in the last year.

Again, in a congratulatory note on Stafford's birthday, Parmoor wrote:

It will soon be time for you to think of the next step in your profession by becoming a K.C. This however is a matter for careful consideration. My own view is not to put this step off, as soon as you think you can take it and keep your work.

I cannot help thinking that it would be good for you and Isobel and the children to have a house in London. This expense is a small matter compared with health and quiet and the blessing of a wife to look after you.

On July 26, 1926, Cripps applied to the Lord Chancellor for silk. "Taking silk" is a risky matter. Once a barrister has become a K.C., he can no longer do the "junior" work which he has done previously. But there usually comes a time when he is so busy as a junior preparing cases before trial that he has to make up his mind whether to take silk or not. "Silks" join a circuit of their own choice. Before taking silk, the barrister must write to every silk on the circuit telling him of his application. This is a form of courtesy and a kind of warning that the barrister is about to join the band. Once he has done that he must wait for the higher sort of briefs to come in. And sometimes they do not come.

The following April, Cripps took silk, becoming the youngest King's Counsel at the British Bar. With him was D. N. Pritt, his fellow student at Winchester though two years his senior, who was later to become one of his most ardent political supporters and an equally ardent critic.

Parmoor's heart rejoiced:

My very dear Stafford,
    I had hoped to see you and give personal congratulations but I have not had a chance. . . . I think that the appointment has come just at the right time and that a move forward is for you a move in the direction of progress. . . . My father and myself were co-benchers at the Middle Temple and I shall hope to be present when your time comes to be called to the Bench of the Middle Temple. I have full confidence in your future and you have only to keep fit to make your way to the head of a great profession. . . . I cannot tell you how much I rejoice and this is quite the right medicine for dear Isobel.
                                        Your very affectionate father,
                                                    Parmoor.

He wrote also to Isobel Cripps on the same day:

My very dear Isobel,
    I am immensely delighted that Staff should have become a K.C. It is a right step, and should bring him in due time to the front of the Bar. May he much prosper and you have health and strength in working with him and encouraging him. He must be taking Silk at about the same age that I did and comes as the third generation. My father and myself were benchers together, which was said at the time to be a record and now there is hope that Staff may become a bencher at the same time as his Father.
    I have full confidence in the future and you should be really proud of Staff's ability and success.
                                        Our dear love to you both,
                                        Your very affectionate father,
                                                    P.

    A photograph of Stafford "taking silk," standing with the rest of the group, smoking, sent to Parmoor by Isobel Cripps, gave him a little amusement. Thanking her in a letter, he remarks, "It seems shockingly modern to have a cigarette in the full dress of a K.C."
    As a King's Counsel Stafford achieved prominence at once and his practice continued to grow in scope and importance. His subsequent patent cases included such noted actions as I. G. Farbenindustrie v. Imperial Chemical Industries (a case of great importance for the British dye industry); Mullard Radio Company Limited v. Philco Radio Company Limited

(the famous "Pentode Valve" case in which his exposition of the history of thermionic valves before the House of Lords took over seven days); and the still more renowned artificial silk case, Courtaulds v. British Celanese. He appeared too for the Lightning Fastener Co. Ltd. (Zipp-fasteners), Crompton Parkinson (frosted glass articles), for Garton Ltd. with regard to patents concerning improvement in the packing of inverted sugar cubes, and for the Westinghouse Company concerning railway automatic signaling. His most important case dealing with trade-mark practice was probably that in which he appeared for the Shredded Wheat Company against the Kellogg Company.

He became a specialist in compensation cases. There was the case of Rosen v. Owner of the Steamship *Quercus*. On the night of February 7, 1931, the *Quercus* was in the harbor of Porto Allegro, Brazil, moored to a quay about six feet away. Rosen, a seaman, had returned to his ship after an evening ashore. The night was clear. He went to the forecastle to sleep. At 2:30 A.M. a splash was heard, and his body was recovered next day. It was surmised that during the night in going to the lavatory he had tripped and fallen overboard. This case reached the House of Lords, and they held that in spite of the fact that he had no duty at the time of the accident on deck, the man's death could be held to have arisen during the course of his employment.

A most exciting case arose out of the unemployment crisis of the early thirties. An organization had been set up called the National Unemployed Workers' Movement. Wal Hannington, an organizer of the movement, made a speech in Trafalgar Square, as a result of which he was arrested on the premises of the N. U. W. M. and certain documents were seized by the police, some of which were retained by them. These documents were used at the trial of Elias, a colleague of Hannington, who was being tried for sedition, but had not been returned to the plaintiffs, among them Elias, at the conclusion of the trial. The plaintiffs claimed damages for trespass to the premises, the return of the letters, and damages for detention. The case caused considerable interest because of its political nature. Cripps, Pritt, K.C., and Mitchison appeared for the plaintiffs, and the attorney general, Sir Thomas Inskip, led for the defendant, the police. The judge ruled that while there was a right to search

all persons arrested, it did not justify seizure of documents belonging to persons other than the persons arrested, and that the
documents had been wrongfully detained.

Cripps rendered an important service to working people by
his clarification of the legal doctrine of "common employment." This doctrine laid down that injuries sustained at work
through the negligence of a fellow workman could not be the
subject of a claim for damage against the "common employer."
In the case of Radcliffe v. Ribble Motor Services Limited,
Cripps appeared for the orphan daughter of a bus driver who
was killed in collision with another vehicle belonging to the
same company. He succeeded in establishing the view that
"common employment" must imply not only the same employer, but the same job or work. Heavy damages were awarded
and the result was of great value to all transport workers.

The only matrimonial case Cripps ever dealt with was in
1938. The case was brought by Captain Cunningham Reid, the
M.P. for Marylebone, against his wife, asking for a declaration that certain deeds by which his wife had assured him a
portion of her income were still effective. The action drew
much publicity because of the status of the persons involved
and the remarkable concentration of legal talent. Mrs. Cunningham Reid was a sister of Lady Louis Mountbatten (now Countess). Cripps was briefed for the plaintiff together with other
K.C.'s. At the end of a week the case was settled by agreement.

One of the last big cases in which Cripps figured and which
ranked high for the complexity of the issues, the amount of
money at stake, and the number of counsel involved was that
of the Westminster Bank v. Liverpool Marine and other Insurance Companies. It arose out of the failure of the Capital
Film Company, and the Westminster Bank claimed £1,000,000
from a group of the leading insurance companies. In all, thirty-
five consolidated actions were heard in the commercial court.
When the hearing began, the judge adjourned for a short while
in order to allow counsel to sort themselves out. The strange
sight was seen of K.C.'s occupying three full rows and junior
counsel occupying the jury box. Cripps took five days to open
the case, and at the end of the opening the case was settled.

When, later, Cripps was appointed solicitor-general, the of-

Illustrated

Sir Stafford Cripps at his home, Frith Hill, on his return from Russia, 1942.

Bassano

Lord Parmoor, father of Sir Stafford.

Parmoor, homestead of the Cripps family, located in the
Chiltern hills near Henley-on-Thames.

Family group showing Charles Alfred and Theresa Cripps
with their children, 1891.

Stafford and his bride, Isobel, on their marriage day, July 12, 1911.

British Official photo (Ministry of Aircraft Production)

Sir Stafford Cripps visits aircraft works.

Fox Photos, Ltd.

Cripps and Gandhi in New Delhi, 1942.

Illustrated

Stafford and Isobel Cripps at their Frith Hill home.

fice naturally gave him added prestige, but it probably did not
make a great difference in his practice, for he would have been
just as successful without it. There is no doubt that he had a
unique position at the Bar, apart from jury cases in which Sir
Patrick Hastings and Norman Birkett had an outstanding reputation. Cripps did not specialize in jury cases. It has been suggested that had he taken part in this branch of the law, he
would have been better prepared for his subsequent political
career through the necessity of "playing to the jury." Be that as
it may, Cripps appealed to jurists because of his particular gift
of thinking on his feet and always dealing at once with questions put from the bench. His voice and manner of address,
when making even the most abstruse points, never lost the interest of the court no matter how long and complicated the
case, and the court was quick to recognize his talent because he
never said, "I will deal with that later."

Gregory Krikorian, a member of Cripps' chambers, writes
that:

Cripps was very free of any mannerism in Court. His manner
was cool and collected and meticulously polite and his voice, which
was well modulated, was capable of keeping the same pitch for days
on end. He relied on a very carefully prepared note for opening and
in a case of any complexity he invariably provided himself with a
pulpit made of legal tomes on which his notes were deposited and
which made it unnecessary for him to crouch down in order to pick
up the thread of his argument. His notes were invariably carefully
indexed with cross references to pages in the Law reports or correspondence and it was sometimes the subject of amusement to see
him waiting patiently at the right page whilst his opponents floun-
dered through masses of paper or whilst their Lordships at their
more leisurely ease withdrew their attention from one passage in
order to fasten it on the other. He relied, too, on carefully indoc-
trinated Juniors behind him always passing to him the right letter
in a mass of correspondence for example or the right passage in the
report. All this gave an impression of formidable competence, which
was only slightly affected in moments of stress by the careful rolling
up and unrolling of the tab on his silksgown. The observer was
sometimes delightfully surprised to notice that the icy calm in court
was relieved on his way to and from the robing room by a gay pro-
peller like action imparted to his keys which he carried on a long
chain.

On one occasion in 1928 after a Parliamentary Committee hearing on certain railway bills, Earl Russell passed Cripps a note: "I prefer listening to you rather than your father—but don't tell him so!" On the refusal of a witness to answer questions, Russell sent Stafford another note containing a brief sentence, "Buy a winkle pin!"

During the years between 1925-1929, in which his legal work took up most of his time and energy, Cripps was repeatedly harassed with intestinal troubles, and time and again he was forced to rest from his labors. It was in these years, when he was making such rapid strides in the legal profession, that he also stepped into the political arena.

IV. The Churchman's Fight for Peace

D
URING his convalescence in the later years of the 1914-1918 war Stafford Cripps had begun to think seriously about political affairs. He writes:

Till the end of the war, I was largely an invalid with much time for reading and thinking. As a result, by the time the war was over I had become aware—indeed very aware—of the appalling and useless tragedy that the world had brought upon itself. At this point my political conscience was born. . . . I was still, however, living in a tradition of conservatism, though the result of the war experience upon my father had very greatly changed his political outlook. His sense of the interference with all liberty of conscience, and of the injustices wrought upon the common people, had convinced him that some new outlook was necessary if civilisation were to be saved from destruction.

The birth of his political consciousness was really an extension of his moral conscience into the world of politics, and not the beginning of an understanding of the political relations of people in a changing, developing society. Instinctively he turned for guidance to those who had helped to mold him in his formative years—to his father and to Doctor Burge, his schoolmaster at Winchester, who had become a close personal friend.

But, as Stafford observes, great changes had taken place in his father. He was no longer the Conservative of the days when Stafford ran his local paper. In the years immediately preceding the war he had been moving away from his old conservative moorings. One of the first things to shake him had been the famous Taff Vale Decision of the House of Lords which had challenged the very existence of the trade unions. Then the Liberal struggle against the House of Lords in 1910-1911 stirred him and he condemned the nonrepresentative character of the Second Chamber. He became aware of the political awakening of the working class, and instead of reacting toward it in a conservative way his religious conscience led him to become more liberal. One day it would lead him into a Labour Government. Hence, when the war came in 1914, to the surprise of everyone, Parmoor was found on the side of the pacifists opposing the war.

He agreed with Erasmus that "war is so pestilent that it blights at once all morality, so impious that it has nothing in common with Christ." As conscientious objectors were persecuted for saying and doing that which Parmoor regarded as in keeping with his own Christian sentiments, he came to their aid. He sought to modify the harsh treatment being meted out to them. Most of them were Christian Socialists. Many were Quakers. It was in this work on their behalf that he met his second wife, Marian Ellis, the daughter of a famous Quaker, the Right Honorable John Ellis.

In 1917 the Government issued an order that no book or pamphlet dealing with the war or the making of peace should be published unless passed by the censor. The Society of Friends felt that this regulation was opposed to the principles of Christian liberty and proceeded to distribute leaflets presenting the facts about the treatment of conscientious objectors. Edith Ellis, twin sister of Marian Ellis, and some other members of the Friends' Committee, were sentenced to six months' imprisonment.

Parmoor became increasingly active. Through Marian Ellis he came into contact with the Swedish Archbishop Soederblum and joined with him in an effort to organize an International Christian Conference "without prejudice to national loyalty . . . to weigh in prayer the duty of the church to resist the passions of war, and to promote that temper which makes for justice and good-will in all the intercourse of Nations." On the visit of President Wilson to London at the end of 1918, Parmoor had led a deputation to the president and presented an address which assured him "of their whole-hearted support of his ideal of the formation of a League of Nations which would present an effective, if not infallible, barrier to future wars, and would do what was possible to insure that justice, instead of force, should be the dominating influence." Parmoor also associated himself with the Lansdowne Peace letter to the press, expressing the demand for moderate peace terms. In March, 1918, he placed the first resolution in favor of a League of Nations on the order papers of the House of Lords.

When his son Stafford began to reflect on these things in the days of his convalescence it was natural that he should begin to respond to the influence of his father and his religious friends. To Parmoor's London house came friends who were deeply interested in the "World Alliance to Promote International Friendship through the Churches" and the "Fight the Famine Council." Stafford was drawn into these discussions and often they were held at Goodfellows. Out of his growing interest, Stafford and Isobel Cripps joined the Alliance and when Doctor Burge was appointed to represent the Church of England at the Copenhagen Conference of the World Alliance in 1922, they went with him to the conference.

Stafford was not approaching the questions raised there as a mere sentimentalist. He knew the legal background of international law and it is possible that from an intellectual point of view his decision to join the World Alliance was not a little due to Hugh Grotius. The masterpiece of Grotius, reverenced as the founder of international law, is contained in an epistle addressed to Louis XIII in which he declared that justice must enter into her own in international affairs in order that the arm of international contract and good faith may be inaugurated; and then, with princes satisfied as to the material and moral expediency of peace, even the widest international difference might be composed, if not by the parties themselves, then by arbitrators, or even international conferences.

After Grotius, a great churchman, had issued his treatise, he turned away from law to a quest for Christian union—to the "visible Unity of Christendom." Many students of history believe that this action was the result of Grotius' recognition that international law, unsupported by the concerted application of Christian principle and doctrine to human society, would be ineffective. There is no doubt that this line of argument appealed to Cripps. He was sure that the Covenant of the League of Nations would not work of itself: motive power was necessary. The only way in which the inefficient judicial machinery for fighting war could be made effective was by anticipating the causes of war, the misunderstandings, the suspicions, the unscrupulousness which both in national and international society lead to strife, and the application of Christian principles thereto. This, according to Bishop Burge, was the work which individuals or bodies professing the religion of Christ, pledged to be His disciples, were called upon to do.

Fired by the enthusiasm of the Copenhagen Conference and its potential promise, Cripps on his return determined to organize the British Council of the World Alliance on more ambitious and determined lines. "Once Stafford Cripps' mind is made up on an issue," a personal friend has remarked, "he expects results the day before yesterday." This is true of him today; it was equally so in 1922. Indeed, Doctor Burge was forced to place a restraining hand on him to approach cautiously the rebuilding of the World Alliance with a powerful British Council.

Burge counseled Cripps against despair at the churches' possible do-nothing attitude, by adding he had reassured Lambeth (headquarters of the Church of England) that it "would be disastrous if anything was done which seemed to be scrapping or superseding the World Alliance." Thus the way was paved for Cripps to buttress the Alliance in Britain. The following spring he was elected to represent the Oxford Diocesan Conference of the National Assembly of the Church of England.

If Cripps is impatient and expects immediate action when a policy has been defined, he is also the hardest worker for it. Between 1923 and 1929 he delivered scores of speeches for the World Alliance. The typical Cripps outlook of this time can best be portrayed by presenting a precis of the pattern of these speeches. They usually began with an account of the endeavors through the centuries to eliminate force from international life as it has been eliminated from national life. The various deterrents are listed; the strong man armed, the balance of power, international police. But all these are unsatisfactory because all are based on force. The only sanction which is stronger than force, and has not yet been tried, is love—love and Christianity. The churches should be the true protagonists of peace; the churches must organize for peace. There follows a brief history of the World Alliance, a sketch of its work on such questions as religious minorities and disarmament, and an account of the special tasks of the British Council. The aims of the Alliance are then stated as the creation of an international Christian conscience and the application of Christ's teaching to our relations with other nations, as we already seek to apply it to our everyday life. The difficulties are listed as "parochialism," unfamiliarity with thinking internationally, ignorance of how the foreigner lives and thinks, and the poisonous prejudices spread by the press against foreign countries. There is no conflict, it is maintained, between patriotism and Christian internationalism. True patriotism does not mean aggressiveness, bullying. Loving our country does not mean hating and despising all other countries—just as loving one's own family does not mean hating all one's neighbors. Family, parish, country, world loyalties, are complementary, not contradictory. To carry all this out needs faith and energy, not lip service. The churches must give a lead, as Bolshevism gives a different kind of lead. Otherwise youth will drift away from Christianity. But difficulties cannot overcome the truly Christian spirit.

Through these speeches Cripps revealed his own credo and his individuality. Sentiments expressed at this time furnish us with invaluable clues to his personality and help us to understand why he acted as he did in subsequent years. His understanding of foreigners might also be due to his many travels abroad and to the fact that many foreign churchmen, legalists, jurists and politicians came regularly to Parmoor during his youth. His advocacy of thinking through a problem and living out the conclusions is his own contribution. That he has insisted on living out his beliefs, that he has been aware of his Christian duty, and that his life is of a one-ness unusual in all life and positively unique in politics, is the result of that mysterious alchemy, personal, indefinable, which distinguishes one individual from another. Inheritance? Being the youngest in a family, dispossessed of maternal affection at the age of four, undue self-reliance, called "Dad" at an early age? These may be psychological indices: they do not explain. Theresa Cripps bore Charles Alfred Cripps four sons and one daughter; aside from a relatively similar upbringing and enjoyment of amenities, Stafford is as different from his three brothers as any stranger might be.

His church activities involved raising sums of money for the

Alliance—which was invariably in financial straits—asking Parmoor for contributions, and contributing goodly sums himself. He was also attending rural diocesan conferences and meetings of the National Assembly, and trying to get the bishops in his own church to take collective action on the burning issues of the day. Although he remained a member of the Assembly until 1929, he became disappointed with the results of his campaigning for the Alliance. The dilatory attitude of both the laity and the clergy depressed him.

Great changes were also taking place in the ranks of the Alliance. Lord Curzon, who had supported Parmoor's motion for the League of Nations in the House of Lords, and Doctor Burge, Bishop of Oxford, both died in 1925. The loss of Doctor Burge in particular was a severe blow to the Cripps family. That he had exercised a great influence on his friend Parmoor, and on the shaping of the outlook of Stafford, is indisputable.

These losses and disappointments caused Stafford to look in other directions. In his earlier speeches he was wont to say that "everyone turns to Christianity on the failure of the politicians." But it was becoming increasingly clear to his pragmatic mind that he would have to turn from the church to politics to apply his Christianity.

And much had happened in the larger world of affairs since 1922 when Doctor Burge held him in leash with kindly warnings. In that year Lloyd George's Coalition Government ceased to cohere. The trade depression was almost at its worst. The trades unions, which had gone through two years of industrial defeats, swung into political action behind the Labour Party. In the December elections of 1923, the Labour vote returned 191 members of Parliament. The Liberals secured 157 seats and the Tories 258. With the consent of the Liberals, the first Labour Government was formed, with Mr. Ramsay MacDonald as the Prime Minister.

This was an event for the Cripps household and relatives. MacDonald wrote to Parmoor immediately after the election:

If I have to try my hand at Ministry making would you be disposed to help me by taking office, say, the Lord President? Or would you come into a more active office like, say, India? Of course this is purely tentative and is by way of sounding you. Perhaps you would be good enough to let me know without delay. . . .

May I add this? I want to gain the confidence of the country and shall suit my policy accordingly. If you could see your way to help me my great personal regard for you would be richly gratified, and I venture to say that you might be doing a useful service to the country. I always remember a talk I had with you by the fire in the Aye Lobby when we sat opposite to each other in the House.

Parmoor replied immediately expressing his deep interest in foreign affairs and sought specific assurance from MacDonald as to their agreement on foreign policy. The outcome was that Parmoor became lord president of the Council and was placed in charge of foreign affairs in the House of Lords. Cripps' uncle, Sidney Webb, was president of the Board of Trade—a post occupied by Cripps himself twenty-one years later. Stafford was greatly interested in these events. On January 24, 1924, he received a letter from his aunt Beatrice, saying:

Sidney was delighted to get your note of congratulation. What a joke it is, your father and he in a Cabinet together. How pleased your mother would have been—I think all the more gratified because it is a Labour Government. She was never keen about Conservative politics, and always looked forward to a re-organised society. It will be very interesting to hear your father's impressions of this strangely assorted group of men coming from all sections of the community.

The Labour Government was short-lived, and was followed by a Tory Government. Domestic events superseded all interest in disarmament and the prevention of another war. The new Conservative administration deemed the time had arrived for Britain to return to the gold standard. That meant, as Mr. Baldwin, the prime minister, put it, "that all the workers of this country have got to take reductions in wages to help put industry on its feet."

The year 1924 had been memorable not only for the fact that for the first time in British history the Labour Party had formed the Government, but also for the renewal of enthusiasm in the trade unions. When, therefore, this new challenge on the economic front came along, the will to resist the demands of the employers and the Tory Government was exceedingly strong. The Government started their offensive against the miners, who labored in a key export industry. To the surprise even of the union leaders, the whole of the Trades Union movement rallied to support the miners. The Triple Alliance of Miners, Railwaymen and Transport Workers threatened to strike together. The Government was not ready to face what would have been a large-scale beginning of a general strike. They retreated by advancing a subsidy of £30,000,000 to the mine owners to cover a period of nine months during which time the mine owners could maintain the existing rates of wages in the industry. In the interim period, known as "the Nine Months Truce," new proposals for dealing with the industry were to be prepared. The day when the Government conceded these terms was called "Red Friday" to contrast it with the failure of the Alliance in 1921 which also had occurred on a Friday and was called "Black Friday."

Of course, during a nine-months truce both sides could have prepared. The only side that did prepare was the Government. Against the day of emergency when the truce should end, the whole country was organized and a strike-breaking body, the "Organization for the Maintenance of Supplies," was set up and trained. Mobile squads of police were prepared and special transport was held in readiness. All was to be set in motion by the one-word telegram from Whitehall—"ACTION."

The situation rapidly became grim and complex. The General Staff of the unions did not want to fight. It never entered their heads that there would be a fight. The fight was thrust upon them. After the Special Conference of Trades Unions Executives had spent two days singing hymns while the leaders "begged and pleaded," seeking for a reasonable way to capitulate without a fight, the delegates were told by Ernest Bevin, leader of the Transport and General Workers Union, that the general strike notices must operate. To their consternation, the spirit of the workers throughout the country was the opposite of that of their leaders. For nine days the strike remained solid. Desperately the General Staff repudiated all "unconstitutional intentions" and all revolutionary implications.

On the ninth day, when the strike was about to extend and the temper of the workers was rising, a somber procession of Mr. Pugh, Mr. Bevin, and Mr. Thomas wended its way to the feet of the prime minister and capitulated—"unconditionally surrendered"—in a fight they had never intended to wage.

On that day, May 11, 1926, one of the most fateful days in British Labour history, a London clergyman wrote to Stafford Cripps:

I am writing of the widespread perplexity among the London clergymen as to what they ought to say or not to say, at the conclusion of the strike, and . . . am trying to get a few level-headed Churchmen together . . . our object will be to formulate some hints as to the best line to be adopted and what questions had better be avoided. Can you spare the time to attend? This effort is well worth while, as our Labour people have generally misunderstood what Church people have said in the past, and with deplorable results.

"And with good reason," Cripps might have replied. He was raising funds to help succor the women and children of the miners. Some years later he expressed himself in very clear terms about this strike:

The most nearly revolutionary incident in our post-war history was the General Strike of 1926. The strike was undertaken for political purposes, though it was expressed in industrial terms. The miners' problem of wages and hours was an industrial problem, but the Government had come to the aid of the mine-owners to assist them in the acute difficulties caused to our coal export trade by the return to the gold standard and the post-war economic conditions of other countries who had been our customers. It was because the demand made was implicitly for some fresh Government action to solve the problems confronting the mining industry, and the mine owners in particular, that the General Strike took place, and necessarily constituted a challenge to the Government of the day. Undoubtedly they who organised and ordered that strike ought to have realised that they were adopting revolutionary tactics. Had it succeeded, it could only have been upon the basis that the workers had compelled the Government by direct, as distinguished from Parliamentary, action to do as they wished.

It failed, not because the response of the workers as a whole weakened, but because those who were responsible for its leadership realised, too late, the full implications of their own actions. It was fear of success and not of failure that caused the strike to be called off.

The miners continued to stand fast for seven months, and then, exhausted and deserted, they gave way. Their hours of labor were lengthened, their wages reduced, and they were thrust lower down in the standards of British industrial wage labor than they had ever been.

The Trades Union Congress met, justified the General Council in the strike and cut off the Anglo-Russian Trades Union Unity Committee because the Russians had denounced their leadership of the general strike as a betrayal of the workers. The working class lay helpless before the onslaught of the Government and employers.

The Government proceeded at once with the Trades Disputes Act, regarded later by Sir Stafford Cripps as the first definite and conscious step in the direction of Fascism in England. The general strike was made illegal; all strikes were made illegal if they extended beyond the limits of a single industry; political strikes were made illegal. The unions of civil service employees were compelled to sever their connections with the Trades Union Congress and the Labour Party; the finances of the Labour Party were dealt a most severe blow. Up to the passing of this act the majority vote of any union favoring affiliation to the Labour Party affiliated all the members with the exception of those individuals who made a written declaration objecting to affiliation. The 1927 act reversed the process. Every member of a union who wished to be affiliated with the Labour Party had to sign a document to that effect.

Nevertheless, the working class recovered from its defeats. The tide turned again and raised the Labour Party to heights it did not expect.

Parliament was dissolved on May 10, 1929. After four and a half years of Mr. Baldwin, who had provoked the general strike of 1926, the British people were looking for a change. In the general election the Labour Party returned 288 members to Parliament. The Conservatives returned 261 members, having lost 139 seats.

Again the Labour Party formed a Government in the precarious position wherein a combination of Tories and Liberals could bring its downfall at will. MacDonald once more was prime minister, and Parmoor became Lord President of the Council and Labour's Leader in the House of Lords. Cripps' uncle, Sidney Webb, now Lord Passfield, was Secretary of State for the Colonies. Arthur Henderson was Foreign Secretary,

George Lansbury, who was to become a close personal friend of Cripps, was the Commissioner of Works. Herbert Morrison, with whom Cripps had become acquainted while conducting cases for the London County Council, became Minister of Transport.

When they thus rode into office once again, full of enthusiasm engendered by victory, they believed that the days of crisis were over. Their outlook was fully in accord with that of the American President Herbert Hoover, who in this same period declared:

. . . the outlook for the world today is for the greatest era of commercial expansion in history . . . unemployment in the sense of distress is finally disappearing; we in America today are nearer to the final triumph over poverty than ever before in the history of any land.

So things would go on from boom to boom with no "slumps." The Labour Government credo was a running buffet providing everything from pure Socialism to impure reformism, from Utopian idealism to sound financial orthodoxy.

It was then that Stafford Cripps became convinced that the changes he most desired in human relations could be effected only by political means, and that in these matters the church had become an effete institution. This is how he stated his position a little later:

I want to address myself bluntly and frankly to that perennial problem of the duty of the Christian Churches towards the great political and economic issues that face us as citizens of our country and the world today. Let me briefly review what contribution Christianity has made to world affairs during the last twelve months.

A thousand Chinese slaughtered in one day in Hankow: . . . the suffering of our people in the distressed areas; the continued starvation of the unemployed; the shooting of people in India; similar tragedies in the West Indies; . . . And what has the organised body of Christians done? Nothing—at least nothing that has had the slightest impact upon the forces of materialism that are responsible for those outrages on civilisation.

Here we have the moral revolt of the conscientious Christian to the church, as an institution, in a state of spiritual inertia.

His experience as a lawyer confirmed his experience in the World Alliance that he must look elsewhere than to the church for an effective means for the practice of his Christianity. He said:

My professional work in connection with the acquisition of land for housing schemes and for new municipal enterprises of all kinds, especially in and around London, took me to slum areas, of the meaning of which I had before been completely unconscious, though I had lived and worked in London all my life! I discovered that in this country of ours the conditions of the workers were appallingly bad. I had long been familiar with the disease-ridden hovels which in many country areas passed for houses, and the tragically low wage levels of the agricultural workers. But for the first time I began to appreciate what the urban slums really signified in terms of suffering, starvation and ill health.

To Herbert Morrison goes much of the credit for bringing Cripps into the Labour Party fold. Writing to Parmoor on April 12, 1929, he said:

For some time I have been wondering if there is any possibility of your son, Stafford Cripps, joining the Labour Party. I have been watching his legal work with interest and admiration and our people admire his splendid work on the London Traffic Bills. It is one of my ambitions to see Stafford Cripps in the Labour Party; I did sound him on the subject some while ago, but he was not clear and I am wondering if it might be useful for me to have another talk with him.

A week later Morrison decided to make the direct approach and wrote to Cripps:

You will remember that some time ago I sounded you on the possibility of you joining the Party. I was aware of the professional considerations which arise but I am personally very anxious to have you in the Party. . . .

Please let me know if and when you would like to join the ranks of the Party and I shall be very happy to make the necessary arrangements, but of course I greatly respect your own scrupulousness in not intending to join the Labour Party until you are quite clear in your own mind that you accept our principles and our policy.

Cripps was conscious that he had now reached a decisive

stage in his career. There was little doubt in his mind that from a practical Christian's point of view the policy of the Labour Party was right and he would support it. But it was another matter to decide that sooner or later he would devote himself exclusively to political work, and one day, not too far distant, leave even his legal career behind him. It was for him an hour of crisis and it reached into his home. There were days and nights of discussion with his wife, Isobel. Together they talked over all that the decision would mean. He was a considerable figure in the legal world. He was high in the councils of the church. He had devoted much attention to the management of Goodfellows farm. And what would become of his hobby of furniture making in the carpenter shop? Then what, too, of the children who were growing up and would need his guidance more rather than less, as they grew? If he decided to enter politics, wouldn't it disrupt the home, take him more and more away from Goodfellows and everything that made up their life there? There were only twenty-four hours in a day, and if he decided in the affirmative *something* would have to go. He and Isobel would have to adjust themselves to entirely new circumstances. His wife's mind was clear enough on the matter. The decision must be Stafford's, and he knew that just as she had been his "good companion" in all phases of their married life, so she would remain in his political life, fostering his ambitions in this direction as she had done in the old ones. They knew that life would never again be the same. But the die was cast. Stafford Cripps became a member of the Labour Party.

V. The New Labour Leader

ERBERT MORRISON, anxious to push Cripps forward into active party work, wrote him again on July 16, 1929:

I did speak to our people at West Woolwich with regard to yourself. I have no doubt you have the electoral history of the constituency since 1918 from which you will see that there has been a consistent growth in the Labour vote and that we nearly won at this recent election. The character of the constituency has changed in recent years owing to the establishment of the Woolwich Borough Council Housing Estate and it is probable that the number of working class electors will tend to increase although there is some middle-class development also.

I am sure you will not mind me reminding you that you are young; that if you do not win a constituency in the first fight you have gained valuable experience and other chances will arise later. I do feel, however, that there is a real substantial chance to win West Woolwich at the next election and that you would be an excellent candidate for the next place.

Cripps accepted the invitation to become the "prospective Labour candidate for West Woolwich." Then suddenly he became the cynosure of all eyes in the Labour Movement. J. J. Moses had been elected member of Parliament, and his opponent tried to unseat him by accusing him of corrupt practices in the election. Moses had to appear as the defendant in a court of law. This was the first time in the history of the Labour Party that an action of this kind had been taken against one of its members, and it was of great importance that Moses should be well defended. Into the breach stepped Cripps, offering his services without charge.

The election law of Britain is not simple. Complexities abound and pitfalls await the unwary. This field of law was not one of

Stafford's specialties, but he marshaled his data and handled his case with masterly ease. Judgment was given in favor of Mr. Moses and the spotlight of another legal triumph fell on the new member of the Labour Party who was the prospective candidate for West Woolwich.

A 1929 Christmas message includes an interesting reminder of Parmoor's continuing interest in his son's political future.

I was introducing Arthur Greenwood and Ramsay MacDonald to the King a short time ago, that they might be made Privy Councillors. This gave me the chance of a talk with them and they both spoke very highly of your law work and progress giving me as a Father, much satisfaction and pride. . . . When Christmas time is over come and have a talk. . . . My own time for public work is running out as it naturally would, but if the Government weathers the various storms, I shall go on with my colleagues, and not desert them.

Parmoor was seventy-eight years of age when this message was written.

Stafford began to make himself acquainted with the people of his constituency. In the speeches of his campaign there is a great similarity of sentiment with that of the earlier World Alliance speeches. But there are new notes. War no longer appears as the primary social evil of the day. Unemployment figures prominently. Through the speeches runs the leitmotiv of "humanization," of unemployment relief, of pensions, of housing conditions, of relations in industry, of international relations. His Socialism at this time was of the kind that appealed to MacDonald, whose ideal was that of the enlightened landowner, who, out of the goodness of his heart, cared for the welfare and raising of the cultural level of the workers.

If all landowners had followed Cripps' example, MacDonald's dream would have come true. For it was in the spring of 1930 that the Witney Rural District Council decided to build four new houses in Cripps' own village of Filkins. They were to be modern houses, built of bricks and mortar, and utterly out of keeping with the native stone architecture of the Cotswolds.

Of all men Stafford loved the Cotswolds. Witness his own poem about them,

O Brave Cotswolds
Rolling hill on hill
Grey in sober strength
Flecked with sun-kissed hamlets
Nestling in deep-furrowed valleys
Pasturing the free-browsing flocks
Whose golden fleeces once
Brought uncounted wealth
And gave your craftsmen power to build
Slender-spired churches and grey grouped homes
Whose beauty yet bedecks your loveliness.

No wonder, therefore, that the proposal of the District Council distressed him. A solution must be found. Afterwards a local newspaper was able to declare that:

Everyone was against it, but what could be done? The Honourable R. Stafford Cripps, K.C., who lives in the village, came to the rescue. He approached the rural District Council, and it was ultimately decided that he should be allowed to erect the houses if he agreed to pay the difference in cost between building them in brick and building them in Cotswold stone. Cripps immediately set to work. The stone was quarried on his own estate; all the labourers, including the foreman mason, were his workers. The architect was Mr. R. Morley Horder. The houses were finally built at a cost of £444 apiece, only a fraction above the price of the vermilion eyesores. They were opened by Mr. Greenwood, Minister of Health, and created a considerable stir in the building world.

That was, for Cripps, practical Christianity and also practical Socialism. But he was soon to be tested in the arena of national politics. Toward the end of 1930 Sir James Melville, the Solicitor General, became seriously ill and resigned. MacDonald appointed Cripps as the new Solicitor General.

On his appointment Stafford was made a knight, as is the custom for this position. But he could not take his place in the House of Commons until elected. Sidney Webb wrote to Parmoor: "We were delighted to see the announcement of the new Solicitor General. I assume that the proper attempts are being made to find him a seat."

Shortly after the appointment, W. T. Baker, the Labour member of Parliament for East Bristol, died. With one accord, the executives of the party sought the adoption of Sir Stafford

Cripps by this constituency. It was not an easy matter to persuade the working class party of East Bristol. The opposition was led by Alderman Hennessy, who was later to become one of Cripps' staunchest supporters. He and others objected to the idea of dumping on them a rich man, an aristocrat, and a knight. Councilor Herbert Rogers writes,

The workers of East Bristol had always been regarded as very radically-minded and there was considerable doubt in the minds of Alderman Hennessy and others as to the reactions of the workers generally, together with his own prejudice, which were very proletarian.

Nevertheless, Sir Stafford was adopted as the candidate, and as soon as he got into his stride in the by-election campaign, he won the whole-hearted support of those who had previously opposed him. On January 16, 1931, he polled 19,261 votes; the Tory candidate polled 7,937 and the Liberal 4,010. Four days later the forty-one-year-old Solicitor General stood before the Speaker of the House of Commons. All eyes were on him as, with Bible in hand, he bowed to the Speaker and swore allegiance to the Crown.

He delivered his maiden speech by introducing the Solicitors' (Clients' Accounts) Bill. With the calm, confident assurance of one who is the master of his subject, he clearly and quietly explained the bill. It was obvious to the members of all parties in the House that in this tall, slim, be-spectacled lawyer a new leader of men was among them.

Parliamentary oratory is quite different from that of the public platform, where one must know how to stir the hearts of the people as well as satisfy their minds; where heat is more essential than light and emotion more convincing than logic. The House of Commons calls for a kind of oratory in which the powers of analysis and logical construction, quick-thinking repartee, and mastery of subject transcend emotionalism. Indeed, emotion must be reserved for the well-chosen occasion, must emerge from deep feeling and conviction and be kept under control. Woe betide the speaker who too frequently mixes too much emotion with too little logic and knowledge of his subject. He will be quickly dismissed as a windbag and find himself speaking to an empty House. The new Solicitor

General was not likely to find himself in this category. Trained to think as an experimental scientist in the chemical laboratory, with years of practice as an exponent of commercial and patent law before the most learned judges of the day, he at once stepped into the front ranks of Parliamentary orators. Lucid in exposition, calm in presentation, with a rich, cultured voice that was at its best in the conversational tones most suited to the House of Commons as an auditorium and debating chamber, Sir Stafford was at home from the beginning. He leaped at one bound into the front rank of the lawmakers. The King's Counsel of the Courts had become the lawyer-politician and leader.

The post of Solicitor General is a lawyer's post. Its holder must fight cases in the courts on behalf of the Crown; he must advise ministers and Government departments on the legality of proposed legislation and guide and direct bills through the House of Commons. As a lawyer, Cripps had to become a politician; as a politician, he was still a lawyer. His briefs were different and his audience was different. It was not he who decided the cases he must now fight in the courts, or the bills he should introduce, or the policy incorporated in them. He had to be, in this apprentice stage of his political career, the voice of the Labour Government, and through it, the voice of the Labour Party, of whose history and social motivation he knew relatively little.

The brief which had given him the opportunity to make his maiden speech was an easy one. His real triumph came quickly afterward when he, with Philip Snowden, the then Chancellor of the Exchequer, piloted the Taxation of Land Values Bill through the House of Commons.

There is probably no country with such a complex system of land tenure as that of Great Britain. Sir Stafford's job was to defend the principle of the taxation of land values. The market value of land increases, whether anything is done to it or not, with the growth of social life around it. It was now proposed that the community should derive some of the benefit thus accruing by placing a tax on the value of land. Cripps had to explain the technicalities of the proposed valuation and the means whereby the new tax would be collected. Introducing the bill, he said:

It was a just means of securing to the community as a whole some part of the wealth which that community has created, and at the same time rendering more free and equitable the sales of land, especially in those cases where land is required for the use of the community.

Everyone who heard this speech recognized the ring of conviction in it. When, on a hot day in July, the bill was accepted by the House of Commons, famous lawyers from the ranks of the opposition paid tribute to the skill of the new leader. Sir John Simon, the famous lawyer-politician, said on behalf of the Liberal Opposition,

The Government in carrying this measure through the House of Commons . . . have had the great assistance of a most notable Parliamentary performance in the work of the Solicitor General.

But a still greater tribute came from Lloyd George, the "father" of the House, another lawyer-politician of high standing. He said,

I should like to begin by saying something with which, I think, the whole House will agree, and that is to join with those who have paid tribute to the extraordinary skill with which the learned Solicitor General has undertaken what I know from experience is an extraordinarily difficult and complicated subject to handle, whether a Bill is right or wrong. . . .
The learned Solicitor General has extricated himself with a skill which has undoubtedly lifted him to the rank of one of the most distinguished Parliamentarians of this generation.

Nor did the tributes end there. As Stanley Baldwin saw Sir Stafford walk into one of the smoking rooms of the House later in the day, he remarked to a friend, "There comes a future Prime Minister."

Cripps was soon to receive his baptism in another kind of leadership. For in these very days in which he turned to account all his legal skill in the service of the Labour Government, Britain was about to receive the full impact of the "economic blizzard" generated in the United States. Probably no government was more oblivious to the oncoming storm than the second Labour Government. When it did arrive, the Government could only explain that it was the victim of "catastrophic developments which could not possibly have been foreseen." Unable to diagnose the real nature of the crisis, the Government had worked out no concerted policy to meet it. As each new blow fell upon them, they simply reversed the engines of social legislation and improvised crisis measures. That which they had promised in the elections did not materialize. The bill for raising the school-leaving age to fifteen was dropped. Promised factory legislation was not produced. The machinery of arbitration was used to lower wages instead of to raise them. The Trades Dispute Bill was withdrawn. The Taxation of Land Values Bill on which Cripps had achieved fame never became law.

Suddenly it was discovered that the budget would not balance. Banks in Europe were closing their doors, the Bank of England was being drained of its gold. The gold standard was in danger. The drain of gold from Britain could be counteracted only by borrowing from France and America; and according to Montagu Norman, the Governor of the Bank of England, the French and American bankers imposed the balancing of the budget as a condition of lending.

The two main suggestions for balancing the budget were tariffs and economies in the social services, especially unemployment relief. The Prime Minister reported that the Bank of England might have to refuse the Treasury the £12,000,000 that was required weekly for the unemployment insurance fund. The story was spread about that actually the French and American bankers determined the issue. As a condition for their lending the £80,000,000 considered essential to maintain the gold standard, it was said that they had insisted not only that the budget be balanced, but that this balance be achieved by cuts in unemployment expenditure. The Opposition parties, Tory and Liberal, were having the time of their lives.

The Cabinet decided to fight. All would stand together to save the unemployed. They would heed Mr. Lloyd George, who had warned them about his own experience, earlier, as Prime Minister:

When I went to the City I was received by the City magnates with frigid and flapping silence, as if they were a row of penguins in the Arctic Ocean. Then they said, "there will be a flight of capital." And there was. These things can be easily arranged. . . . I beg the

Government not to be nervy and jumpy when the City of London threatens.

But Mr. MacDonald had a new shock in store for them. At a Cabinet meeting held on August 23 he put before its members another ultimatum, this time his own—either accept the cut in unemployment benefits or resign from the Cabinet.

When he had their resignations in his hands, MacDonald rose hastily from the table and announced that he would at once seek audience with the King.

The members of the Labour Government naturally assumed that Baldwin would be asked to form a government. But Mac-Donald had something quite different in view. Without a word of consultation with his Cabinet colleagues, without even informing them of his intention, MacDonald proceeded to set up a National Government with himself as Prime Minister— the culmination of a well-thought-out plan.

There was an amazing scene when the Cabinet assembled next morning. MacDonald came in and announced that a new Government had been formed—in short, he was in and they were out. He went on to explain that he had consented to be head of a Government which included members of the Conservative and Liberal parties.

At this time, the period of the summer recess in Parliament and the courts, Stafford Cripps was in a sanatorium in Germany receiving treatment for his intestinal ailment and complications arising from it. He was suffering considerably and was expecting to stay on longer.

On Wednesday, August 26, a telegram reached him with the following message: Hope you are progressing Stop Would you like to go on—Ramsay MacDonald.

Sir Stafford returned to England immediately.

On Friday, August 28, from the Royal Automobile Club in London, he addressed a letter to MacDonald.

It was very kind of you to offer me the opportunity to continue in my post as Solicitor General under the new Government and I am sorry to have had to delay my answer until I came back to this country. I arrived back last night and immediately took steps to acquaint myself with the political situation. I had a long talk with the Attorney General last night and this morning the Lord Chancellor has been good enough to spare me an hour to explain the whole position. It is with very great personal regret that I find myself unable to accept your kind offer.

May I be allowed—without being considered impertinent—to say that I admire immensely the courage and conviction which have led you and other Labour Ministers associated with you to take the action you have taken. My own personal hope is that the rift in the party may be quickly healed and I shall do all I can to attain that end. I should like also to take this opportunity of thanking you most sincerely for your personal kindnesses to me during the past year—kindnesses which I shall always remember.

It would be unprofitable for me to waste your time with any long explanation of my reasons for not accepting your kind offer and I will content myself with saying that I disagree with the policy of the Labour Party taking any part in a National Government having the programme of the present Government.

How little there was to admire of courage and conviction in the decisions of MacDonald and Snowden and Thomas he was soon to learn. But that letter ended chapter one of his political career.

He had hitched himself to the Labour star and he went with the party of his choice into opposition. To this new position he would apply himself as thoroughly and competently as to the old.

There was no doubt that the affairs of Britain and the world were in a state of crisis. The "economic blizzard" had accentuated every problem left by the war of 1914-1918. Unemployment was growing enormously. Foreign trade was slumping. Not only did the budget not balance, but imports and exports did not balance, and the drain of gold to pay for the imports was knocking Britain off the gold standard. Nor could its free-trade economy longer stand the strain. The Tories and Liberals combined to recover at the expense of the social services and the wage earners and to change Britain from a free-trade country to a tariff country. So profound were the crisis conditions and so clearly defined were the class issues that the Labour Party leaders began to speak the language of class war and of Socialism. There was a feeling of revolt throughout the Labour Movement against the policy of "gradualism," that is, the slow reform of capitalism into socialism, personified in the leaders

who had deserted the movement. Everybody agreed that the
Labour Party must formulate a new policy for the new circumstances.

Stafford Cripps was now to contribute to the shaping of the
policy of the party. Hitherto he had expounded high principles
of brotherhood in international affairs and Christian ethics in
social relations, and when he became a member of the Labour
Government he had followed the policy already established by
the party. Now every leader had to think out questions of
policy afresh.

That Cripps was profoundly stirred by the course of events
there is no doubt. In a letter to a friend he said:

The moment had arrived when reformism had to be abandoned.
It had necessarily increased the difficulties of the capitalists with
their rapidly contracting markets, and would no longer be tolerated
without the danger of a complete collapse of the whole system. Two
paths were open: to allow reaction to take charge and to give up
concessions which had been extracted from capitalism; or to proceed to risk the breakdown while making a rapid change-over to
socialism.

He soon got to grips with the technicalities of finance, party
doctrine and economic history, as if he had been handed a new
brief to prepare for the courts. He had a special regard for
William Graham, the extremely able ex-Financial Secretary of
the Treasury. Graham was a member of the Executive of the
Labour Party which would make the new policy. Therefore Sir
Stafford wrote to Graham:

There are three things in the present situation which give me
serious cause for alarm as regards the future of our party and the
country. . . .
The attitude of the rank and file of the Party seems to me to be
extremely dangerous at the moment. There is a strong tendency to
disregard the realities of the situation and to do that for which our
Party has shown such an inclination to do in the past, that is to use
a number of half-digested slogans in place of arguments and to try
to avoid the responsibility of putting forward concrete proposals
for putting into force the ideas which lie behind the policy of the
party in the circumstances in which we find ourselves today. I think
a great deal of the future of the Party will depend upon the expression of opinion in the first few weeks of the new Parliament. If our

back benchers get up time after time in the House and reiterate the vague non-constructive statements which so many of them seem to like, the impression upon the country will be fatal to our future success, and I am afraid that with nothing but a single Party meeting, probably of no great duration, before the Parliamentary fight begins, there will not be time to impress upon our people the absolute necessity for a constructive socialistic plan of coping with the financial situation. I do hope that you and all our other leaders will be able to impress this upon the party. . . .

We are undoubtedly going to be attacked heavily as you will have observed from some of the National Government speakers' speeches on the score of the length to which ex-Cabinet Ministers were prepared to go for the purpose of reaching a compromise. This, it seems to me, unless we are extremely careful, will lead to the impression in the country that there is nothing between the policy of the Labour Party and the National Government except certain details as to how to raise the necessary money to balance the Budget, and, as of course you noticed at the Party Meeting, the Independent Labour Party will take full advantage of this to attack the ex-Cabinet Ministers.

If it is a fact that a General Election is likely to be upon us during the winter it seems absolutely necessary to throw off once and for all the attitude of compromise which was impressed upon us by reason of the minority position in which the Labour Government found itself, and to come out boldly with a slap-up Socialistic policy for dealing with the whole industrial and financial situation. . . . We must, I feel, completely divorce ourselves from the past on the basis that we are now unhampered by the necessity of a compromise with the Liberals and that the recent crisis had shown us that there are only two possible solutions to the difficulties, either a frank reversion to capitalism with its concomitant denudation of social services or a reorganisation of finance and industry on fundamentally socialistic lines and an emergency programme ready to deal with the crisis which will inevitably arise if we come back to power after the General Election. . . .

Here Cripps the pragmatist is getting to work on new problems in the old way—as the lawyer and the experimental scientist. From the study of every brief he had always come forward with a plan of action. He would do the same in the field of economics. He would examine the facts, produce a plan, and seek to apply it with all the fervor of the missionary. It would lead him into strange company, but that would not perturb him. He would show how to bring order out of chaos. The *planner* was on his way.

The letter to Graham is obviously that of a politically mature person who is thinking his way forward and is not afraid to follow the logic of his thinking. But the crisis was not yet spent. Before ever it would be possible to shape the new long-term program for which he called, quick decisions would have to be made on the direction which the new policy of the Labour Party would take.

On September 8, Parliament reassembled to a scene unparalleled in its history. The very structure of the House of Commons lent drama to the occasion. The House was an oblong chamber. A gallery for distinguished visitors was located at the speaker's end and a gallery for the general public at the other end. A gangway separated the tiers of benches upon which sat the members of the rival parties, facing each other. At the top end of the gangway was the speaker's chair upon which sat the speaker, in wig and gown. On the front benches sat the rival leaders, the Government leaders on one side, the Opposition on the other. There were six hundred and fifteen members of Parliament. Every seat was taken, and since there were not enough seats for all, the members crowded into the gangway. The galleries were full to capacity. Face to face on the front benches sat the betrayed and the betrayers.

On the Government bench were MacDonald, Snowden, Thomas, side by side with Baldwin, Chamberlain, and Simon. Incredible! On the Opposition bench Arthur Henderson sat in the place formerly occupied by MacDonald. To him, the defection of his old colleagues was a tragedy from which he would never recover. He had believed in these men, relied upon them as brothers sharing common ideals, serving a common cause, laboring for a common purpose. He sat waiting for the proceedings to begin, not as one ready to leap into the fray, but as an old man, sad at heart, steeling himself for an ordeal. With him sat J. R. Clynes and William Graham, Arthur Greenwood, Herbert Morrison, and George Lansbury. To every one of these, the rupture in the ranks of the leadership of the party had been a deep, personal blow. Beside them sat Sir Stafford Cripps. While the defection of the leaders was a sad disappointment to him, no long personal association was broken. His thoughts turned upon tomorrow, as, upright in his seat, he waited composedly.

Behind the front bench the dense ranks of Labour men stared across the House with mixed feelings of anger and pathos. Behind the Government benches the greater throng of Tories and Liberals rejoiced with mocking smiles and cynical expressions. They waited to cheer MacDonald as he rose to explain the Government's policy and the reasons for his desertion of the Labour Party and the formation of the coalition.

Although long past his prime as an orator, MacDonald was a man of commanding presence and picturesque appearance. His naturally rich voice gave added power to his words. Now he was truculent and challenging. It appeared that he was throwing down the gauntlet of battle to the party he had done so much to build. The somberness of the Labour ranks disappeared the moment he began to speak. Anger and indignation became vocal. But the fight was not yet on. Arthur Henderson, "Uncle Arthur" to the Labour movement, rose to reply and his supporters cheered him as he rose. He waited for the cheers to subside, obviously with considerable emotion, and out of accord with the feelings of those behind him. Quietly yet with great dignity he began:

I hope the House will accept it from me that never on any previous occasion during the eight and twenty years that I have been a member of this House have I risen to address it with a greater feeling of embarrassment than I do today. No one who knows anything about the history of the Party with which I have been so long associated, and who knows anything of the day-to-day collaboration between the Prime Minister and myself, will expect me to have any feeling other than of a difficulty in finding myself called upon to reply to his speech.

MacDonald never once in his speech had referred to his past associations or showed the slightest discomfort about the change in his position. Henderson proceeded:

He and I have occupied the most important offices—shall I say— of the Labour Movement in this country. It has only had two secretaries in thirty-one years. The Prime Minister was secretary for eleven years, and, at his request, I became his successor, a position which I have held just upon twenty years. We have been in two

Governments. Now, I find myself in a position which I never sought, called upon to reply to his first speech under exceptional conditions. May I say that the personal aspect of the case appeals to me very strongly? By the change that had taken place, we had lost three if not four of those who have been in the forefront of the battle, and who, especially in two cases have been associated with the building up of the Movement. It is no use hon. members interrupting me—I shall deliver my speech in my own way. The loss must be felt especially by one situated as I am. I want to say this: whether the withdrawal of our colleagues be long or short, whether it is temporary or permanent, it is a direct loss to the Labour Movement.

Whatever else MacDonald may have done he had delivered a deadly blow to a lifetime friend.

MacDonald received his vote of confidence by 309 votes to 250. Twelve of the majority consisted of former members of the Labour Party. Now the battle had really begun.

VI. Left Turn

IN THE few weeks after the fall of the Labour Government, Ramsay MacDonald encouraged the feeling of panic in the country and posed as the savior of the nation from the calamity of inflation that would follow if England went off the gold standard. That Cripps was not taken in by this is clear from a letter to his father on September 12:

> The position of this country is becoming more and more critical every day, and best opinions we can get all tend to the view that whatever the Government in power, National, Tory, or Labour, it will be absolutely essential to devalue the £ within the next six months, unless strong and immediate international action is taken. There has been a strong swing to the Left in the Party and a general feeling of relief that we have shed a number of members who were on the extreme Right. Opinions differ very much as to what the effect would be of an Election in November, but most people seem to think that if the Election is delayed till next Spring, Labour will have a strong chance of coming back into power. The difficulties as regards the financial position are so complicated and technical that I do not suppose that 1% will even appreciate what they are. On the other hand, they will appreciate that the next Election is a direct fight between Socialism and capitalism. The tariffs issue will no doubt very much complicate the situation, and I am afraid that we as a Party shall have great difficulty in arriving at an agreed policy on this matter.

Hardly had it been possible for the credulous to return thanks for their salvation from "disaster" than one fine morning in September, England slipped off the gold standard. A pound note could no longer look the sovereign in the face without shame and dishonor.

Nevertheless this did not stop Mr. Snowden from re-introducing the "National Economy Bill," with its wage cuts and reduction of unemployment pay as the means to balance the budget and keep England "on gold." There had been several days of debate when Sir Stafford rose on September 29 to move rejection. The House was full. Everybody expected Cripps to make a speech of great merit, but it is doubtful whether even those on the Labour side of the House anticipated a speech so forthright in its denunciation and so revolutionary in its implications. He began:

It is a curious reflection upon the mentality of the Government of this country that they are today pressing forward the final stage of a Bill which, barely three weeks ago, was introduced into this House as an emergency Measure to accomplish one purpose. That purpose was to save the Gold Standard. Intervening circumstances have completely defeated that object; yet the Government are, apparently, wholly unconscious of the failure of their one purpose, and the one object of their existence. Whatever justification there may have been for this Bill when it was first introduced, and up to ten days ago, that justification vanished at the hour in which this country went off the Gold Standard.

Having hammered the point home, he accused the Government and its supporters of a class campaign to depress the standard of living of the workers while the going was good. He roused the anger of the Tories and was often interrupted.

Then he turned his attention to MacDonald. Debating skill and clarity of thought and expression had never been specialties of the prime minister. He was a master of emotional words, the dramatic incident, the sonorous and the sentimental, the colorful dream and splendid peroration. For Sir Stafford, with his rich experience as a lawyer, MacDonald was an easy opponent who had in recent days made himself exceedingly vulnerable.

"Let me remind the House of the words which were used by the Prime Minister on the 8th of September," continued Sir Stafford, looking directly at MacDonald. He described how on that occasion the whole world was waiting with anxiety to hear a statement as to the financial position of the country and its power to stand up against any further drain of gold. The prime minister had said: "One day it (the pound) would have been twenty shillings and the next day ten shillings, and it would have tumbled without control."

He assured the House, said Sir Stafford, that he was not scaremongering. Again he repeated the prime minister's words:

I am not scaremongering; I am not scaremongering; I am giving you some history. That happened in Berlin. What then would have happened? . . . War pensions, old age pensions, health and insurance benefits would become worth, as they became in Germany, only the price of a newspaper. In Germany and Vienna people rushed to convert their whole life-savings into some tangible article, or offered everything they had for one square meal.

Cripps added:

The "talkies" too, were called to his aid. The day before this House met—on September 7—a picture of the prime minister was shown throughout the country holding an envelope with stamps amounting to eighty billion marks, and, at the same time he explained the picture with these words:

"I hold in my hand an envelope of a letter posted in Berlin and sent to England at the time that the German credit was smashed. You will observe that the postage stamps upon it amount to the colossal sum of 80,000 million marks, a sum which was once equal to £4,000,000,000. That is the result of a smash in the credit of a country. Those of us who are now in power are not going to allow this country to sink into that deplorable position, and so I appeal to you all to do your bit."

That [said Sir Stafford] was a perfectly fantastic comparison which every financial authority in this country knew to be wholly unwarranted, but it was well and truly calculated to raise an atmosphere of panic in which legislation of this type might be passed without question or criticism, and, unfortunately, too well calculated to inspire those in other countries who had but a small knowledge of our financial position with a complete lack of confidence.

Now, turning toward Neville Chamberlain, the Minister of Health, Cripps said:

On September 14th, the Right Hon. Gentleman, the Minister of Health, made this statement to the House: "It was the duty of the foreign bankers when approached, to state under what conditions they thought it possible to raise the money." . . .

If money is raised on conditions, as the House knows, the borrower is generally bound, morally at least, to carry out those conditions. I do not think that anyone has yet told us what those conditions were, or whether we are morally bound by them; and I ask the Right Hon. Gentleman to tell us categorically what are the conditions that he mentioned in his speech of 14th September, and how far we are bound morally to see that those conditions are carried into effect.

He now gave way for the reply. Chamberlain rose and said:

The Hon. and learned Gentleman is confusing the issue. It is perfectly obvious to what my observations referred on that occasion. The conditions were not the conditions of a bargain; they were the conditions under which the bankers who had to raise the money thought it would be possible to do so in their markets.

This answer was not precise enough for Sir Stafford. So with the urbanity of the well-poised lawyer he pursued Chamberlain,

I am only too happy to accept the Right Hon. Gentleman's answer if he means this, and this is what I as a lawyer do not quite appreciate: you ask a lender the conditions upon which you can get money from somebody else. He is to help you to raise the loan. He tells you that there must be certain conditions, and you say, "Go on and raise the loan." Does the Right Hon. Gentleman suggest that in those circumstances you are not bound to observe those conditions—not legally bound, but morally bound to observe them?

Chamberlain tried again. He answered,

The conditions were merely the conditions under which it would be possible to raise the money. What the late Government had to be sure of was that there would be sufficient confidence in foreign circles in the determination of the British Government to set their house in order and to balance their Budget.

Sir Stafford continued,

I am afraid that it would be improper for me to continue the cross-examination of the Right Hon. Gentleman, so I must accept his answer as meaning that we are not bound morally or otherwise by any conditions whatsoever as regards this £80,000,000 credit. The Right Hon. Gentleman acknowledges that statement by nodding his head. Therefore we can both, as regards this House and the country at large, remove that hedge behind which the Government has sought to take refuge.

He went on to tell the House that the major question they had to solve was not the balancing of the budget, but the far more serious question of how to balance trade. The conclusion of the speech was of great significance as a pointer to Cripps' own future policy and the Labour Party's turn to the left. He wound up thus:

We on this side of the House have long predicted that capitalism as a system would fall. We now see that it has brought the whole structure of finance and industry to ruin, inflicting fresh miseries and sufferings on the workers throughout the world. We shall fight this Bill to the end.

We believe that instead of trying to rush through a Bill of this sort the first vital matter to be attended to is the reorganisation and reconstruction of the financial machinery and industries of this country, so that the full benefit may be derived from them, not by those who own the capital, but by the nation as a whole, and to this end the financial and industrial machine must be brought under public control.

This speech roused enthusiasm in the depleted ranks of Labour. But the Labour Party was not to enjoy a respite. The Government dissolved Parliament on October 7, while the thirty-first annual conference of the Labour Party was being held in Scarborough. The election was set for October 20.

The 1931 conference of the British Labour Party "sat throughout in an atmosphere of challenge," said Arthur Henderson. According to Henderson:

All parties to the decision of dissolution had realised the overwhelming importance of inflicting upon the Socialist Party a crushing defeat. All the world over . . . (capitalism) has broken down. You have said with emphasis that you refuse any longer to tinker with its patent inadequacies. On the other hand is Socialism, which is now definitely recognised as the only alternative to the present chaos.

Everybody talked Socialism at this conference. J. R. Clynes, the little, able, elderly, staunch gradualist, declared:

We are no longer frightened by the term Socialism. We must affirm it more than ever in this coming election as an alternative to the crushing burdens of the vicious and foolish system of capitalism which has produced poverty in the midst of plenty, and in the face of these facts I ask you unanimously to confirm your Socialist faith.

A resolution by F. W. Pethick-Lawrence, the experienced

financial expert of the party, demanded the nationalization of
the banks and credit system. It was in this atmosphere that Sir
Stafford Cripps made his first speech at a party conference.
Speaking on "unemployment cuts," a ringing debut for the
rich lawyer, Cripps remarked that "The one thing that is *not
inevitable* now is *gradualness*." Attacking relief cuts and the
Means Test, he said:

The unemployed problem in this country is one of the main
symptoms of the breakdown of capitalist organisation. It is their
duty, as it is the duty of any system of industrial organisation, to
supply work; and if work cannot in any special circumstances be
supplied, then maintenance must be given in its stead.

These measures and maintenance, necessary as they are in a
period of transition, are mere hospital work, and we are not to do
hospital work for the Juggernaut of Capitalism. We are here to
stop that Juggernaut from his progress through the world.

The recent crisis, . . . I think, brought home to all of us that the
time has come when we can no longer try with one hand to patch
up the old building of Capitalism and with the other to build
Socialism.

Thus the defection of hitherto beloved leaders pushed the
surviving Labour leadership into a wave of uncompromising
Socialism. In the demure words of Mr. Attlee, some years later:

. . . the revulsion from MacDonaldism caused the party to lean
rather too far toward a catastrophic view of progress, and to em-
phasize unduly the conditions of crisis which were being experienced.

Stafford Cripps was in the forefront of this "swing to the
left." He created a profound stir throughout the country by
his by-election speech at Hull, when he bluntly stated that
Labour had a "complete scheme to take over the Bank of England, to be followed by the control of the joint stock banks, the
discount houses, and the complete financial apparatus of the
city." He announced that all foreign securities would have to
be mobilized with a view to ensuring the stability of the currency. There would be a national investment board, a reorganization of the basic industries, power, transport, iron, and steel
as public services, and nationalization of the land.

As the election drew near, Sir Stafford's relatives were watching the scene and his part in it with the greatest interest. Beatrice Webb wrote to Parmoor on October 20, 1931:

On the whole I rejoice in the crisis as I think it will clear the issue and purify the party. Sidney and I were so glad at Stafford's attitude towards things and to see the ease with which he gets on with the other leaders and with the rank and file of the Labour Party.

I wonder what is your forecast of the results of the election: Sidney and I estimate a loss of 100 seats owing to the withdrawal of Liberals in three-cornered constituencies. . . . However, as I want the Labour Party to have more time for thought about the future I am not keen on it taking office for another five years.

The spokesmen of the "Nationals" (Tory, Liberal, "Labour" Coalition) were in high glee. Since the end of the war in 1918 they had succeeded, in every election, in raising a panic issue. Now they caricatured Labour's program as "bolshevism run mad" and put out the story that "Mr. Henderson's hooligans" planned to seize the deposits in the Post Office Savings Bank.

It is doubtful if, in the history of British general elections, the reactionaries have ever conducted a more despicable campaign. Sir Stafford, now notorious for his revolutionary speeches, received the full impact. Herbert Rogers, Sir Stafford's election agent in Bristol East, writes:

During the General Election of 1931, a vile campaign was conducted against Sir Stafford Cripps, and his opponents adopted the most unscrupulous methods. The following is an instance: There is one area (which usually polls 75% to 80% Labour) in which a large factory is situated, employing in normal times upward of 1,000 hands, and in recent years this had been converted to the manufacture of artificial silk. With the slump in the artificial silk industry, the whole district had been reduced to poverty, aggravated by the fact that many of the workers had invested their small savings in the industry. Three days before Polling Day, huge posters appeared on the boardings—"Return National Government and Silk Mills will be reopened." This was followed on the eve of the Poll and during Polling Day itself with the lighting of certain fires, smoke being visible through the tall chimney stacks. One can appreciate the effect this might have had upon the voters in such a district where poverty had been widespread since the closing down of the factory. However, in spite of a terrific barrage he did increase his poll over that of the By-election by 200 votes, and won with a majority of 429.

The election returned 471 Conservatives to Parliament and gave the Labour Party only 46 seats—a loss of 219. Parmoor was astounded by the results. He wrote to Stafford:

What a crushing blow. There it is, and the only moral is to look forward to a resurrection. I never thought that our late Prime Minister could give such a blow to his own party, but he and Snowden have done their best to crush us and have so far succeeded. Thank goodness you are saved out of the wreck, but this will mean a great deal of anxiety for you. . . . God bless you and yours, my dear boy, and let us start again together.

Nevertheless Parmoor deemed it the right moment for him to retire from the leadership of the Labour group in the House of Lords.

Replying on October 31, 1931, to a double-edged note of congratulation from his former housemaster at Winchester, a Conservative, Cripps wrote:

It is very kind of you to write me so understanding a letter, and I agree with you that from a purely personal point of view it would have been more comfortable to have been out of the House at present. I naturally take a rather different view as regards the present situation to that which you express in your letter, but these differences I feel can have no effect upon a friendship between people who are both anxious to do their best for the country. . . .

Our fundamental difference of outlook is, I think, that you envisage a possibility of the permanent continuance of our present social order, while I do not. Once you have educated the population with the franchise, I believe it is inevitable that the overwhelming majority of the people which consists of the working classes will insist upon controlling the affairs of this country in their own interests, and my desire is to assist them to do this in the wisest possible way.

Back to the House of Commons came Sir Stafford. But what a scene was there! The Labour Party had only forty-six members to wage its fight. Gone too were all but three of the leaders who had graced the front Opposition Bench. Only George Lansbury, Clement Attlee, and Stafford Cripps were left. The Tories had a free hand. MacDonald and his erstwhile colleagues might occupy front seats on the Government benches, but it was obvious that Baldwin would call the tune.

That the fall of the Labour Government had given the whole Labour movement a jolt to the left is unquestioned. The striking thing about all the debates at this time is that everyone either fought shy of the most significant features of the situation or became lost in generalities about the crisis of capitalism. Nobody had drawn attention to the fact that Britain's being forced off the gold standard in the war of 1914-1918 signified the beginning of the eclipse of the British Empire, the emergence of the dollar standard, the rise to world power of American economy, and the regrouping of the powers in the struggle for control in various parts of the world.

The leaders of Britain were frightened by the Russian Revolution but oblivious to the significance of the development of the United States. Their outlook was "back to normalcy," which meant back to 1914. It never dawned on them that Britain's pre-eminence was gone forever and that the real challenger had overtaken her even while she was busy settling accounts with Germany. Nor had it dawned on them that the gold standard rose and fell with the peculiar conditions which accompanied the transformation of Britain into the "workshop of the world." It became a workshop with an agrarian hinterland only developed enough to feed half her people. Once there appeared on the horizon a greater power than she, which could export to her and to others on a scale unprecedented, and this power *could not sufficiently take payment in goods* but only in dollars or their equivalent in gold, the days of the gold standard were numbered, and so was the pre-eminence of the British Empire.

The crash of 1931 shook Britain from end to end. The Conservative leaders dropped all their efforts to restore the gold standard, slipped into the fluid realms of "managed currency," and desperately sought to pull the Empire together. But this was no British renaissance. Old men were in the saddle. MacDonald was old and gray. Snowden was old and soured. Baldwin was looking forward to his retirement, when he could leisurely browse among his books and stroll around his country grounds. Chamberlain sat on the Government front bench with the vision of a Birmingham cashier and the demeanor of a permanent depression. They were not merely physically old. They were spiritually old. It was they who began the process of adaptation to the twilight of the British Empire, snarling at the social revolution and retreating before the rivals of their empire in the name of "peace" and "safety first." They had seen the rise of Mussolini in Italy and were rather pleased with the way he had handled the labor problem. They were not unhappy at all about the advance of Hitler in Germany. They never dreamed that these new powers emerging from the ruins of war would leap at the British Empire and threaten its very existence. They still thought of Japan as an old ally who could be relied upon as a friend in the Far East against the encroaching power of the United States and the Russian Revolution. They regarded the shifting of the headquarters of finance from London to New York as only a temporary dislocation that would be set right when things became "normal" again.

Such was the position when Sir Stafford Cripps and his forty-five colleagues assembled for the opening of the new Parliament in November, 1931. They had to elect the leader of the Labour Party. Here was an extraordinary situation which, had Sir Stafford been a man of careerist ambitions, he could quickly have turned to account; he could have stepped into the shoes of Arthur Henderson as leader. Although his political experience had been very short, in most of the qualities of leadership in Parliament he was well ahead of any of the forty-six.

The two others with front-bench experience were George Lansbury and Clement Attlee. Lansbury had the qualifications that Sir Stafford lacked. He had behind him a long experience of the Labour Party. He was known throughout the length and breadth of the land. He was elderly but still a man of great vigor and youthful spirit. He had the human touch. His ruddy complexion, surrounded by his white hair and chopped beard, and his affectionate bearing toward his fellow men, were familiar to every group of Labour people. It would be no exaggeration to describe him at this time as the best-loved leader of the British Labour movement. His election to the leadership of the party was therefore natural and almost automatic.

Next came the election of Clement Attlee as Deputy-Leader.

Again, Attlee was an older man than Sir Stafford, with more than a quarter of a century of party experience behind him. Also, he could give all his time to the job. Cripps was still practicing at the Bar and his services as a leading lawyer were in great demand. The fact is that he did not strive to supersede either Attlee or Lansbury, whose Parliamentary fellowship meant much to him. Within two years Attlee succeeded Lansbury, and personal conditions arose which caused Attlee to contemplate resigning in favor of Sir Stafford. Instead of taking advantage of this, Sir Stafford organized the solution of the difficulties and persuaded Attlee to continue.

So there was no struggle for leadership in these first days of the new opposition. On the contrary, there began a warm friendship between the three men. They had much in common. None of them was an iconoclast of the revolutionary seizure of power. The revolution they sought was the Christian revolution of the heart and the mind of the individual, which would bring the economic and social revolution through the peaceful ways of constitutional change. Never were three men more fundamentally in accord, and their friendship became deep and enduring.

There were, however, differences among them in temperament and personal history. The two elder men were seasoned party members with an abundance of patience derived from long years of persistent struggle against the stream. Sir Stafford was young in party history, highly intellectual, and impatient for results. He had examined the crisis which had brought about the fall of the Labour Government as if it were a lawyer's brief, had come to sharp revolutionary conclusions, and was ready with his plan for quick fundamental changes in the structure of society.

But the effect of the heavy defeat of the Labour Party was twofold. The more conservatively minded of the party, and the trade unions, now blamed the leftward turn for the defeat. The party had gone too far to the left and frightened the people, they declared. Sir Stafford and others were still of the opinion that there could be no return to gradualism, and, as the small contingent of Labour M.P.'s lined up behind Lansbury for the battle to begin in the House of Commons, there began also a struggle in the larger Labour Movement outside of Parliament. In this, Sir Stafford sought to capture the mind of the Labour Party and secure it for a revolutionary socialist economic policy. But it is a dangerous thing when a "gentleman" embarks on revolution, however constitutional it may be in its conception, if he is armed only with high ideals and great principles.

VII. The Gathering Storm

URING these autumn days of 1931 in which the "economic blizzard" from the United States reached increasing ferocity, a bomb exploded on a railway in far-off Manchuria. The Japanese invasion of China had begun. Less than thirteen years after the end of the First World War came the first bomb of the Second World War.

At the end of the war of 1914-1918 the victorious powers Britain, France, and the United States had set up a new regime. Its pillars were the Versailles Treaty in Europe, the Nine Power Pact in the Far East, the League of Nations, the Kellogg Pact to outlaw war, and a Disarmament Conference. Outside the framework of this system stood Soviet Russia, the organized embodiment of social revolution unleashed by the war and against which the "peace system" was also organized. Then, simultaneously with the economic crash in the West, Japan tore up the Nine Power Treaty and the Kellogg Pact—a foreshadowing of what Germany and Italy would do with the Versailles Treaty as the League of Nations went into a state of dissolution. But no one in the House of Commons on the day when the work of the new Parliament began thought of this background to the speeches.

It fell to Sir Stafford to challenge the King's speech with an Opposition amendment. On behalf of the Labour Party he moved that at the end of the address be added the words:

but regret that Your Majesty's advisers have no policy for the planning and co-ordination under public ownership or control, of the principal industries, including agriculture and the banking and financial machinery of the country . . . and all the factors which are at present constituting economic barriers against the free flow of international trade . . . and further regret that there is no mention in Your Majesty's gracious speech of any intention of reversing the unjust economies imposed upon the unemployed and other classes of persons, or of restoring and developing the social services.

Sir Stafford was facing a packed and hostile House. The distinguished strangers' gallery and the gallery for the populace were full and the floor of the House was packed. Government supporters filled both the Government side and the Opposition side, except for the small corner behind the front Opposition bench, in which were squeezed the few Labour supporters.

Cripps told the House that the Government had "no policy whatever to put forward" and proceeded to show the kind of program he thought was necessary. He urged

the summoning of an international conference to deal with international economic difficulties . . . war debts, reparations, their relationship to subsequent commercial debts and municipal loans . . . to deal with disarmament, currency and exchange problems . . . to make a real big effort to break down the economic barriers against the free flow of international trade.

To relieve the economic distress in Britain he called for "a definite plan for the co-ordination of industry, agriculture, and finance, so that the national resources may be pooled and used in the best interests of the nation as a whole."

He wound up his much-interrupted speech with a plea that the Government relieve the unemployed. Neither this appeal, nor another which he made before the Christmas recess, had any effect other than to call from the prime minister, Ramsay MacDonald, the accusation that Cripps was being swayed by "the genial humor of human sympathy."

But there was not much genial humor in the way Sir Stafford handled MacDonald in those days. The prime minister, speaking in Luton, had denied his responsibility for reducing the allowances of the unemployed. Sir Stafford dealt with him as a prosecutor deals with a prisoner in the dock. Standing erect, facing the Government front bench, his arm outstretched and his accusing finger pointing at MacDonald, he said, "I should like to give the Prime Minister an opportunity of answering a question."

He stopped for a moment as the attention of the whole House became riveted on the scene. Then he went on, "He said at Luton that the Government were being accused of responsibility for reducing the allowances of the unemployed and that was not true. Would the Prime Minister kindly say who was responsible?"

Seeing no signs of response from MacDonald he continued, "I am prepared to give way if he will answer the question." Still there was no answer. MacDonald sat looking down frowningly at the treasury table before him.

"The Right Hon. Gentleman is apparently incapable of stating whether his own statement is true or not," Sir Stafford taunted. Still no answer.

Pointing again at MacDonald, he said, "When I speak at Luton on Thursday, I shall tell the people he was unable to answer the question in the House of Commons. Will the Right Hon. Gentleman wish to say something?"

He paused again, still poised erect, pointing his finger at the gloomy figure before him. "Apparently, no," he concluded. "He is trying to shelter himself against some vague suggestion of responsibility in some other quarter. Surely a rather despicable piece of conduct."

But nothing would draw out the frowning MacDonald, and Sir Stafford turned from him with contempt.

At the end of the session in December, 1931, Stafford wrote to his father:

The Session ended quite satisfactorily I think, but the atmosphere of the House forebodes a full Tory administration very shortly, unless the Liberals give up every principle they have. The atmosphere in the country, so far as our Party is concerned, is I think improving, and people are beginning to realise that the National Government is not an unmixed blessing when it means reaction."

When Parliament reassembled in February, 1932, Neville Chamberlain, now become Chancellor of the Exchequer, went into action. The struggle of Britain to find her new place in the stormy scene of world affairs was his responsibility.

Chamberlain announced a general duty of ten per cent on all imports, except, be it noted, on wheat and meat. He announced an Import Duties Advisory Committee, which would have the power to remove articles from the free list to the tariff list without reference to Parliament for approval. The next step was to move toward Empire free trade and the famous Ottawa

Conference, which established a system of imperial preferences and quota schemes for wheat and meat.

This was economic nationalism in full swing, whereby the National Government, with the aid of the depreciated pound, hoped to win back the markets lost since the beginning of the great slump. Chamberlain took up Sir Stafford's suggestion about a world economic conference but held it over until after the Ottawa Conference. Whatever chance there may have been of a world economic conference achieving success before the Ottawa Conference, there was none afterward.

When Neville Chamberlain, official spokesman for British big business, addressed the World Economic Conference in 1933, he referred to the "economic warfare which has arisen between us and other countries," and added,

We must maintain that warfare, so long as it is the other countries who have taken the aggressive and are unwilling to make any sort of reparation or restitution for the wrongs they have done us.

Such injured innocence, in this sophisticated age, can only be admired; but it was surely a little ungenerous of Chamberlain to identify virtue so completely with his own cause. Sir Stafford suggested that the National Government pursue a policy such as President Roosevelt was then advocating in America

to inject purchasing power in the system by means of forced expenditure of some sort or another, and it is by means of pumping in the consuming power to start with in order to meet production that a revival of the price level will be brought about.

The suggestion made no headway. The World Economic Conference was a dismal failure. Instead of the stabilization of currencies, the lowering of tariff barriers, and the like, the conference was followed by a currency war, more tariffs, and intensified competition.

Meanwhile there came a sequel to the explosion of the bombs in Manchuria. The Chinese appealed to the League of Nations and the signatories of the Nine Power Pact to stop the Japanese invasion. Not only the Chinese, but all the world, looked to the League to block the path of the aggressor. The principal powers involved were Britain and America. In this case America was prepared to honor the Nine Power Treaty, for thereby she could put a spoke in the wheel of Japan. The British National Government was not prepared to join with America in that purpose or to stand by the pledges to the League.

The conservatives of Britain had never forgiven America for forcing upon them the abrogation of the Anglo-Japanese Treaty at the Washington Conference of 1922. That treaty had been signed in 1905 with a twofold purpose. It was designed to stem the advance of Russia and America into China. Without an ally in the East, Britain's pre-eminence in the Far East was gone forever. Japan was her hope against the two-way encroachments. When China pursued her appeals to the League, Simon, Britain's foreign secretary, was applauded by the Japanese Minister, who testified that Sir John had made out a better case in justification of Japan's invasion of China than he could himself have made. When Stimson made the declaration that the American Government would not recognize any Japanese gains from aggression, and declared again for the validity of the Nine Power Treaty, Britain refused to join with America. When Lord Lytton, on behalf of the League of Nations, headed a mission of investigation into Japan's actions in Manchuria, the Government made it clear that it would take no action to implement the Covenant of the League against Japan.

The cynical duplicity of the British Government with regard to League obligations marked a decisive turning point in Stafford Cripps' attitude to international affairs. When the report of the Lytton Commission was discussed in the House of Commons in 1933, he said:

It is important to notice that the findings of the League of Nations are based upon a series of breaches of faith by the Japanese. Since this is true, the question now arises, what are we to do as a sequel to Japan's action upon the League of Nations' report? . . .
Are we merely going to put ourselves into the position of performing what we would call the centuries old ceremony of kowtowing to the bullies of the world, or are we going to say that the theory of sanctions is a real theory, and it, indeed, is a theory and a practice that was invented for the purpose of assisting in keeping peace, and are we going to apply it? Probably the Foreign Secretary will not answer that question tonight, but sooner or later this

House will have to come to a determination as to whether they are to treat Article XVI as a mere scrap of paper.

It was a pity that he left the Foreign Secretary free to dodge the question! Although he regarded Sir John Simon's actions as morally indefensible, he did not yet see the full significance of Japan's invasion of Manchuria in relation to the world situation as a whole. In leaving Simon free to reply at a more convenient season, instead of forcing him to be explicit, he left the Government with the benefit of the doubt, and the interpretation of its policy toward the League to be determined by implication and future events.

Sir Stafford could not himself dismiss the League and its Covenant so cynically. He had idealized the League since it was launched in 1919. It had become part of his religious equipment, had been to him the means for Christian practice in international affairs as the Labour Party was in home affairs. Now he felt himself driven to the conclusion that to hope for sanctions or any collective action to stop war or to secure disarmament was futile as long as a capitalist government controlled British affairs. This was a negative decision but a very important one for him in this period when the Labour Party was re-shaping its program.

Those who had been outspoken against the old gradualist policy saw the need for a new statement of policy. They saw also the possibility of another financial crisis should the Labour Party be returned to power. How should they prepare to handle such a crisis? The House of Lords stood in the way. Therefore one of the first things the next Labour Government must do would be to clear the House of Lords out of the way. Then by means of emergency powers it would quickly nationalize the banks, take control of the financial apparatus, and put into operation a program of nationalization of coal, electricity, gas, transport, banks and key industries, and the land. This group planned to persuade the party to adopt their "alternative to gradualism."

They formed the Socialist League, which brought together a number of able people, the most "left" of the Labour Party's intelligentsia. The first chairman was Mr. F. E. Wise, an economist and business adviser. Sir Stafford Cripps was on the executive committee, which was a galaxy of intellectual talent comprised of Christian Socialists, pacifists, variants of Marxists, ex-Communists, and ex-members of the Independent Labour Party. All were ready to join the leftward drive. At their first national conference, held at Leicester in the same week as the national conference of the Labour Party, they drew up a program which was in reality an expansion of the program Sir Stafford had been formulating and advocating since 1931.

Sir Stafford was later to be accused of organizing and financing the Socialist League as his means of winning the leadership of the Labour Party. That he was the main source of financial aid was true, but that the Socialist League had anything to do with a fight for leadership was untrue. He was fighting for ideals, not leadership. The fact is that his activities with the Socialist League proved ultimately to be the cause of his loss of leadership in the Labour Party.

Beatrice Webb had written to him at the end of 1931 expressing her solicitude for his position. She said:

I am afraid you must be feeling rather lonely on that Opposition bench, though Lansbury seems to be doing well in his own way and creating a certain impression of directness and honesty as well as good humour.

I am also afraid that you will find it rather difficult to combine a busy professional career with leadership in the House of Commons and that even solicitors may be frightened off by some aspects of your public work. However, that is the penalty of taking up the cause of the bottom dog—the upper dog will not love you!

She had really no need to be afraid on either count. His professional work was flourishing more than ever, while on the Opposition bench there was close friendship among the three leaders and especially between Sir Stafford and George Lansbury. They were frequent visitors to each other's homes and they discussed together their personal problems in relation to their politics. A letter from Lansbury to Stafford written on July 17, 1932, after a visit to Goodfellows where they unburdened themselves, reveals how greatly shaken Lansbury had been by the confusion in Labour's ranks:

I have wanted to talk or write to you ever since we had the talk during which I said I felt like joining the Communists and you replied if I went wrong you would lose faith in everybody.

The fact is, life becomes more and more difficult for me, everything gets so mixed, persons, causes, tumble into each other and form such a hotch potch of ideas that truth or what seems like truth gets quite smothered. Sometimes my daily tasks come and go quite easily, at other times my whole being gets overwrought. At other times I am not certain of my own action because sometimes you others see the right course different from myself. One day the party seems all important, the next day quite unimportant because its interests seem to conflict with truth. Then I find myself smothering my own mind and thoughts because others think a certain way better than mine, but over-riding everything is the simple fact that full of guile of sorts as I am, my wickedness is not of the kind that can stand up to the guile of men like Simon or J. R. M. I hear words from them which mean certain things to the ordinary men and something else to the men who use them. Consequently I am often on the wrong tack.

But my chief thought is the multitudes outside who *trust* us, those thousands who pin their faith to our assurance that given power, big things will be attempted. I think of myself, even if I live to see us in power, will it be possible for me to keep my faith. *The thought of leadership does not enter, it is as one of the 350 in the House* and then when the others come under review, what a mixture of personal ambitions and ignorance confronts us and this appals me. . . .

Somehow, in ways it is impossible to describe, I get bewildered by the fact that though we cannot live without bread, it is equally if not more true we *cannot* live with it alone. I have striven hard to make myself and others see that we must each lose our lives in the life of the Community and while fighting for bread and rights for ourselves, we must never forget the common weal, but the last has been buried in words and as a result our movement is full of men and women who measure success by what it brings to them. This is not a fault of mine, it is perhaps the only decent thing that has remained firm and fixed since my earlier enthusiasm. . . .

I believe the world, and our people especially, need a purely religious message, not theological, in fact the world needs this more than anything else. . . . Yet there come days when my want of faith both in our actions and our courage and discretion worries me to distraction. I laugh and keep as stout a heart to the hills of difficulty as is possible, but often my heart fails and my soul seems to cry out within me whether I am spending my old age in the way that is

best. At the start I felt God had given me a task to do, it may be
He has, my doubt is whether I am good enough to do it or whether
the way is right. You must not imagine there is self-righteousness in
what I say now, but it is true my mind does not allow me to see
more than a very few who see the impersonal side of life as I know
I do, yet if we cannot within the framework of our party get together a body of men and women, especially young ones, who will
see the cause of Socialism as a religion to be served as St. Francis
and Tolstoi served their faiths, all our work is hopeless. . . .
   It is me and my own faults and shortcomings and misgivings
which perplex and baffle me and make me so tiresome in thought
and action. Don't answer.

   What reply Sir Stafford ever gave to that letter in conversations, I do not know. But the significant recalling of "if I went
astray you would lose faith in everybody" is a touching evidence of the admiration Cripps had for Lansbury. To find
that Lansbury, who talked the same language of Christianity as he, and held the same fundamental beliefs, had
such doubts and fears that he "felt like joining the Communists" was a shock. Such a decision would have struck at the
very foundations of Sir Stafford's beliefs. Lansbury did not join
the Communists, and together they traveled the revised Fabian
way.
   Shortly afterward, Lansbury had a talk with "Uncle Arthur"
Henderson, who had become very worried about their "left"
agitation. Now he was afraid lest the Labour Party move too
fast for the economically minded trade unionists. Lansbury
wrote to Stafford:

   I saw Uncle Arthur yesterday. I do not think he is very well
though he says he is. I found him a bit upset with the sort of forward policy we aim at. He talked of miners and others demanding
something to go on with and not being content to wait for Socialism.
This seems like our old friend Gradualism with a vengeance. I
reminded him that at Scarborough all our speakers deliberately and
after due consideration declared we could not deliver the goods re.
Social service etc., within the capitalist system. He is not anxious
for us to be too definite about big Socialist measures as our first
objectives. Put them in our programme, but be sure when we come
to power to keep our line of least resistance. He is not dishonest
or to be blamed for this attitude. Like me he has spent his whole
life doing small things while advocating big "changes." You must

make him see the movement he has done so much to foster will perish if once again it gets lost in the morass of gradualism.

I send you this note because he told me he is seeing you this week-end. . . .

In December 1932 Lansbury and two others went on a deputation to Ramsay MacDonald which called forth from him sad observations on his old colleague of earlier days. He wrote to Cripps:

I must tell you about J. R. M. when we meet. He is a terrible mixture of sanity, cowardice, and utter lack of principle. He is like a rudderless vessel, just drifts, does not attempt to see an argument. . . .

But I came away terribly distressed that a man with his mentality should have led us all for so many years. He never could have believed in civil liberty or socialism. His whole mind is one web of tortuous conservatism. He has no solid root of belief anywhere except perhaps a lingering kind of protestant faith as expounded by John Knox. The sort of individual liberty best expressed in the words, "what I believe is of God, what you believe in a contrary sense is of the Devil and as such must not be heard in the land."

In his efforts with the Socialist League Cripps was following the urge of his Christian idealism. He was conscious of the conservatism and the economics of the trade unions and their leaders, their insistence on squeezing out concessions rather than making fundamental socialist changes, their lack of idealism, and their great power in determining the policy of the Labour Party. The function of the Socialist League was to be the means of recapturing the spirit of the pioneers of militant, idealistic, yet Fabian, Socialism.

Bitter feelings were created among trade-union leaders, however, by the demand for change in the structure of the Labor Party. Nothing disturbs the trade-union leaders so much as criticism from people who are outside the unions, particularly if it comes from the intellectuals.

"At present," Sir Stafford argued, "the agenda of the national conference are not discussed by the union branches and many unions cannot even have the guidance of their own national conferences because they are held biannually. By the means suggested the rank and file of the trade unionists would be able to discuss the resolutions and help to shape the policy of the party."

Had the Socialist League contented itself with propaganda for its program, it might have flourished without coming into fatal conflict with the party. It was not content so to do but sought also *to shape the policy of the party on current issues.* Here the Socialist League had failed to learn from the history of the Independent Labour Party and its attempt to function as a rival party within the Labour Party. No party can long tolerate such a rival within, as Stafford Cripps was soon to learn from his own experience.

Nevertheless his campaign for the Socialist League made him the most popular Labour Party leader in the country. He could fill the halls when most of the other Labour leaders could not get an audience. What he had to say certainly angered his political enemies inside and outside the Labour movement. The Attorney General of the National Government, Sir Thomas Inskip, accused him of becoming an advocate of violent revolution. This was too much for Stafford and he wrote to Inskip on March 15, 1932:

The enclosed cutting was brought to my attention in Glasgow. It formed part of the report in the "Glasgow Herald" of your speech at Bearsden.

I should be obliged if you would inform me whether it sets out correctly your statement about myself, and if so would you be so good as to let me know when I "told them the day of evolutionary socialism was past *and* the day of revolution—according to the manner of the Russian revolution was now the political creed of the Party, etc."

The newspaper report of the speech by Inskip at Bearsden said:

The Socialist Party today stood for red hot revolution. That was not an exaggeration or an imaginative effort of his party, because a gentleman who stood very high in the leadership of the Labour Party—Sir Stafford Cripps—had lately told them that the day of evolutionary Socialism was past and that the day of revolution, according to the manner of the Russian revolution, was now the political creed of the party which with one or two others he led.

The reply came:

My dear Cripps,

In reply to your note, the enclosed report of my remarks is an accurate report so far as I can remember. The speech I had in mind was one delivered in Edinburgh on January 17, to a Labour Party Conference.

Yours sincerely,
T. W. H. INSKIP.

Back to the Attorney General went the following:

Thank you for your note. I am afraid the account that you saw of my speech must have been entirely different to any of those that I saw and can have no relationship to anything I said, as I have always condemned revolutionary means and the Communist movement which relies on such means. Will you be so good as to give me the reference to the report of my Edinburgh speech which you saw and which contained the passage to which you referred at Glasgow.

The Attorney General was quite sure he had not misrepresented Sir Stafford. He replied:

If you will look at the report of your speech in the "Times" I think you will see I did you no injustice. I am told there was a much fuller report in the "Scotsman."

I accept, of course, your disclaimer of revolutionary means and of the Communist movement. But your repudiation of "gradualness" (which I called "evolutionary socialism") and your reference to the Russian revolution and its result, and your final statement about pulling down the building, justified me, I think, in my observations. At any rate, a great many of your friends read your remarks as an indication of your view that your party should adopt and indeed was going to adopt revolutionary plans, instead of the old and as you thought obsolete methods of "gradualism": something sudden and drastic in fact like pulling down a building instead of repairing and enlarging and improving it.

I write at length so that you may know what I have in mind and I do most respectfully think that there is no ground at all for the feeling which I gather you have, that I have treated your speech unfairly. If I have misunderstood you—as is possible—I am very sorry, but if I may say so, your language seemed to me very plain.

Inskip was nothing if not stubborn and Sir Stafford was nothing if not tenacious.

My dear Attorney General,

Thank you for your full and frank reply.

I of course join issue with you on the interpretation you put on what I said at Edinburgh. I do not object to your strictures on the policy I advocate, but I think you must realise that it is hardly correct to say, "I had told them . . . that the day of revolution . . . according to the manner of the Russian Revolution was now the political creed of my party" when I had said precisely the opposite.

There can only be one meaning in the minds of the public to the phrase "according to the manner of the Russian revolution" and that is the use of force and bloodshed in bringing about a change. I have uniformly stated—as I did at Edinburgh—that I abhor such an idea and will have nothing to do with it.

I have stated that I believed in a very rapid change of the present system by the method of Parliamentary Democracy. You may term that a "revolutionary" change in the same sense as one speaks of a "revolutionary" change in fiscal policy, but I am sure you must appreciate the difference between this use of the term revolutionary and the use you made of it by adding the qualification—"in the manner of the Russian revolution."

Yours faithfully,

R. STAFFORD CRIPPS.

No amount of argument would budge Inskip. Determined to have the last word he wrote:

We cannot carry on indefinitely a correspondence, but perhaps I ought to send a final reply to your last letter. It never occurred to me to suggest that you advocated bloodshed, but when you said that "the experiment in Russia taught them that, however Utopian it might be to imagine a state in which they had equality, at least it was a matter which could be put to practical experiment" I think I was justified in understanding you to mean that confiscation and wholesale nationalisation of a thorough going and drastic character was the policy of yourself and your Party. Nor do I think that my paraphrase substituting "evolutionary Socialism" for "gradualness" and speaking of "revolution according to the manner of the Russian revolution" was an unfair one.

You and I are perhaps not likely to agree as to what is the fair inferment from your language, but I entirely accept your statement that you are opposed to bloodshed.

The Conservative and Liberal press were so exasperated by Cripps' speeches at this time that they became scurrilous in the extreme. One day he spoke of the obstruction likely to come from Buckingham Palace and that raised a howl which echoed round the world. He had said,

When the Labour Party comes into power they must act rapidly and it will be necessary to deal with the House of Lords and the influence of the City of London. There is no doubt that we shall have to overcome opposition from Buckingham Palace and other places as well. It is absolutely essential that it should be made perfectly clear to the people exactly what it is we ask for the power to do. There must not be time to allow the forces outside to gather and to exercise their influence upon the Legislature before the key points of capitalism have been transferred to the control of the State. I look upon these two points myself as being land and finance. If other people become revolutionary then the Socialist Government, like any other Government, must take steps to stamp out the Revolution. The Socialist Government must not be "mealy-mouthed about saying what they mean."

The right wing of the Labour Party and the Trades Union bureaucracy were as outraged by this as were the Conservatives and the Liberals. The implication read into the speech was that Sir Stafford was a republican preaching the abolition of the monarchy. The personal popularity of the British royal family in Britain is such that republicanism is identified with communism and is consequently "un-British." Naturally Sir Stafford rejected the imputation. Whatever class war speeches he may have delivered in the course of the years, the action he sought never reached beyond passive resistance, beyond individual refusal to do this or that. He advocated that all political changes be made through Parliament, which he believed to be capable of being reformed into a more democratic and efficient political institution.

These ideas ran through the publications of the Socialist League. Sir Stafford himself wrote one of its pamphlets entitled "Can Socialism Come by Constitutional Methods?" He answered emphatically in the affirmative. Clement Attlee wrote another entitled "Local Government and Socialism." These were but two of a series.

Suddenly the attention of the British Labour movement was shifted from the shaping of a program for the next Labour Government to immediate history in the making. Hitler had come to power in Germany and the Socialist and working-class movement there had been overwhelmed almost without resistance.

VIII. The Storm Bursts

HITLER'S accession to power in Germany in 1933 cannot be said to have come as a shock to the leaders of Britain. Certainly not one of them—Churchill, Baldwin, MacDonald, or Chamberlain—showed the slightest alarm, or thought of this new force as "a symptom of the decay of capitalism," or foresaw that it would tear up its treaties and leap at the weakened British Empire.

That the triumph of Hitler was a shock to the British Labour movement there is no doubt. But it was in no position to react as it had done to earlier challenges. The splitting of the labor movement of the world into rival political internationals inhibited united action. Torn asunder in Germany, the Social Democrats and the Communists hated each other more than they did the common enemy, and down they went like ninepins before the Nazi onslaught. In Britain, the membership of the Communist Party had never exceeded ten thousand, but it had succeeded from time to time in exercising its influence within the trade unions and the Labour Party, and its working-class politics influenced many outside its organizational bounds. The effect of the Russian Revolution on the British working class had been far-reaching. But since the General Strike of 1926, the Labour Party had pursued a relentless ideological war against the Communists and purged its membership of them. Hence, when Hitler's blow fell, the Labour Party and the trades-union leaders issued a manifesto "Against Dictatorship from the Right and from the Left"—a philosophical dissertation which left the reader to imply that British labor was opposed both to Nazism in Germany and to Communism everywhere.

The effect on Sir Stafford was quite different. He had had nothing to do with this division of the Labour movement into rival camps. All this had happened before he became a member of the party. He had joined the Labour Party because he believed in Socialism as the best means of living a Christian life and as the fulfillment of human brotherhood in the organization of society. His brief experience in political leadership had taken place in extraordinary circumstances during which time party warfare in Britain had resolved itself dramatically into open class conflict. Tories, Liberals, and a fraction of the Labour Party had formed themselves into a class bloc against the Labour Party and the trades unions. He had seen this combination shatter the Labour Government of 1929-1931 and, without the slightest scruple, ride roughshod over the working class. He had heard it express its hatred of Soviet Russia in unmeasured terms. He observed the difference of attitude toward the rise of Hitler.

Only a month after Hitler became chancellor of Germany, the Reichstag building was fired and the Communist leaders were arrested and charged with complicity in the burning of the edifice. Sir Stafford acted promptly on behalf of the five accused Communists. Writing to Dr. Heinrich Ehlers, a German lawyer, he said, "The suggestion is current here that they [the accused] will be unable to get a fair trial as no lawyer will dare to go forward whole-heartedly with the defence. Three of the lawyers originally engaged have withdrawn."

Within a few days he drew together prominent lawyers from eight countries and formed them into an unofficial legal commission in London to inquire into the burning of the Reichstag. Sir Stafford himself opened the inquiry and declared that it would be a "political trial in the fullest sense of the word." The inquiry proved that the Nazis themselves had set fire to the Reichstag with the object of creating a state of hysteria in the public and discrediting their opponents.

Shortly after this he was called upon to show his full personal qualities against a House of Commons hysterical with anti-Soviet rage. Six Englishmen, employed by the Metropolitan Vickers Company and working on contracts in Russia by invitation of the Soviet Government, were arrested on March 11, 1933, charged with sabotage and espionage. That Englishmen should be engaged in such activities, and that a foreign government, particularly the Soviet Government, should arrest them was unthinkable! The British Ambassador in Moscow was in a panic. Without stopping to make any inquiries whatever he telegraphed to the British Government saying,

It is inconceivable that the Soviet Government can produce credible evidence of any criminal malpractice on the part of the company.

... On the assumption that the Soviet Government do not at once liberate the prisoners I am inclined to suggest at the risk of His Majesty's Government incurring an accusation of participation in prejudging an issue of which legal remedies have not been exhausted, that the Soviet Ambassador, London, should be frankly warned that if his Government wishes to continue to entertain friendly relations with His Majesty's Government they must refrain from being drawn by an excessive zeal on the part of the police into permitting the trumping up of frivolous and fantastic accusations against a friendly and reputable British company. Otherwise it will obviously become impossible for any subject to conduct business in Russia, and conclusion of trade agreement will be pointless."

On March 15, Mr. Baldwin the Prime Minister stated in answer to a question in the House of Commons:

"His Majesty's Government are convinced that there can be no justification for the charge on which the arrests were made. Sir Esmond Ovey has been instructed to represent in strong terms the grave view which they take of these proceedings against British subjects of high standing engaged in normal commercial pursuits to the benefit of both countries, and the unfortunate consequences to Anglo-Soviet relations which may follow unless it is rectified."

On March 20, 1933, Mr. Eden (Under-Secretary of State for Foreign Affairs) announced in the House of Commons that as a result of the arrests the negotiations for a new Anglo-Soviet Commercial Agreement had been suspended. Two of the accused, Nordwell and Monkhouse, were released on bail after forty-eight hours detention. On April 4, 1933, three others, Messrs. Thornton, Gregory and Cushny, were released on bail but MacDonald was kept in custody.

On April 5, Sir John Simon asked the House of Commons for authority to ban all Russian imports into Britain. It was most appropriate that it should be Simon who asked for this power, for he was the foreign secretary who had declined to ask for such power against Japan when it had attacked China.

Rarely has there been such a scene as that which the House

of Commons presented. It was packed, hostile, hysterical, almost uncontrollable. M. P.'s were standing around the sides of the House. The galleries were full. When Sir Stafford rose to speak he had to wait several minutes for the Speaker to quiet the howling pack of Conservatives. He stood calmly, waiting, and gave a glance to the ladies' gallery where his wife sat quietly and intently, watching the ordeal below. At last he could begin. He spoke with that quiet, reasoning precision with which he argued his cases before the judges of the courts:

The House is being asked to grant powers to the Government as against a particular foreign nation—powers which, as far as I know, are unprecedented in any recent years in the history of this country. . . . Beyond the right to make the fullest enquiry and obtain the fullest information, international law recognises no right of interference in the internal affairs of a foreign country, unless certain specified states of affairs can be shown to have arisen with regard to the nationals of another country.

The House did not want to listen to legal arguments. Interruption followed interruption. Time and again the Speaker had to remind the House that this was a debate. Sir Stafford criticized the Ambassador for prejudging the guilt or innocence of the arrested men. He turned on the Government because of their instructions to the Ambassador. He finished with the declaration:

I feel convinced that if we continue to pile up ill-feeling in Russia by the statements that are in the White Paper and by this sort of emergency action, which is being taken to treat Russia in a way in which no country has ever been treated before, and by this House of Commons, we are seriously jeopardising the fate of the men who are still in their hands, and whom it is for them to deal with and not for us.

At the end of his speech, of an hour's duration, against a continued barrage of interruptions, the Labour Opposition was overwhelmingly defeated.

The trial began in Moscow on April 12, 1933. All the Russians who had been arrested at the same time as the accused British, pleaded guilty. So, also, did MacDonald, who had been refused bail. Thornton, who had pleaded guilty in the preliminary examination, now pleaded "not guilty." The other British-

ers pleaded "not guilty." The outcome of the trial was that
Monkhouse, Nordwell and Cushny were sentenced to deportation from the U.S.S.R., MacDonald to two years imprisonment,
and Thornton to three years imprisonment. They decided to
appeal to the Supreme Court as was their right.

Without waiting for the result of the appeal, the British Government on the following day issued a proclamation prohibiting
the importation of eighty per cent of the Soviet commodities
which Britain had recently been importing. The Soviet Government answered in kind. There was considerable excitement
for some weeks and the British Government did not fare well
in the eyes of the public. Criticism mounted against it, especially after the reports of the trial were published. Soon the
Government retreated and Simon took advantage of the opportunity presented by the presence of Litvinov at the World Economic Conference, held in London at the end of June, to
negotiate for the re-opening of trade with the Soviets. On July
1st, the Soviet Embassy issued a statement announcing that the
petitions of Thornton and MacDonald had been commuted
to deportation. On the same day the British Government
announced the end of the embargo and a date for resuming
the negotiations for an Anglo-Soviet Trade Agreement. During the whole of this period Sir Stafford's prestige in the
House of Commons stood exceedingly high. But it was obvious
that had the British Government been in a position to make
war on Soviet Russia it would have done so.

The rise of the Nazis in Germany and the reactions of the
National Government to it, along with their hatred of Soviet
Russia, convinced him that the world was moving toward war
and that the only force which could resist it was a *united working class movement*. For this he was now prepared to work
with all his might. It is at this moment that Cripps and the
Socialist League began to play the role of a left opposition
within the Labour Party.

It was 1933 when, for the first time, Stafford Cripps led the
Socialist League into action at the national conference of the
Labour Party. The first resolution of the League was sponsored
by a local Labour Party whose spokesman was Sir Charles
Trevelyan. It was a lengthy resolution, remarkable mainly for

the policy it advocated. It assumed that war was on the way as an inevitable product of capitalism. It saw in Fascism a logical development of capitalism and also saw how directly it was related to war. No one was clear as to whence the war would come or what the character of the war would be, except that it would be a capitalist war. What then should be done? The Socialist League declared that its function was:

To work within the Labour and Socialist International for an uncompromising attitude against war preparation; to pledge itself *to take no part in war* and to resist it with the whole force of the Labour Movement and to seek consultation forthwith with the Trade Union and Co-operative Movements with a view to deciding and announcing to the country what steps, including a general strike, are to be taken to organise the opposition of the organised working-class movement in the event of war or threat of war, and [the League] urges the National joint bodies to make immediate approaches to endeavour to secure international action by the workers on the same lines.

This was the mind of Sir Stafford Cripps too, and was to be the basis of his actions for some years.

Elderly Sir Charles Trevelyan, an orator of great power, let loose torrential eloquence in the tradition of Jaures. He declared,

At no time has there been such a black outlook in the world. The great instrument for keeping the peace, the League of Nations, some day will be the machinery for international safety, but it will be when hearts are different and when Governments are different. . . . This resolution is one of action. . . . The rulers must know that if war comes they will fight with a divided nation. They can make their bourgeois war themselves but they will make it without the workers. Until we reach that point, until there is a workers' movement bold enough to say that and to say it so that it is trumpeted throughout the world, there is no safety for the workers of any land.

Percy Collick, a leader of the Locomotive Engineers and Firemen's Union, followed with the declaration,

All the work of this Conference this week, all your aspirations and all your resolutions are of no use unless you are perfectly clear and certain about the one that is before this Conference at this moment.

H. L. Elvin, a member of the Executive of the Socialist League, went to the platform after Collick, declaring, "I believe that war is the acid test of Socialist conviction," and added passion to the rising temper of the conference.

Then the tall Dr. Dalton, on behalf of the Executive of the Party, rose and in stentorian tones said, "I rise to say that the Executive Committee accepts the resolution that has been moved. We rejoice to see the rising flame of hatred of war."

The resolution calling for a general strike against an unspecified war was carried unanimously. But it did not end there. Arthur Henderson, chairman of the dying Disarmament Conference, capturing the spirit of the occasion in an historic oration, sought to restore the faith of all in the League of Nations. So impressed was Sir Stafford that he rose and asked that the Executive immediately issue Henderson's speech in pamphlet form for widespread distribution.

From this conference Sir Stafford went forth and campaigned the country. His energy seemed inexhaustible. With almost fanatical persistence he expounded his theme—working-class unity against war and Fascism. In the succeeding months he wrote his book, "Why This Socialism?" which explained the reasons for his faith. His contacts with Socialists of other countries extended. As Austria became increasingly subject to the pressure of Hitler, he wrote to Parmoor on March 6, 1934:

I have seen a great deal of people from Austria and the position is very bad indeed. We tried to put some pressure on the Government here to help and it may have had some restraining influence, although it looks as if conditions were getting worse. The Trade Unions are doing their best to give some help to the Socialists.

The international situation generally seems to be getting worse, and with the increase of our air and navy estimates the position seems to becoming more hopeless.

This did not mean he was turning to pacificism. It meant that he distrusted the capitalist governments. He did not think they would use arms for the right purpose and was accordingly opposed to such governments having arms.

His popularity in the Labour movement increased month by month and in 1934 he was elected to the Executive of the Labour Party. The fears of the more conservative Labour Party and trade-union leaders mounted in almost equal ratio to Cripps' popularity, since his new role threatened their leadership. More than that, they feared the deeper political and social implications of his crusade.

Parmoor, who was ambitious for his son, was exceedingly pleased, and never slackened in his good advice. After a meeting with George Lansbury, he wrote to Stafford in October, 1934:

G. Lansbury spent yesterday at Parmoor, much to the delight of Marion and myself. . . . You know that I have a great admiration for him and his book (*My England*). It is a powerful work having regard to the conditions under which it was written.

He spoke most kindly and generously about you. I hope that you will see much of him and help him in his position as Leader in the House of Commons.

His views on the general outlook are and always have been similar to my own. I do not mean on every point, but in the main directions, and collective team action, to be successful, must have a certain element of give and take. Please think of this and of your father's and Lansbury's views. "More haste less speed" are not counsels of despair but a just appreciation of the conditions of stable progress. I am not afraid of the future in this world or elsewhere, but I want the time to come when you will be chief pilot of a strong Labour Party.

Your v. affectionate father,

P.

To this Stafford replied on October 17, 1934:

Very many thanks for your letter. I heard from G. L. I very much hope he will remain on as leader in the House of Commons, as I think at the moment it is very vital. I entirely agree about the "give and take" that is necessary. If I did not I should no longer be in the party, but I propose to stay there as long as the Party will have me. I am quite certain that the one thing that is essential above all others at the present moment is unity.

Just about this time there occurred one of the greatest mining disasters in the history of the British coal fields. A terrific explosion at the Gresford Colliery in North Wales resulted in a death roll of 265. All Britain was staggered. Naturally, an official inquiry had to be held before the Chief Inspector of

Mines. Sir Stafford Cripps was asked by the miners' North
Wales Association to conduct their case.

The magnitude of the disaster demanded the most exhaus-
tive investigation. Such an inquiry requires not merely a knowledge of the laws governing the operation of the mining industry,
but also an intimacy with the whole technique of mining.

The inquiry opened at Wrexham in October, and Sir
Stafford appeared, free of charge. The Miners' Federation of
Great Britain, not believing that a mere lawyer would know
the right questions to ask about a pit, was represented by its
officials. Geoffrey Wilson writes:

Sir Stafford arrived in Wrexham the night before the inquiry
opened without, as far as anybody knew, any detailed knowledge
of the technical side of mining. But he was fortunate in having as
his technical advisor Mr. D. R. Grenfell, [subsequently Minister of
Mines in the Churchill Wartime Coalition Government] one of the
South Wales Miners' Members of Parliament, and a fully qualified
mine manager. Within thirty-six hours of his arrival in Wrexham,
Sir Stafford began a cross-examination of the manager of the mine,
which continued mercilessly for two and a half days. The cross-
examination took the form at which Sir Stafford has no superior.
So skillfully were the questions selected and put that the manager
had no option but to agree with the course of the argument put
forward by the questioner, and there was universal admiration for
the grasp of technical detail which Sir Stafford had acquired.

Day by day the newspapers gave the greatest prominence to the
proceedings and everybody was shocked by the revelations which
Sir Stafford's ruthless cross-examination brought forth. He extracted
from the management that a considerable time before the explosion
dust samples had contained combustible matter verging on fifty per
cent; that miners were firing sixty-three shots a shift even when
it was acknowledged to be dangerous to fire more than forty-five
and the management had done nothing to prevent this; that there
had never been a measurement of the air in the three districts where
the explosion occurred. The Junior Inspector of Mines had to admit that although twelve days before the explosion had occurred it
had been reported to him that there was gas in the pit, he had
taken no steps to verify the report but had been content to accept
the manager's explanation that the gas was in a cavity.

As a result of the inquiry, which lasted thirty-five days, a
manager of the mine was imprisoned and the Government

had to respond to the indignation of the people by setting up a Royal Commission to inquire into the safety of the coal mines throughout the country.

Sir Stafford was increasingly in the public eye. When he was not attacking the Government from the front Opposition bench, he was holding public attention by his criticism of Labour policy from the platform of the Socialist League. Time and again he was hitting the news headlines with his handling of a case in the courts, and he was winning the confidence and admiration of great bodies of workers by the way in which he used his professional skill on their behalf. Lord Sankey wrote to Parmoor:

Stafford is making a great name for himself. I admire him for his courage. It is a great tribute to him that everybody recognises his selflessness and honesty of purpose. I hope he will not overwork, that is his only danger.

Shortly after the Gresford inquiry, Sir Stafford had a brief interlude in the form of a visit to the United States. While at sea, he wrote to Parmoor:

This is a very nice simple clean steady boat and very empty. Its only disadvantage is a rather trying disregard of punctuality. We are 24 hours late and unless everything goes according to plan may be 48 hours late, which will probably upset all our plans hopelessly but we shall not know until we see John at New York. [His son was at this time traveling in America as a member of the Oxford debating team.]

I have read Laski's new book on the State which is really *excellent,* also George Soule's "The Coming American Revolution" which is good too, and one or two other books on economics, and a number of articles and pamphlets.

The rather vague news on the wireless about Stressa doesn't look too good. Its the old story of agreements which no one trusts and which mean nothing but words. Every day makes me realise the more the futility of attempting any sort of permanence of agreement within Capitalism. It is very depressing. . . . I hope to see Roosevelt in Washington this week.

His trip could not be described as a holiday visit. He went to Washington, New York, Montreal, Ottawa, Toronto. He talked with President Roosevelt, Henry Wallace, then Secretary of Agriculture, Frances Perkins, Secretary of Labor, the British Ambassador, newspaper editors, Averill Harriman, Justices of the Supreme Court, leaders of the American Federation of Labor, members of the American Socialist Party, officers of the Labor movement, ministers and lawyers. In Canada he visited the Prime Minister and many of the leading personalities of Canadian politics. He returned to England after a few weeks.

Meanwhile he had posted an interesting abstract of his conversation with President Roosevelt to his father, Lansbury, and Attlee. He wrote it on April 17, 1935, immediately after his visit with the President from his quarters at the Mayflower Hotel in Washington, D. C. It read:

I lunched today alone with the President in his office, spending just an hour with him.

He was extremely charming, frank and friendly and spoke both of American domestic affairs and international matters. He was oppressed with the difficulties of the situation and the international exchange and monetary situation troubled him. He was working towards a stable price level in terms of wholesale commodity prices in America trying to get back to the average level of 1924-27, when the bulk of the private indebtedness grew up in America. The index was 55 when he took office compared to 100 for the average of 1924-27 and it had now risen to 80 and he hoped to get it back to 95-100 gradually, and then keep the dollar value fixed in terms of a commodity index. He was most anxious other countries should do the same, at whatever level suited their internal economy, especially England. He deplored the storing up of gold in U.S.A. and stated that every dollar bill now had a backing of gold 1.55 dollars, silver 25 cents, whereas 33 cents in all would be sufficient backing. The U.S.A. would be only too glad to exchange this gold for foreign paper if gold was required elsewhere and countries would stabilise their monetary values on wholesale commodity prices. "It doesn't matter much what the list of commodities is" so long as it is stabilised on some list.

As to the expenditure of the 4½ billion dollars granted by Congress he was puzzled as to what permanently effective form this expenditure could take. Housing he looked upon as a temporary expedient. Afforestation and soil erosion work was useful but would not absorb it all. He is most anxious not to create a large body of *semi-skilled* workers and then leave them with nothing to do when the money is spent.

He was very pleased with the work that had been done in the camps for the younger men, whereby 350,000 had been put to work and were contributing twenty-five dollars out of the thirty dollars paid them per month to the upkeep of their families.

He was hankering after "small town" development, that is, a small urban centre working in with surrounding rural areas and in effect exchanging their commodities—the workers doing part time in the factories and part time on the land—but realises that this can of course be no solution for the large industrial centres.

He likened the problem of the diversity of climates, populations, races and creeds in America to that in Russia.

He was very antagonistic to Father Coughlin and Huey Long. He said that he had told Upton Sinclair he would back him if he would limit all his schemes to strictly state matters, but that his suggestions as to currency and credit were impossible to inter-state commercial dealings.

He hoped to get a measure of control over both monetary and credit policy through the new banking bill which would be sufficient to enable the value of the dollar to be controlled.

It was not possible to get any distinctive impression as to general policy which one got the idea of being experimental, with its sole positive objective the monetary idea outlined above.

On the international side the fear of Japan was obviously quite real and there was a total disbelief in any pacific intentions of Germany. When I suggested—to test the effect—that Germany might not really be so warlike as he suggested he said "I hope you won't become a second Lord Haldane!"

We discussed the necessary economic basis for peace and he agreed on the necessity for some economic arrangement as to war materials in the world generally but thought it no good suggesting any internationisation scheme "as it would only be laughed at," though he agreed nothing could be done as to disarmament till this was settled. "It's no good having another World Economic Conference" showed that he was thoroughly disillusioned by that attempt.

He was not very polite about Simon! who is obviously not persona grata in this country any more than he is at home. He was rather despairing as to peace prospects, though he agreed as to the widespread and sincere desire of the people. I pointed out that this was ineffective and hopeless as there was no lead of a realistic kind given to it, pointing out the economic necessities of the situation, and that I believed if someone in his position could enunciate the proposition it would, although not immediately accepted, create a great impression and provide a rallying point for peace-loving people to make their work effective.

He was taken with the idea but said it would require a lot of detailed working out and that he had at present nothing but the vague general conception of necessity. If I could get a scheme or plan in broad outline worked out, it would interest him very much to see it and study it. Before I left he was, I think, struck with the possibility of making some such proposal.

These are the general lines of the talk which covered a great number of other incidental matters. My whole impression was of an honest anxious man faced by an impossible task—humanising capitalism and making it work. A man full of charm with whom it would be possible to discuss anything and settle most things if he trusted you.

In this period the Labour Party geared its policy on foreign affairs to the League of Nations more ardently than ever before and forgot about its resolution of 1933. But not so Sir Stafford and the Socialist League. The Italians invaded Abyssinia, the developing war was coming nearer home and an answer had to be given to the question: "What are we to do about it?" The Labour Party, not influenced by the dubiety of the Government's attitude to the League of Nations, urged that the League apply sanctions to force Italy to cease her war on Abyssinia. Sir Stafford and the Socialist League opposed this policy. Stafford's views differed from those of his father, to whom he wrote:

You will probably have seen that I spoke in the House on this matter. It seems to me that the position is getting very serious, but in spite of their large majority I think the Government was probably shaken up a bit as a result of the debate and the obvious interest which is being taken in the country on the Peace question. . . . I had a very long talk with Maisky the other night on the whole matter and he is very much alarmed at the Eastern situation and thinks that the only chance at the moment is to get an Eastern Pact of Mutual Assistance, but it does not look as though our Government is really going to press this on the Germans, and short of this nothing I think can even temporarily appease the Eastern difficulties.

Later he wrote more specifically on the question of sanctions. His father replied:

We are delighted to hear that Lansbury is with you, and I only write further on the political outlook, because I think you have not quite understood my view from your letter. You say that you agree with me that we should not support the National Government in regard to sanctions, although our reasons for this differ. I think that this puts my view rather too high. My objection was intended to be levelled against military sanctions because I believe myself that the difficulty can be overcome without them, and that if it comes to a question of military sanctions, there will be considerable difference of opinion.

Sir Stafford held the view that

If war comes before the workers in Great Britain have won power, that war will be an imperialistic war. A "National" Government may claim to be fighting on behalf of the League system, in conjunction with the U.S.S.R.; it will in fact have led the country into war to preserve the interests of British Imperialism.

Visualizing that the coming war would be a war of the capitalist states against the U. S. S. R., he declared,

A socialist Government, when it comes to power, should make it clear to the world that it will do everything possible to support the U.S.S.R. . . . negotiate a Treaty of Mutual Assistance with the U.S.S.R. and with any other Socialist States.

But he warned the workers "not to be misled into support of a war entered into by a 'National' or capitalist Government in the name of the League of Nations, nor to overestimate the effect of the entry of the U. S. S. R. into the League."

When the Labour Party Executive announced its support for League sanctions against Italy, Sir Stafford resigned from the National Executive in order to be more free to expound his own views. This meant that he would cease to be an Opposition leader and would break his partnership with Lansbury and Attlee.

His action was a disappointment to Parmoor who wrote:

Many thanks for your letter and the report of your speech. I do not disguise my disappointment at the resignation of your position on the governing body of the Labour Party and wish that I could have a talk with you. The decision whether to resign on an inability to uphold the whole programme of a party, though agreeing with a **great part of it, is** always a difficult one, and must be decided by the person interested with courage and sincerity. I do not doubt the choice but still regret it.

Stafford maintained his position and replied:

Thank you for your letter. I thought the matter of resignation over very carefully and I was quite convinced at the present moment, with so much uncertainty and differences of view in the Party, it was wiser to get out of the Executive in order to show people where I stood.

I quite realise that the smaller Nations at Geneva have a great desire for protection, but it has become more and more obvious every year that the League is being run by France and England for purely imperialist purposes, and I think the people must be made to face up to this or else we shall be led under the banner of the League to another imperialist war.

Momentous changes were afoot. The time had come when it would no longer be possible for a pacifist of the type of Lansbury to hold the reins of leadership. When the Labour Party Conference met at Brighton in 1935, the party was nearer to a split than at any time since the departure of the I. L. P. The Italian war on Abyssinia was the issue of the day. The Brighton Conference therefore saw Sir Stafford in bitter conflict with others in the leadership of the party. Two men would hold the center of attention, Cripps and Lansbury.

Hugh Dalton opened fire for the Executive. He made it clear that the Labour Movement of Britain was "firmly united in its opposition to the policy of imperialist aggression" and made a most powerful speech justifying the policy of the Labour movement in favor of sanctions against Italy.

Sir Stafford promptly followed Dalton. Without any preamble he said:

Let me go straight to the heart of the controversy so far as I am concerned. To me the central factor in our decision must turn, not so much upon what we as a country should or should not do, but upon who is in control of our actions. I cannot rid my mind of the sordid history of capitalist deception. The empty hollow excuses of 1914, which I was then fool enough to believe, echoes through the arguments of today, the "war to end war," the need to fight to save democracy, the cry to crush the foul autocracy of Prussian militarism, all have their counterparts in today's arguments. . . . When economic sanctions are applied, a state of war automatically exists, and we must be prepared to defend these sanctions against military attack. We must envisage the possibility of war. Whether we call it military sanctions or war, matters not; it is the same thing. That means the use by our Government of the workers for military action against the workers, in this case, of Italy. . . . If the attack on Italian Fascism turns to an Italian revolution as some people hope, our "National" Government will not use its forces to assist the Italian workers to freedom. I certainly do not and cannot trust the capitalists; and I have heard no arguments which would convince me that it is right to trust them not to misuse their military power in the future as they have always done in the past. . . . Had we a workers' Government in this country, as they have in Russia, the whole situation would be completely different. Then, with a Socialist Government there would be no risk of imperialist and capitalist aims being pursued, as today it is certain they are being, and will be pursued. . . .

No League system has a reality within imperialism. . . . I have been accused of changing my views on this topic. I have changed them, because events have satisfied me that now the League of Nations, with three major powers outside it, has become nothing but the tool of the satiated Imperialist powers. France and Great Britain determine its use. . . .

I wish to God the workers were in control in this country and so could make their power effective as the Russian workers can do today in their own country.

A voice called: "Through the League."
Not to be sidetracked, he retorted,

Through their own Government which they control. That is the vital factor. If we feel a desperate urge to do something at all costs in the present situation, we must fall back on the attempt to use working-class sanctions. These at least we can keep within the workers' control.

Marchbanks, the leader of the Railwaymen's Union, would have nothing to do with this talk of workers' sanctions and shouted, "Let those who will not observe the decision of the Annual Conference . . . get out."

A miners' leader referred to Sir Stafford as the "most colorful figure which the workers of this country have produced since Mosley!"

Clement Attlee, one-time supporter of unilateral disarmament and of the 1933 resolution for a general strike against

war, turned on his erstwhile colleague. He did not think that
sanctions against Mussolini would lead to war. Then came
George Lansbury to deliver his pathetic swan song, reaffirming
his renunciation of force.

There was not a man or woman in that conference who did
not realize that Lansbury's declaration was the end of the
career of a remarkable man in the leadership of the Labour
movement. There was not one who did not realize that he
could no longer remain in the leadership of the party and that
he would resign immediately. But that was not enough for
Ernest Bevin. This short, physically powerful, somber figure
whose whole career had been full of personal grievances,
ambled to the platform to mouth the obvious and boot the
aged leader as he fell from grace. Bevin accused Lansbury of
taking his conscience "round from body to body asking to be
told what . . . to do with it." That of course was not Lansbury's
"crime." It was just the opposite of that. Lansbury had pitted
his conscience against the conference and had refused to be
told what to do with it. Having disposed of Lansbury, Bevin
turned his attention to Sir Stafford:

People have been on this platform talking about the destruction
of capitalism. The middle classes are not doing too badly out of
capitalism and Fascism. Lawyers and members of other professions
have not done badly.

This was not the first time Bevin and Cripps had been in
conflict. They had faced each other in 1932 when Sir Stafford
stood for the nationalization of all the banks and Bevin opposed the nationalization of the Joint Stock Banks. Bevin, too,
resented the existence of the Socialist League, which he regarded as Cripps' personal organization of political power
within the Labour Party. Bevin had also all the class prejudice
of the conservative workingman against the intellectual. He
proceeded to mobilize this prejudice, which is strongly entrenched in the trade unions, instead of dealing with the issue
of Cripps' antiwar and antifascist policy. He accused Cripps
of willfully staying away from Executive meetings, and, referring to one occasion on which Sir Stafford was absent, said:

And so vital was it to you, that Cripps never turned up. If I feel bitter, please understand it. I cannot play with my members like this.

He then charged Cripps with trying to split the party:

And who am I to let my personality protrude as compared with this great Movement? Who is any man on this platform? I do sincerely ask this Conference to appreciate the Trade Unionist's position. Sir Stafford Cripps said there would be no split. He has done his best.

He said that Cripps had delivered to the Executive of the Labour Party a "cowardly stab in the back" by his resignation from that body when he could no longer agree with it on policy. The bitterness with which Bevin waged his fight against Cripps revealed that the two men had little in common beyond their membership in the same party. It almost appeared that Bevin was intent on driving Sir Stafford out of the party. Great changes had to take place in the political history of the Labour movement before these two would be found walking in step as leaders of the same Government and party.

As the debate continued, poor George Lansbury tried to explain how wrong Bevin was in his personal attacks upon him. Cripps ignored the personal attack. It appeared at one moment as if the Labour Party were on the verge of a great "purge," until Herbert Morrison, adroit as always, wound up the debate with a plea for toleration, calculated to calm the troubled scene. Nevertheless, the conference supported the Executive and defeated Sir Stafford's policy. Lansbury departed from the leadership. But Cripps held to his view and decided to fight back.

IX. In and Out

UNPERTURBED by Bevin's exhibition of mass power, Sir Stafford went his independent way. But the political mood of the country was against him. The Labour Party's advocacy of collective security through the League of Nations was exceedingly popular. The League of Nations Union, ostensibly a nonparty organization founded after the First World War to popularize the League, cleverly harnessed the feeling throughout the country and carried through what became famous as the Peace Ballot. By the ballot, 11,500,000 people almost unanimously voted that the British Government should carry out its obligations to the League, including the use of economic sanctions, collective security, and the reduction of armaments.

After first scoffing at the Peace Ballot, the Government, with an eye on an imminent general election, suddenly made a tactical maneuver and appeared to accept the "will of the people." It even led the League of Nations to apply limited sanctions against Italy. This gave some substance to the idea that after all the National Government did really stand for the League of Nations and all it implied.

Baldwin and MacDonald were old hands, not infants, in electioneering and preparing for elections. They trimmed their sails to the result of the Peace Ballot. They also seized upon the twenty-fifth anniversary of King George V's coronation, to make it into a fine Conservative Party "Silver Jubilee." So Sir Stafford Cripps again hit the headlines of Britain's newspapers at Caxton Hall in September 1935, when he said:

The new phenomenon in our national life of a 25-year Jubilee has been sedulously surrounded by the politicians with a well-cultivated ballyhoo from which they hope and indeed boast that they will derive electoral benefit. . . . It is understandable and reasonable that the people should express their loyalty to their nation through the medium of a titular sovereign on appropriate occasions. Apart from that aspect of the question, there is every reason in the tragic and depressed circumstances of the workers today why they should accept an opportunity for the relief and escape of a national jollification.

But neither of these matters offer justification for a ruling class utilising the loyalty of the people for the purpose of assisting them in an electoral campaign. The expenditure of large sums of money up and down the country to this end cannot be justified. The Conservative Party have claimed as their own the National Flag and the National Anthem, and they desire to monopolise for their own purpose the national loyalty.

That speech raised a storm. Description of the celebration as "ballyhoo" shocked the conscience of every newspaper editor, and it was at once linked with Cripps' earlier speech about Buckingham Palace. Once again he had "put his foot in it." But he was seeing things a little clearer than were his Labour Party colleagues. He saw that Baldwin was skillfully outmaneuvering them for the election.

In a broadcast on October 25, 1935, Baldwin said: "We do not want and no one will propose huge forces for this country." Three days later he emphasized this by declaring, "There has not been, there is not, and there will not be any question of huge armaments or materially increased forces."

So well did Baldwin pursue his campaign that he completely took the wind out of the Labour Party's sails. On October 15 the Labour newspaper, *The Daily Herald,* had as good as handed the election to the Government. It reported:

The General Election will be fought on domestic issues and not exclusively on foreign policy. Six months ago it looked as if foreign policy would dominate the election. Between Labour and the Tories there was a gulf that seemed unbridgeable on foreign policy. Now incredible as it would have seemed six months ago, the Government is supporting the League.

The Government issued its election manifesto, saying:

The League of Nations will remain as heretofore the keystone of British policy. . . . We shall continue to do all in our power to uphold the Covenant and to maintain and exercise the efficiency of the League.

Sir Stafford was taken in neither by the "ballyhoo" of the Jubilee nor by the cooing of Mr. Baldwin. He saw that a trick was being played, and in a speech at Birmingham he said,

Why it is that the Government have rushed the present election upon the country, right on top of the Municipal elections? Because the Government are afraid that if it took place any later the crooked bargain which is going to be made with Mussolini whereby a "sphere of influence" over Abyssinia will be given to the Italians, will be flung back in the Government's own face. The acid test of the Government's sincerity will be whether Ethiopian independence emerges from this scuffle as it was last January.

The election came on November 14, 1935. Campaigning had by now become commonplace in Cripps' political life. He flung himself into this campaign with all his usual ardor. This time it was to be a straight fight between himself and a Major Church who stood as a "National Labour" candidate, that is, a supporter of the Macdonald group. The Major was defeated from the start. Sir Stafford was unsparing in his efforts. Isobel Cripps joined in to campaign among the women of the constituency. Sir Stafford was returned triumphantly with a 7,000 majority.

The Tories polled ten and a half million votes to Labour's eight and a half million. The National Government won 387 seats as against 154 seats for the Labour Party. Promptly, the Hoare-Laval double-cross of Abyssinia, as foretold by Sir Stafford, was put through. The Labour Movement protested against the outrageous betrayal of League principles. Sir Stafford wrote:

The world will get tired of "perfide Albion" and we shall be set upon one day and left an isolated carcass to be picked by the new imperialist vultures. Robbed of our Empire and with no socialist confederation to take its place, we shall indeed be the victim of a most unhappy end.

Early in 1936 he wrote to his father:

I am afraid the Labour Party leadership at the present time is extremely unsatisfactory. It is both hesitant and weak and the Party in the House of Commons are not at all satisfied with it, but things will just have to go on as they are for the present, as the trouble is that the Party itself has no clear idea of its objectives or strategy.

I fear we are moving towards a capitalist concentration of power in this country which is likely to draw the Trades Union and Labour elements with it. I agree with you that it is essential within Democracy to have a party form of Government with clear cut distinction between Party policies. . . .

I am busy doing meetings in the country, but I am not taking any particular part in the House of Commons work as it is very difficult to do without making an apparent line of cleavage in the House which I think is unwise to develop at all at the present time.

He was getting further and further away from his father's policy, although Parmoor approved much of what he said. Parmoor affectionately followed every move his son made with deep interest and concern. On reading an interview which Stafford gave in August, 1936, on the new extension of the war to Spain, he wrote:

I am delighted with your interview today in the "News Chronicle." It does not place the danger, underlying the present spread of Fascism and war, too high. Blum's policy deserves the support of every right thinking man and places freedom and peace as the mainstays of the progress of civilisation. There can be no compromise such as the present Government appears to desire.

Shortly after the Franco revolt in Spain, George Lansbury, whose friendship with the Cripps family had grown with the years, visited Parmoor. The two elderly men spoke to each other of their concern for the course Stafford was taking. Parmoor wrote to Stafford:

Lansbury spent yesterday with us at Parmoor, and we talked a good deal of your future. He is evidently very anxious that you should resume your place on the Executive Committee of the Parliamentary Labour Party, and stressed the view that it was a real drawback to the Labour Party Executive that you were not a member. Naturally I agreed with him and I hope you will think the matter over. One point was especially in his mind, that the Labour Party ought to make a move now, and press the Government to declare what they intend to do in the existing Spanish crisis.

I should like to bring about a meeting of you and Lansbury, as soon as it can be conveniently arranged, and I am sure if you make a move, you will find a ready response from him.

Franco, openly backed by Hitler and Mussolini, had struck a military blow at the new Republican Government of Spain.

The Liberal Government of Spain had been accepted into the League of Nations. Its representative had taken his place at the Assembly of the League. Public opinion was shocked. It was obvious that the world was rapidly being driven toward war. And the question was asked, "what should Britain do about it?" There was no panic in the ranks of the Government. The pattern of its policy since 1931 had become clearly defined. As it had aided the Japanese and Mussolini, and had made a deal with Hitler, so it would facilitate the triumph of Franco and would use the League for the purpose.

The question this time was not that of the application of sanctions, but whether the constitutionally elected government of Spain, recognized as a member of the League of Nations, was entitled to obtain arms from other countries in order to restore law and order in its own territory. Franco was getting arms galore from Hitler and Mussolini. The democratic Republicans were getting none. The League governments declared for "non-intervention" and, behold, the Labour movements of Britain and France echoed the non-interventionists.

When the Spanish Fascist revolt began, Cripps was naturally on the side opposite to that of the Government. When the Edinburgh Conference met in October he was ready for the next stage of the struggle with the Labour Party Executive. What a scene! Real war was on the agenda of the Conference. There was no time now for Jauresian flights of oratory about war in general. The trades-union leaders were to be put to the acid test. They had already lined up the Labour movement behind the policy of non-intervention. Now they had to get endorsement from the conference. It was known that two delegates were on their way from Spain to the conference. On with the debate, then, and get the endorsement before the delegates arrive! Arthur Greenwood, deputy-leader of the Parliamentary Labour Party, led the way. He struck the right chords of sympathy:

All of us feel alike in our hearts about the tragedy of Spain today, and in what I have to say I want you to believe that those who have spent many weary hours and many sleepless nights over this problem feel as you feel about the events of the past two months. . . .

I admit and have said in public, and I have written that I regard this policy of non-intervention as a very, very bad second best.

But that was the only policy he had to recommend. Grenfell, an M. P. and miners' leader, followed and finally got himself into the position of accusing those who disagreed with the policy of non-intervention as being "warmongers."

Bevin advised the conference delegates "not to vote . . . as if this report confirms non-intervention, but confirms the active work that the National Council is trying to do, and back its efforts to assist Spain to the best of its ability." How to vote for non-intervention and against non-intervention with one and the same vote, he did not explain. They voted for non-intervention.

Two days later the Spanish delegates appeared on the platform. They moved the conference profoundly and made the delegates feel ashamed. The Executive then sent Attlee and Greenwood by night train to London to see Neville Chamberlain. After a chat with him they took the train back again and told the conference how moved Mr. Chamberlain was too, and how he had promised to look at the documents concerning the legal validity of the accusation against Hitler and Mussolini. That started the argument again, but once more the emphatic Bevin came down with his full weight, not for ending the disastrous policy of supporting "non-intervention" but in favor of "his officers sitting on the doorstep of Downing Street until a satisfactory reply was forthcoming." Sir Stafford managed to persuade the conference to accept a change of words in the resolution which would make it clear that at least the conference itself was convinced that the Fascists had broken the non-intervention pact. Having expressed that conviction and having enthusiastically sung the "Red Flag" to show how their hearts had been moved, and having voted to send bandages and cigarettes, it sent Bevin's two-way resolution out to cheer Franco on his way. Non-intervention had won and the war rolled on with Britain in retreat all along the line.

When Stafford Cripps left that conference he knew what he wanted and how he thought he could get it. He wanted a *British United Front of the Working Class* against the National Government. He was still interpreting politics from the point of view of class struggle in opposition to the Labour Party Executive. He regarded the Government as the arch enemy and he now set forth to make a joint campaign with the Socialist League, the Independent Labour Party, and the Communist Party. But before his plans could mature he was thrust into the forefront of public attention by a sensational event which stirred the entire country.

On December 10, 1936, King Edward VIII abdicated his throne in order to marry the American woman, Mrs. Wally Simpson, who had previously divorced her husband. The proposed marriage shocked the church conscience. There was some question as to whether such a marriage would be in conformity with the constitution. The press asked the constitutional lawyer, Sir Stafford, for his opinion. He answered thus:

Granted that we are to continue with a constitutional monarchy in this country, I personally cannot see any sufficient reason for forcing the abdication of the King because of the choice he has made. The only way in which the position could be altered would be by the passage of a law at the request of the King and in a form assented to by him. Mr. Baldwin has stated that the Government will not initiate any such legislation. With this attitude I agree, as it seems to me to be quite unnecessary to deal with the present case as exceptional. It is important that people should realise that there is no such thing known to our laws as morganatic marriage. The King's wife—whoever she may be—is the Queen Consort. The more vexed question that is raised is whether in this matter of his marriage the King is bound as a constitutional monarch to accept the advice of his Ministers. The answer to that question indubitably is, "Yes, he is bound."

King George VI succeeded his brother, and the Coronation came some months later. Again Sir Stafford protested against the extravagance of the celebrations and their exploitation by the Tory Party. He said:

In all this Coronation bunting or bunkum the Government appear to have overlooked the essential nature of the struggle which is proceeding in this country. I have no objection, let me say in parenthesis, to people celebrating if they wish on any proper occasion. . . . But the present circus which is being carried on and organised, for which the Government, incidentally are paying three quarters of a million out of national funds—apart from the millions which are being spent municipally all over the country—is simply being run as a political stunt by the Conservative Party.

That set every newspaper in the country after Cripps, in spite of the fact that he has always been a supporter of a constitutional monarchy in Britain.

Meanwhile, in January, 1937, with the plans well laid for the new Unity campaign, Cripps joined with William Mellor, Aneurin Bevan, G. R. Strauss, and Ellen Wilkinson in launching a new journal called *The Tribune*. For its first number he wrote an article in which he said:

It is the business of every one of us by some means or another to bring back to the Labour Party that courage and self-belief which is the basis of victory. . . .

We are often urged to make good resolutions on the first of January. They seldom last long, if made, because so often they are about small things that concern our private welfare. Today I ask you to write this resolution: I pledge to my fellow workers throughout the world my faith to strive increasingly to work for unity as a step to power, by which power the workers shall control their lives in peace and security.

This set the tone of the new campaign. The essence of the campaign, which was anathema to the Labour Party leaders, was co-operation between the Socialist League, the Independent Labour Party, and the Communist Party. They had agreed to cease attacking one another and sought to make an alliance with the Labour Party in rousing public opinion against the foreign policy of the National Government and for the unity of the three parties in the next election. When that campaign started there was no doubt whatever as to who would be its leader. Sir Stafford Cripps was the man. Remarkable meetings were held in the great industrial towns and cities. Cripps, Pollitt, Brockway, Bevan, Strauss, and Gallacher appeared on the same platforms calling for the "United Front of the Working class to fight Fascism and War."

Neither Sir Stafford's father nor the Webbs were at all happy about his new venture. Sidney Webb expressed their views in a letter to Parmoor:

We are perturbed about Stafford's recent action in getting the Socialist League to enter into alliance with the I. L. P. and the Communist Party in flat defiance of the Labour Party ruling. We have had no opportunity of talking it over with Stafford, and do not even know whether he had led the action or been outvoted.

I can't see any advantage in what is called the "United Front" where unity is most necessary, namely, in elections, as there can be no allocations of constituencies among the several sections (the example of France is misleading as there the second ballot makes things easier). In Great Britain the alliance with the Communist Party serves *only* to swell, by a small fraction, the numerical strength of a meeting or demonstration; and that only at the cost of lessening its effect on a hostile Cabinet or on employers or other classes prejudiced against Communism as being unchristian!

I wrote two articles in "The Tribune" at Stafford's request for the second and third issues, on "The Future of the British Labour Movement." I wrote them before hearing anything of the move for a "Popular Front." Feeling that their effect was against this I submitted the articles in typescript to Stafford suggesting that if they were not "in tune," he should return them to me as unsuitable. But to my bewilderment both he and Mellor welcomed them. Now I am more bewildered than ever as to what Stafford's line is. He may be right in giving up his position inside the Labour Party and taking on the role of a preacher or prophet, in the wilderness, if he is convinced of the ultimate rightness of his gospel. But I am a pedestrian accustomed all my life to be in a minority; and looking for nothing but being outvoted, and nevertheless going on smiling and willing to talk—relying I must confess, on my confident assurance that the majority will, whatever they now think, "come my way" in the end! The *facts* will ultimately convince, either me, or the majority.

Nevertheless, Sir Stafford proceeded securely on his way. The campaign waxed fast and furious. Tremendous meetings were held up and down the country and the press and the heads of institutions reacted according to their political bias. Sir Stafford sought to stage a great United Front meeting in the Albert Hall, London, but the trustees refused him the use of the auditorium. Promptly, he countered their refusal with an effort to bring political pressure to reverse the decision. He wrote to Stanley Baldwin, John Simon, Ramsay MacDonald, Winston Churchill, Lloyd George, Archibald Sinclair, and Clement Attlee, saying:

I am writing to ask your assistance in a personal matter which I believe to be of some importance. I know you have often expressed yourself in favour of freedom of speech in the past and I therefore ask you in the concrete case mentioned below to put these beliefs into practice by using your influence as a well-known public figure in the political life of the country.

I applied for use of the Albert Hall on a date upon which I had ascertained that it was free, but the Trustees have refused it to me without offering any reason. The only conceivable reason can be that they disapprove of my political views.

I would ask you therefore to write a letter to the Trustees, in your personal capacity, protesting against the action that they have taken and thus help in making a reality of the professions of freedom of speech of which this is a most flagrant denial.

The Prime Minister acknowledged receipt of Cripps' letter but declared:

The matter of the use of the Albert Hall for a meeting is quite outside my province and I should not think it right to intervene in the matter in any way.

Ramsay MacDonald, from the Privy Council Office, wrote:

It is quite impossible for me to divide myself into a private person and the Lord President of the Council in any relations I may have with the Trustees of the Albert Hall.

From Lloyd George came support for Cripps. He wrote:

I think the conduct of the Trustees of the Albert Hall is monstrous and that a protest ought to be registered against it by all those who believe in liberty of speech. I will either write direct to the Trustees or send a letter to the Press in the course of the next few days.

Sir Archibald Sinclair, Liberal Party Leader, and Clement Attlee, Labour Party Leader, supported Cripps's request. From Winston S. Churchill came a characteristic reply:

I cannot feel that right of free speech is directly involved in the inability of a particular person to procure a particular hall. I do not therefore feel myself impelled to come to your assistance. You are, unless I am misinformed, working in political association with the Communists at the present time. And it has always been their rule whenever they have the power, forcibly to suppress all opinions but their own. This also would make the case you mention by no means a good occasion on which to make a protest to the Public. Most people will think that the Communists have a pretty good run over here, certainly much better than they are given by the German

Nazis, by whom, if I remember rightly, you declared it would be a good thing if we were conquered. Excuse my frankness in dealing with the points you raise.

Cripps answered Churchill on March 13, 1937:

Thank you for your letter of the 12th of March. You are quite right that I am working in political association with the Communists at the present time in order, not to obtain power for the Communists but in order to obtain power for the Labour Party, who like myself have always expressed the view that freedom of speech is essential to Democracy, even to the extent of supporting your belief that you should be allowed to use the broadcasting.

I do not appreciate your reference to the Communists being allowed a pretty good run over here. They are as entitled in a democratic country to a good run and the use of a recognised Public Hall as are the Fascists, yourself, or Mr. Baldwin.

If you will take the trouble to refer to the press and the correction which I issued as regards my Stockport speech to which you refer, you will see that you are misquoting me.

I am delighted at your frankness because it shows as I suspected that you are keener on downing the Communists than in supporting freedom of speech.

I shall probably be sending to the press the whole of the correspondence with respect to the Albert Hall.

The Labour Party Executive acted quickly. It declared that membership in the Socialist League was incompatible with membership in the Labour Party. This was a clever tactical move. The members of the Socialist League had now to choose between continued membership in the Labour Party or becoming a dissident and ineffective group outside the party. They chose to remain in the party and dissolved the Socialist League. That ended part one of the Labour Party's suppression of the United Front campaign.

Sir Stafford and his colleagues had now to make up their minds on how to continue the struggle. Should they continue, as individual members of the Labour Party, to campaign publicly as before and risk personal expulsion? This they decided to do. One fact the Executive of the Party could not escape was that Sir Stafford had established himself as a Socialist leader of renown and undeniable ability. Right in the middle of the United Front campaign, when they were most anxious

to dissociate themselves from him, the Parliamentary Labour
Party were compelled to ask Cripps to lead the debate in the
House of Commons on the report of the Royal Commission on
the Gresford mining disaster. Anyone else would have been
completely eclipsed the moment Sir Stafford rose to speak.
They had no option but to ask the back-bencher to lead for
the party in that debate. And of course he did so.

A few weeks later the Labour Party Executive decided to
crush the United Front campaign. They announced that any
member of the Labour Party who appeared on the public platform with any member of the Independent Labour Party or
the Communist Party would be expelled automatically. What
had Sir Stafford and his friends to say to that challenge? Some
of the leaders of the Labour Party were hoping that they would
promptly jump for expulsion. But not so Herbert Morrison
who, anxious to keep the leader he had brought into the party,
wrote to Stafford a long letter in which he said:

No one has regretted more than I the difficulties which have
risen between yourself and the Party. You may remember that I
was among the first, if not the first, to urge you to join the Labour
Party, way back in the days when we ran across each other in the
proceedings of the Railway Rates Tribunal. . . .

I do not believe that there has been any desire to prevent your
playing a full part in the great work of the Party; I do not need
to assure you that there is no such desire so far as I am concerned.
But I should be less than honest if I did not say that there is, I
think, a responsibility on you to make your contribution to a rapprochement, and that many of your public statements and activities
have been a source of embarrassment to the Party and hardly conducive to that Labour Party unity which is so essential to the success of our work. An unfortunate result has been, I think, that
what might have been a valuable and desirable influence from your
point of view has been weakened within the ranks. . . .

Forgive me for writing this plainly, but I have a high personal
regard for you and I am terribly anxious that it may be possible
for you and others so to reshape your political future work that
you may play that bigger and closer part in the work of the Party
that I would desire.

The campaigners for the United Front of the working class
decided to refer the matter to the annual conference of the

Labour Party, which was near at hand. Again Cripps led the fight and again he was overwhelmingly defeated. That ended the first "unity" fight. But a surprising thing happened. Structural changes were made in the Labour Party which gave the local Labour parties the right to elect a specified number of their own nominees to the Executive of the party. The day following the defeat of the United Front proposals, Stafford Cripps was again elected to the Labour Party Executive as a nominee of the Local Labour parties along with D. N. Pritt and Harold Laski, both of whom had supported Sir Stafford in the Unity Campaign.

He was again on the front bench in the House of Commons, in the forefront of the attack on the Government. Early in 1938 the "non-intervention" supporters brought in a new measure for the withdrawal of volunteers from Spain. Sir Stafford made one of his most savage onslaughts on the Government. In the House of Commons he said,

> Whenever any restraint has been put nominally on both sides it has been effective against the Government of Spain but never effective against the Rebels. . . . They decide to stop munitions, but they stop them for the Government and not for Franco. They decide to stop volunteers, but they stop them for the Government and not for Franco. . . . This plan of the moment is the plan to give the greatest help to General Franco and be the most damaging to the Spanish Government. . . . We are not ashamed to say that we urgently desire the Spanish Government to be victorious. It is only the other side who are ashamed to say, what is a fact, that they anxiously desire to see the victory of General Franco.

Despite all protests the bill went through, and one December night it was Sir Stafford's fate, along with Clement Attlee, to meet a train in Victoria Station, London, bearing three hundred British members of the International Brigade, withdrawn from Spain. Attlee and Cripps welcomed these men as the first Britishers to fight the war of liberation against Hitler and Mussolini on foreign soil. It was a sad momentary ending to a great adventure.

By the middle of 1938, the drama of Europe began to reach its most decisive stages. Czechoslovakia was about to be first carved up and then handed over completely to Hitler, with Britain violating her treaty obligations and abandoning every principle upon which the League of Nations had been founded. The last pillars of the League were crumbling to bits and the old "peace system" which had risen from the ashes of the First World War soon would be no more.

The "man with the umbrella" flew to Berchtesgaden and there fixed the Sudetenland sellout, and flew again to Godesberg. He returned in a panic and cried "Get your gas masks!" On September 30, he and the French Premier, Daladier, signed the Judas document of Munich without consulting the governments of either Czechoslovakia or Soviet Russia. Waving a bit of paper, like a child with a new toy, he stepped out of an airplane in England assuring the gaping crowd of "peace in our time."

In the House of Commons, on October 5, Sir Stafford rose to speak for Labour. Never had he been so deeply stirred by the turn of events. He accused the Government spokesman of conscious dishonesty and cynical indecency:

All the time they have been afraid to expose their true policy to the people of this country, because they know that the people would not accept it, as Lord Baldwin, in the appallingly frank speech which he made after the last election, admitted to the House. They have spoken of collective security and of the Covenant of the League of Nations, but have never believed in the efficacy of either of them. . . .

They have uniformly failed and purposely failed, to give that lead for strengthening those organisations of peace which might have given real effect to them as implements for securing the salvation of this country and other democratic countries.

After this critical onslaught, a new note appears which indicates that some great change had taken place in his orientation. He continued:

What is required for a sound foreign policy are two things: First of all, the strength to maintain the rule of law internationally, and secondly, and no less important, . . . the courage to initiate a complete re-organisation of the international economic life of the nation, even, I add, at the price of sacrificing some of our imperial interests, if need be. I do not and never would suggest the handing over of any Imperial possessions of this country to any other Imperialist nation. . . .

Maybe today we have staved off war by the sacrifice of other people's national interest. That is a comparatively easy way of buying peace. Never has this Government been prepared to throw into the pool of international co-operation, vital British interests or possessions in any part of the world. . . . As long as policy is based on the conception of what Britain has Britain holds, there will be no solution possible of the economic problem of the world, a problem which lies at the very root of the grave dangers of the last few days. . . .

You will not forever satisfy rival imperialisms by handing over to them the smaller nations of the world. The time will come when the clash will be at your own door. . . . Sweet reasonableness which consists in giving away the property of others and building up huge armaments to protect what is your own will never resolve the problem of peace; yet such is the policy of His Majesty's Government today. From such a policy we dissent with all our power.

From the time when he had helped to launch the Socialist League he had pursued a policy based clearly and firmly upon the need for *working class unity* in a *class fight* against the *ruling class of Britain*. On all international questions he had taken his stand upon the principle of fighting the class enemy in one's own country. In this period he had been as tenacious as the Labour Party Executive in refusing to have political association with Liberals and Tories, had refused, indeed, any semblance of alliance with other than working class parties.

Now the duplicity and utter incompetence of the Government, led by Chamberlain, had created so ominous a situation that he was convinced that at all costs the people of Britain must force the resignation of the Government and replace it with an antifascist coalition or Popular Front Government. To secure such a change he determined to throw his energy into the support of the agitation already started for a "People's Front." An election was due at the end of 1939. It was obvious to any observer that if an immediate election were to be held the Labour Party could not secure a majority on its own account. The Conservatives would be returned unless there was unity of action among all the opponents of the Government with three-cornered fights avoided, and a general concentration of democratic forces against the Conservatives.

Already there was a widespread movement favoring this course. Sir Stafford was a member of the Executive of the

Labour Party. How then should he act? On January 9, 1939, he sent to the National Secretary of the party what was shortly to become famous as the "Cripps Memorandum." In this he declared,

If the Labour Party were to come out boldly as the leader of a combined opposition to the National Government, such a step would, I am sure, enormously increase its prestige and popularity in the country.

The Popular Front should be formed by

the Party issuing a manifesto inviting the co-operation of every genuine anti-Government Party, or group of individuals who would be prepared to give support to:

(1) The effective protection of the democratic rights, liberties and freedom of the British people, from internal and external attack.

(2) A positive policy of peace by collective action with France, Russia, the United States of America and other democratic countries for the strengthening of democracy against aggression and a world economic reconstruction based upon justice to the people of all classes and nations.

Sir Stafford's memorandum came before the Executive of the Labour Party. The discussion was most revealing. Mr. Attlee said in effect:

We can't run counter to Conference. I am doubtful about the feeling in the country. The proposals are wrong in their conception of the sort of Government that could act. Only a positive Socialist programme could get us through. You can't oppose the Government all out and unite all anti-Government forces. People are more likely to be attracted by a clear-cut programme of Socialism.

James Walker, the leader of the Steel Smelters' Union, wanted to know what all the fuss was about. He thought Chamberlain had done good work at Munich and that Cripps was still in his political childhood. Herbert Morrison did not think the Popular Front proposals were practicable. Dalton accused Sir Stafford of making personal popularity out of his opposition to the Executive. And so the discussion proceeded as if the political situation were that of a year far removed from the imminence of war. In the outcome, the memorandum was rejected by seventeen votes to three. The three in favor were Ellen Wilkinson, D. N. Pritt, and Cripps himself.

He had the satisfaction of knowing that the memorandum had the approval of his father. Parmoor had written to him:

> I have read with great interest your memorandum submitted to Middleton, with your letter stating clearly your views on the present political outlook. I may say at once that I am in close general agreement with your statement as expressed in the memorandum and the letter.

Now once again he was in conflict with the party machine. Had he accepted that defeat as final, nothing more would have been heard of it. But he regarded the situation as too serious to let matters rest there. He claimed the right to issue his document to all Labour organizations and to get it before the conference of the Labour Party. He issued it to the press to make sure that the world should know his views on the urgency of the times. That meant, to the Executive, that he had again begun the organization of forces around a rival center of leadership. They determined to put an end to the matter.

Then came another meeting of the Executive, at which there was presented a lengthy counter-memorandum which listed all Cripps' demeanors and "irresponsible speeches of the last seven years." He was accused of what appeared to be the crime of crimes: "had publicly indicated his view that the Labour Party is incapable of returning a Government by itself," which, of course, at that time it could not. He was asked to withdraw his memorandum "by circular to the persons and organisations to whom it was addressed." He refused, and was promptly expelled from the party. So at last Labour Party headquarters could breathe freely and hotly. The most disconcerting leader they had ever known in their ranks was out of the party if not out of the way.

This precipitate action instead of bringing the dispute to an end, succeeded in creating a national sensation. The newspaper headlines told the world that Cripps was out. Newspapers that had belabored him in and out of season now declared that he was far and away the most able man the party possessed. Indeed one newspaper talked of the Labour Party "blowing its brains out."

Sir Stafford did not let the grass grow under his feet. He was not to be disposed of easily. He was still a member of Parliament. He had the full support of the East British Labour Party and the backing of his constituents who had elected him. After consultation with friends, he decided to launch a petition which would be the basis for his People's Front campaign. It was a direct appeal to the people of Britain to support his views and it asked the Labour Party rank and file to insist that the forthcoming conference reverse the decision of the Executive. The petition said:

We British Citizens, looking out on a world threatened as never before by War and Fascism, call upon the parties of Progress to act together and at once for the sake of peace and civilisation.

We ask for a Government that will:

(1) Defend Democracy, protect our democratic rights and liberties against attack at home and from abroad;

(2) Plan for Plenty, multiply the wealth of the nation by employing the unemployed on useful work; increase Old Age Pensions; ensure a higher standard of life; educational leisure for old and young;

(3) Secure our Britain, organise a Peace Alliance with France and Russia, that will rally the support of the United States and every other peace-loving nation and end the shameful policy which made us accomplices in the betrayal of the Spanish and Chinese people to Fascist aggression;

(4) Protect the People's interest, control armaments and the vital industries, agriculture, transport, mining and finance;

(5) Defend the People, provide effective protection against air attack and starvation in the event of war;

(6) Build for Peace and Justice, and the exploitation of subject races and lay the foundations of a lasting peace through equality of opportunity for all nations.

In the face of the perils that confront us, we urge you to combine every effort to drive the National Government from office and win for us the Six Points of our Petition. To a Government of your united forces we pledge our whole-hearted support.

At once strange things happened. Ellen Wilkinson and D. N. Pritt, who had supported Cripps and voted for his memorandum, declined to go further. Three Labour M. P.'s rallied to him—G. C. Poole, Aneurin Bevan, and G. R. Strauss. Other former leaders of the Socialist League joined in the fray. Petition committees were formed in all parts of the country.

John Maynard Keynes, later Lord Keynes, wrote:

I am in full sympathy with what you are doing. It seems to me very important not to split existing Parties but to capture them. . . . I had a talk yesterday with Violet Bonham-Carter and agreed to sign the petition of which she had a copy, though I made some suggestions about some additional words to it. . . .

And G. B. Shaw, as young as ever, crashed into the *Daily Herald* with characteristic verve,

Sir Stafford Cripps proposed a Holy Alliance to get rid of the present Government as Napoleon was got rid of at Waterloo, by a mixed force of British, Belgians and Prussians under an Irish General. If a Labour Member may not propose this he may not propose anything. But the Labour Party Executive, taking a leaf out of Herr Hitler's book, promptly expels Sir Stafford, who, whether right or wrong, will presently wipe the floor with it for being so silly.

Fast and furious went the battle. The Labour Party Executive claimed to be the custodian of Socialism in all its purity. They asserted that association with other parties in a People's Government would mean the abandonment of Socialism. But what annoyed them most was that in this campaign Sir Stafford proved to be the biggest recruiting agent the party had had in many years. Thousands joined the Labour Party at the meetings which he addressed.

The Labour Party threatened further expulsions, and with that crack of the whip Mr. Poole and Will Lawther, the miners' leader, retreated. Ellen Wilkinson resigned from the editorial board of *The Tribune,* which was backing the campaign. An ultimatum was issued to Aneurin Bevan, M. P., G. R. Strauss, M. P., Sir Charles Trevelyan, Lieutenant-Commander Edgar Young, and Mr. Robert Bruce to cease support in the campaign or be expelled. They were expelled. H. N. Brailsford wrote to the Executive and told them to expel him, too, as he was with Sir Stafford.

The fight was waged with great bitterness. Ridley, an Executive member of the party, wrote:

By accident of birth, and a privileged capacity to earn a fabulous income, a privately controlled political machine is being created that gravely menaces the authority of the Party.

Herbert Morrison talked of Sir Stafford as possessing "an indelicate manifestation of egotism." There appeared to be no limits to the innuendos. D. N. Pritt wrote to Cripps:

Whether it is part of a whispering campaign emanating from Transport House or just independent malice, there is a story being sent around about you to the effect that the men you employ at Filkins are (a) not members of a Trade Union, and (b) not being paid Trade Union wages. I have actually got one case where I can fasten on a definite individual who has spread this story and put a stop to him. Could you tell me the facts when you have a moment to spare?

Sir Stafford replied:

Many thanks for your letter about the men employed at Filkins. The facts are as follows:
(a) After a struggle of some years against the apathy of the Trade Unions, I managed to get a branch of the Transport and General Workers' Union started in the village, and I have since made Trade Unionism compulsory so far as any of my jobs are concerned.
(b) It is therefore obvious that anyone employed by me is paid Trade Union rates of wages. They also get a holiday with pay.
If you have any cases of absolute libels of this kind, you might let me know, as they are interesting.

He toured the country from end to end. The meetings everywhere were large and enthusiastic but they did not influence the mass of the trade unions who would decide the issue.

When the time came for holding the annual meeting of the Labour Party at Southport, Sir Stafford asked to be allowed to face it. The question which dominated the great gathering was the position of Sir Stafford and the other expelled members. There they sat in the public gallery, Sir Stafford and Lady Cripps, Aneurin Bevan, the stormy petrel of the party, George Strauss, and Lieutenant-Commander Young. Sir Stafford was given twenty minutes. As his erect figure walked quietly to the rostrum there were storms of applause and booing. Quietly he waited, and then, speaking as if he were addressing a court,

he stated his case. He limited it to a justification of his course
of action as a constitutional procedure, claiming the right of
every member of a party not only to state his views, but to
take whatever measures he might deem necessary to organize
support for them. It was of no avail. The unions had decided
how they were going to vote long before they had heard what
Sir Stafford had to say. The Executive's act of expulsion was
endorsed by 2,100,000 votes to 402,000. A similar vote also
sealed the fate of the People's Front resolution.

So Stafford Cripps had become, by the action of the Labour
Party, an Independent Labour M. P. for East Bristol, a back
bencher without a party. It was a strange position for him and
not a little ironical. All his opposition to the Labour Party Executive up to the Munich crisis had been based upon *class
struggle* principles which the Labour Party rejected. From the
time of the signing of the Munich Pact he proceeded to aban-
don them also in favor of the national principles of the Labour
Party. The difference between Sir Stafford and the Labour
Party now was not a difference of principle but of application
of principles they held in common. And this had led to his
expulsion! The Labour Party wished to organise the support
of all people irrespective of class, who accepted their program.
Stafford wanted this, too, but went further than the party, in
that he wished the Labour Party to *unite with other parties
irrespective of class* against the Government of the day in order
more effectively to fight Fascism and War.

This was a significant turning point in his career. From this
time onward he left behind him the *class struggle* principles
to resume the course he had been taking before the crisis of
1931. Then he was in full accord with the Cripps-Potter tradition, working in harmony with Parmoor, the Webbs, and their
theory of the progressive organic development of society without abrupt breaks. The events of 1931 shocked him, as they did
the whole Labour Movement, from this mode of thought. All
society was torn apart into rival class camps, the Labour Movement in one and the old parties of Liberalism and Toryism in
the other. He moved in conjunction with the Labour Party and
promptly rationalised the situation in accordance with the logic
of that division. This led him to the "extravagant criticisms" of
Buckingham Palace politics, the institutions of Government

and rival parties, although at no time did he become a republican or a nonconstitutionalist. All that was behind him in 1939 for the new crisis did not lend itself to the same simple alignment of forces. Now all classes were involved, along with the very existence of the institutions which he had previously criticised, "Monarchy," "Parliament," "democracy" itself. Nation was about to fight nation. That he saw and understood. All his native, traditional patriotism demanded of him that he follow the logic of these circumstances as fearlessly as he had followed the other. Hence, in his judgment, the claims of the nation began to supersede the claims of any class.

Thus once again Cripps moved into the main stream of his forbears.

World War Two was on the doorstep.

X. The Independent

WHEN Cripps and the others who had been expelled met on the day following their expulsion, all agreed to apply at once for readmission to the Labour Party. By return of post came a most amazing reply which said that the applications could not be considered for some time because, in view of the gravity of the international situation, no meeting of the National Executive would be held during the summer; a strange decision in view of the serious circumstances of the time. The gravity of the situation is evident, for the date was June 2, 1939.

The conference had passed a resolution in which it expressed "its deep concern at the prolonged delay in concluding a definite and unequivocal pact with France and the Soviet Union for mutual defence," condemned the "shameful record of the so-called National Government, advised it of the principles it should adopt, and adjourned. It rejected every proposal for attempting to force the Chamberlain Government to resign, content to wait for an expected general election some time before the year's end.

Fortunately, expulsion from the Labour Party did not carry with it expulsion from Parliament. Cripps knew also that he had the full support both of the Bristol East Labour Party and the people who had elected him. Neither he nor Aneurin Bevan and George Strauss, the other expelled M. P.'s, gave a moment's consideration to the formation of a new party. That, they knew, would only have obscured instead of clarified the main issues.

Sir Stafford had to think quickly. Suddenly it dawned on him that what he could not do as a leading member of the Labour Party he could do as an individual. He would speak in Parliament and out of it as an independent Socialist. Unable to organize a Popular Front, he would use every personal contact he possessed among the supporters of Chamberlain to disintegrate their support. He was convinced that as soon as war embroiled Britain there would have to be a "government of concentration"—a coalition which would include the Labour Party. He would therefore aim to make it impossible for Chamberlain and the other "Men of Munich" to be the leaders of such a government.

It is necessary here to recall the developments of the months before Britain's declaration of war on Germany. On April 14, 1939, after Britain's unilateral guarantees had been given to Poland and Rumania, Russia was asked to give similar guarantees to those two countries. On April 17 Russia replied, proposing a triple pact of mutual assistance among France, Great Britain, and Russia, a military convention reinforcing such a pact, and a triple guarantee of all the border states from the Baltic to the Black Sea.

The British and the French were afraid of the implications of the proposed alliance, and, as the *Times* put it, thought that "a hard and fast alliance with Russia might hamper other negotiations and approaches." In other words, it would rule out a continuation of the Munich policy. So, on May 1, Chamberlain declined the Russian proposal. But on May 9 he repeated his proposal for a unilateral guarantee for Poland and Rumania, with the novel suggestion that the guarantee should become operative only upon the decision of the British Government, without making the slightest mention of any reciprocal assistance to be accorded Russia by Britain and France. Russia replied by repeating her original proposals and ignoring the British Government's stupidity. But the Soviet Government had noticed the character of the British proposals. Indeed, they regarded the proposals as one more attempt on the part of the Chamberlain Government to turn Hitler's face toward the East. When, therefore, the British Government notified the Soviet Government of its readiness to negotiate a pact, Count von Schulenburg for Germany was already in Moscow to negotiate a trade agreement. Should it happen that once again the British and the French proved to be playing for time, rather than really coming to equitable terms of common defense against the Fascist powers, the door was wide open for the Soviet Government to step aside and defend the Soviet Union by other means.

Lord Halifax was invited to come to Moscow to negotiate the pact. On June 8, Halifax made a speech in the House of Lords, expressing his distaste for the division of Europe into politically hostile groups, and offered to Germany the idea of a conference for the adjustment of rival claims. This appeared to the Russians to be writing off their proposals as of no account. Nevertheless, they waited for the British and French delegation, which arrived in Moscow on June 15. Conversations proceeded without arriving at any decisions, until Zdanov, a member of the Russian delegation, wrote an article in *Pravda* telling the world it was his opinion that "the British and French Governments are not out for a real agreement acceptable to the U. S. S. R. but only for talks about an agreement whilst facilitating the conclusion of an agreement with the aggressors." To the Russians, this appeared to be the fact.

But by July 25 it was agreed that staff talks should begin. The Joint Staff Mission of the British and the French Governments left London on August 5, traveled by slow boat, and arrived in Moscow on August 11.

These were the highspots of world war developments from the time of the Labour Party's expulsion of Stafford Cripps to the end of his first efforts to undermine the position of Chamberlain and change the Government by personal persuasion. Sir Stafford's diary records that the first step in his new offensive was to write to Baldwin arranging a meeting with him on June 19. Of this meeting he said:

> We had a long conversation. . . . I gained the impression that I could not expect anything from him in the way of action, though his political sense and observation were obviously acute. However, he promised to consider all I had said and to see whether he could do anything.

On June 22, Cripps conferred with Winston Churchill at his flat. Churchill inveighed strongly against the Prime Minister and told how he and Eden had been ready to join the Cabinet ever since Hitler had entered Prague. But Chamberlain would not have them because their entrance into the Government would have put an end to his policy of appeasement. Churchill expressed the view that had not Chamberlain appeared to have changed his policy after Hitler's march into Prague, the movement for a Popular Front would have swept the country and he would have supported it. He agreed that an all-in government was necessary but despaired of convincing Chamberlain and could not see how to get rid of him.

On Friday, June 23rd [says Cripps] I sent Kingsley Wood a draft of the sort of speech I should have liked to make over the wireless to the German people—including a strong repudiation of imperialism and the acceptance of international co-operation as the new basis of world development. I suggested if Halifax would like to see me I would gladly go to see him. I had an immediate response that the letter had gone to Halifax, and he would be glad to see me.

On June 28, he wrote:

I fixed an appointment for 4:30 P.M. at the House of Lords. I found Lord Perth there and discovered that Halifax had discussed my memorandum with Ogilvie (BBC) beforehand. I developed the scheme for broadcasting on a much wider basis of a really strong and broad attack. I had discussed the matter with David Astor who had been working on the broadcasts. . . . During the discussion, I had the opportunity of raising the second point as to an all-in Government. . . . Halifax agreed that it was the right policy. . . . The same evening at 10:15 P.M. I had an hour with Oliver Stanley, and completely convinced him of the urgent need of an all-in Government. I told him who I had already seen and begged him to start doing something. . . . Before I left he promised he would discuss it at once with others and see what, if anything, could be done.

On June 29, Cripps wrote:

I arranged a lunch at which three Trade Unionists, Ben Smith, Jim Griffiths, Will Dobbie, should meet Colonel Count Schwerin of the German General Staff in order to impress on the German Colonel that the British working class was really serious in its attitude. I dined with Aneurin Bevin and was glad to find his reactions the same as mine.

Cripps had now got the idea going in many quarters that an all-in government was essential, but he says:

The difficulty is to replace the Prime Minister to make it at all possible. This can only now be done by intrigue from within the

Cabinet itself. It remains to be seen what will eventuate from that. If nothing occurs within the next week, I shall consider launching a press campaign to try and bring the result about—as the situation is so desperate that something must be done. I have been appalled in these and other conversations to feel the hopeless bankruptcy of ideas and initiative in the highest quarters. There seems to be just a hopeless resignation to the inevitable disaster.

On June 30, the day after the Zdanov article appeared in *Pravda,* now anxious above everything to see a pact between Britain and Russia signed, he wrote in his dairy: "I rang up Kingsley Wood and offered my services to go at once to Moscow to get the Russian agreement concluded, as I felt I could do this if I was given the authority."

Halifax thanked him for the offer but could not make use of his services. He learned the next day that the negotiations had reached the stage of qualified acceptance by the Soviet Union, subject to three points: (1) that aggression should include direct and indirect; (2) that military talks should follow at once on the signing of the pact; (3) at the last moment Britain had raised the question of including three new countries, Holland, Switzerland, and Luxembourg. Soviet Russia could not agree on the third proposition without further consideration. The third proposal appeared to Cripps sadly like sabotage. Anxiously he went to the House of Commons in search of ministers to beg them to take action on the matter. But it was a Scottish night and none of the ministers could be found. He even wrote to Winston Churchill urging him to make a public statement offering his services. But Churchill replied on July 8, 1939, from his home at Westerham, Kent:

Many thanks for your most kind letter which I have carefully weighed.

I am sure that any such demarche on my part would be unwise and weaken me in any discussion I might have to have with the gentleman in question.

Coming to the conclusion that there was nothing more he could do at the moment, and Parliament having risen for the summer recess, Cripps went to Goodfellows. Ever since 1920, Goodfellows had been the treasured home to which he returned as frequently as possible. From here he drew strength and confidence in his life with Isobel and his children; here, during the nineteen twenties, he rested from his legal battles; here, exactly a decade before, he had decided to embark on his political career, after long discussions with Isobel during which they recognized "that life would never be the same." The thirties, with his increasing involvement in the legal and political world, cut a mighty swathe into the time for domestic life. But the life of Goodfellows went on under Isobel's direction; the house echoed to the sounds of growing children and their school and university friends. Of life at Goodfellows, a schoolmate of John's at Oxford, Geoffrey Wilson, who became a close family friend and professional associate, writes:

Stafford used to get to Goodfellows on Friday evenings in time for dinner after his day's work in the Courts, and leave again very early on Monday morning. But that was only during the summer. From October to April his week-ends were spent in addressing meetings throughout the country, and he rarely saw his peaceful and soul-restoring home. So week-ends at Goodfellows really meant summer week-ends.

The beauty, the comfort and the sense of general well-being could be repeated in countless homes. It was the spirit of Stafford and Isobel which pervaded the whole place that made Goodfellows different. They were the life and soul of all that happened there. Several of their four children and two adopted sons were generally around.

And there was Miss Hill, Stafford's secretary, and Miss Lawrence, universally known as Nannie. The guests, generally three or four at a time, were a miscellaneous lot—distinguished politicians and some less distinguished, youthful proteges, relatives, old friends of the family, and people that Isobel just thought would be all the better for a few days rest in the country. Among the politicians George Lansbury and Jawaharlal Nehru stand out particularly in my memory, perhaps because their simple humanity and friendliness fitted so well into the general atmosphere.

There was little routine. But you were expected to turn up in time for 8:30 breakfast unless you had a good excuse, to rest when you were told to, and to go to bed when Stafford announced that it was time, usually about 10:30. If you felt so inclined you could go for half an hour's walk—always the same walk—before breakfast with Stafford, accompanied by a selection of the family, three dogs and a goat. In the evening after dinner, you would sit in the library and talk at random about anything and everything while

Stafford and the ladies of the family knitted jerseys for themselves and each other. When the weather was particularly good you would sit out of doors by the "Moat," a stream that ran through the well-ordered garden.

Otherwise the time was your own. You could go for walks or play tennis which was robust rather than expert, and read and talk in the library or garden. You could browse through the collection of special editions whose number grew steadily as each birthday passed. On Sunday you would probably be taken on a conducted tour of the village and shown the museum, the new cottages, the village centre, the swimming pool, the children's playground, and be introduced to George Swinford, the mason and foreman builder. At some stage you would find yourself engaged in a long talk with Isobel, which somehow always left you feeling more at peace with the world than you had been before. If you were lucky enough to strike a week-end when a birthday—your own or one of the family's —was being celebrated, you would be bundled into one of a fleet of cars and taken for an all-day expedition with a picnic lunch to the Black Mountains. Or it might be a Shakespeare play at Stratford. If you felt so inclined, you might go with the girls to see if there was anything to report from the fields where the earliest fritillaries or bee-orchids or anemone pulsatilla or some other wild flower were normally to be found. Or you could just mooch around and take life easy, turning up for meals at the appointed hour.

I don't recollect any great preoccupation with "problems," unless a group had been specially invited for the purpose. That was not the way things worked. It was not that "problems" were avoided, if the conversation happened to turn that way. But Stafford's life in London was busy and he usually had to spend a good deal of the week-end working. When he was not working he relaxed and he relaxed as wholeheartedly as he worked. The result was a lot of leg-pulling and uproarious laughter, and a tendency to boisterousness at mealtimes which Isobel sometimes seemed to fear might get completely out of hand. We were not there to set the world to rights. Stafford and Isobel knew that they had created at Goodfellows a place where not only they but all who came there could draw inspiration from the peace and beauty and serenity which surrounded them. So those who had arrived from the city on Friday jaded and careworn would leave on Monday loaded down with flowers that Isobel had plucked and spiritually refreshed to face the problems that awaited them in plenty in the world outside.

So once more, in this atmosphere, Stafford talked things over with Isobel. The children having attained their majorities, the home was no longer the tie which it had been when they were young. Isobel was now free to begin a new period of collaboration with Stafford in his political life. The responsibilities of this partnership were to be well shared between them. In a few short months Isobel's burden of representing Stafford in England would begin as he set out on his journey around the world.

But that was to be for the future. The time was now July, 1939. Believing, incorrectly, that a pact would be duly signed between the Russians and Britain despite delays, the family packed their bags and sojourned to the south of France for what they thought, correctly, would be their last summer holiday abroad for a long time to come. Reflecting on the situation, Cripps wrote on July 27:

It seems as if Chamberlain might be going to the country in the autumn as the Saviour of the Peace, by getting the Russian Pact and doing an appeasement with Germany, in which case the prospects of the Labour Party will be poor in the extreme, as they will really stand for nothing in particular. There may well be an electoral debacle if there is not a war before the year is out.

But events did not take that course. On August 15, Count von Schulenburg informed the Soviet Premier, Molotov, that Germany was prepared to negotiate a pact of non-aggression with Russia. The British-French Military Mission in Moscow was without instructions. The Russians were convinced that nothing could come of continued conversations. The Poles refused to agree to the assistance of the Red Army or to sign any agreement with Russia. On August 23, the Soviet-Nazi pact of non-aggression was signed, and the Soviet Union had a free hand to plan her defense in depth and to secure the regions on her frontier from the maneuvering of Hitler's left wing. Hitler had secured his forces against a two-front war and was ready to turn westward as soon as he had rubbed Poland off the map. And for that he was ready to strike. He struck immediately.

Cripps and his family had just returned to England when, on September 3, 1939, Chamberlain announced that Britain was at war with Germany.

There was no doubt in Sir Stafford's mind as to what he should do. The question of the use of force had no relevance to his Christian conscience under these circumstances. All his family traditions, his centuries-rooted patriotism, his political convictions—which were integral with his Christian ethics—his whole nature as a man of action, combined to impel him forward as an active participant in the war against Nazism. There were no half measures to his commitment. He wound up all his personal affairs and placed his services at the disposal of the Government. This was not an application for membership in the Government, but an expression of his readiness to serve in any capacity whatsoever. He was scientist, lawyer, administrator, ex-manager of the largest chemical factory in the war of 1914-1918. But his services were not required!

Now he was in a unique situation—"purged" from the Labour Party; his services rejected by the Government, and his country at war. He was a back bencher serving the Labour movement which did not want him, yet outshining its leaders every time he spoke in the House of Commons or on the public platform. He was a leader without an army. If ever there was a man who could now afford to wait on events it was he.

But he could not wait on events passively. Events of world significance were following one after another at great speed, and he was alarmed by the isolated position into which Britain had drifted. Fortunately he did not lose his wits as so many of his old colleagues had done when the German-Soviet pact was signed. He saw that, whatever ultimate objective the Russians might have, it was of paramount importance for Britain that the pact of non-aggression should not be allowed to develop into a German-Soviet military alliance, by default on Britain's part. The latter, he considered, could be avoided if, instead of sulking about the German-Soviet pact, the British Government promptly set about establishing improved trade relations with Russia, as the beginning of better political relations. The day before the Red Army had marched into Poland he had written to Lord Halifax in furtherance of this idea:

I am so desperately worried by the development of the Russian situation that I am taking the liberty of writing to you and giving you my impressions on it for what they are worth.

You may remember that in the first note that I sent you through Kingsley Wood last July I stressed the possible danger of the

German-Russian alliance if we were not more active in pursuing our own alliance with the U. S. S. R.

This unfortunately for us has materialised and the policy of Russia in this matter is quite understandable from the point of the real politic that Russia has been pursuing ever since the dismissal of Litvinoff. . . .

The hostility of Poland to Russia, largely due to the fear of Sovietisation, has its reciprocal in the attitude of Russia to Poland which is now in evidence. This reaction on Russian opinion combined with the fear of Japan makes it natural that the Russians should look at the European scene with very different eyes to our own.

The Russian Government today has not the least sentimental attachment to the Western Democratic powers.

They regard both the regime of the western Imperialisms of Great Britain and France as equally undesirable as the regime of Germany and as a consequence are prepared to take either side in the contest judging their position solely from the point of view of their own advantage. . . .

I think that the extent of the hostility that is thus developed towards this country in Russia is not yet finally determined and that it is possible yet for something to be done to allay the danger of our finding a new and very powerful enemy arrayed against us in company with Germany.

It is not necessary to stress the extreme danger of such an eventuality. The question seems to me to be, can anything be done at this stage to prevent such a tragic development.

Could not something be done at once on the line that was adopted during the last war for America when there was a dangerous development of anti-British feeling in that country? Or if that is not the appropriate technique in this case, could not an all-party delegation fly to Moscow at once in order to try to influence Russian opinion in our direction?

I realise very fully that these are unusual steps to take, but I regard the situation as so full of menace that it seems to me that no step, however unusual, should be neglected in the present circumstances, to prevent so serious a development of the situation to our most grave disadvantage and to our imminent danger.

He saw Winston Churchill who, at the outbreak of war, became First Lord of the Admiralty. The only points of agreement between Cripps and Churchill on this occasion were the needs to crush Nazism and to separate Russia from Germany.

Although Churchill was still interested in discussing Government changes, he was now praising Chamberlain. In all the comings and goings, Cripps found Maisky, the Russian Ambassador in London, personally keen for better relations but emphasizing that his Government were indifferent one way or the other. They would be ready to receive a trade delegation if Britain wanted to send one, provided it was sufficiently influential. They would receive no more delegations headed by "office boys." At the same time he denied all possibility of Russia fighting with Germany. Cripps was not impressed by the denial. Nor did he rest content with agitating ministers. He suggested concrete ways and means in a memorandum which he sent to Halifax:

NOTE ON RUSSIAN TRADE TALKS

I suggest that the best way in which to put the matter forward would be to propose that you should be authorised to start upon conversations with Maisky on the following basis to be laid down by you at the commencement of the negotiations:

(1) The negotiations to be concerned with the practical arrangements of the next twelve months' trading with Russia.

(2) Negotiations to be carried on with Maisky in London in the first instance.

(3) A statement to be made by you at the beginning that if the following conditions mature in the course of the negotiations then you will go to Moscow to conclude them, but that you are not prepared to give any kind of undertaking at this stage that you will go to Moscow.

The conditions to be as follows:

(i) That a point is reached in the London negotiations when you are satisfied that there is enough substance in them to merit your going to Moscow.

(ii) That it appears necessary for you to go to Moscow on the ground that the negotiations cannot be finalised in this country.

(iii) That Maisky will give you his assurance and that of his Government that in a stay of not more than one week there is every chance of a final decision being come to.

As you know I regard this offer to go to Moscow in certain events as of the very essence of success for the following reasons:

(1) Russia is in the position of having a number of competitive customers for her exports of whom the most importance from

our point of view at the moment are Great Britain and Germany, in the sense that everything we can take will not only be to our advantage, but will also be to the detriment of Germany. . . . In these circumstances Russia, having no great preference for either individual customer, will naturally deal with that one which takes the most trouble about the matter. Germans are continually sending people of importance to Russia to do deals of all sorts, and in consequence Russia is prepared to deal with them in preference to a customer who sends no one, or only the office boy!

(2) Russia is still smarting under the treatment that she received in the summer and in her hurt state of mind the compliment of sending an important personage to Moscow will be invaluable in smoothing the way to an arrangement.

(3) The offer in certain contingencies to send a Cabinet Minister will demonstrate, as nothing else can, that we are anxious to establish better relations and in the light of that atmosphere it will be easier to solve the difficult points that will arise in the negotiations.

On September 22, Lord Halifax replied:

I am grateful to you for offering to go out to Moscow to sound the Soviet authorities and am quite prepared to facilitate your journey, on the understanding, of course, that you would be travelling as a private individual.

Here was born an idea which would soon evolve into a plan for the full use of the waiting time which became known as the "phoney period" of the war. Cripps had long wished to visit India, China, and America in order to learn from them and to discuss their affairs and their relationship to Britain. The existing "absence of relationship," or as it was defined "hostile neutrality," between Britain and the Soviet Union, plus the state of affairs in India, led him to decide that he would strive to go to Russia by way of India and China.

But try as he might, he could get no decision on his project of trade negotiations with Russia. The days went by without news. Cripps was of the opinion that the holdup was due entirely to political matters outside the range of the proposals. This turned out to be the case. The Russians were convinced that the stubborn resistance of the Finns to the Soviet proposal of a pact was due to British pressure upon them. They were concerned too with the appeasement policy being pursued by the British Government in relation to Japan.

Meanwhile there was another aspect of the situation with which Cripps felt called upon to deal. When Hitler replied to Britain's declaration of war by a so-called "peace offensive," Cripps held the view that Britain could not answer merely by a flat rejection of the proposals made both by Hitler and the Soviet Union. He insisted that it was necessary to give a precise answer as to what should be the basis of peace. He himself answered in two ways. He submitted a memorandum to Chamberlain, the Prime Minister, and made his first speech in the House of Commons since the outbreak of war. He set out his views in these words:

We on this side of the House have certainly been consistently opposed to the regime of Hitler in Germany. It would indeed have been to the great benefit of our country and the world as a whole, if that antagonism had been shared by the Government during the last five years. I am as unwilling as any Hon. Member in this House, to place reliance upon the promises of Hitler or of any similar Government in any part of the world. . . . Yet it would, in my view, be the height of unjustifiable folly merely to turn down his proposals without putting forward in clear and precise terms our own objective.

Any definitive world settlement must envisage democracy and freedom, if that is our true aim, not only in territories that have been conquered by the Germans, but throughout the world. Our care for India must be as great as our care for Poland. Our readiness to re-establish the map of Europe must be equalled by our readiness to reconsider the whole question of the Imperial conquests of the past. We cannot, without laying ourselves open to the charge of cynicism, select the territories of others for the benefits of democracy and freedom while withholding those benefits from territories from which we derive economic advantage. To go forward with a war upon such a basis would, in my view, invite disaster.

He went on to outline the reforms at home, which were essential to give social security and well-being to the workers of Britain. Then he declared:

The true solution is, therefore, not to give any particular country any colony, but to pool the whole of the colonial areas as territories which the European countries should share in developing with the object of their attaining maturity and self-government as soon as possible.

The memorandum he sent to Chamberlain formed the basis of an article in *The Tribune* of October 6 which ended with the following:

The answer stated in colloquial terms should be:
If Germany is prepared to give up her conquests of non-Germanic peoples and to deal with minorities under a true international system in which all the nations shall partake of the administration, then we are prepared to do the same as regards the British Empire, and enter into an economic arrangement, whereby all the resources of our various countries are pooled for the benefit of the people of the world, through the control of an economic general planning staff, drawn from all countries, by a scheme to be worked out by the nations forthwith, as a permanent basis for world peace and to be accompanied by rapid disarmament on all sides by successive stages.

Chamberlain replied:

Many thanks for your letter and for sending me your Memorandum on Hitler's proposals. I am greatly obliged to you for the trouble you have taken in setting out your views so fully, and there was certainly no need for you to apologise for the length of your note. The problems we have to consider are of immense importance and great complexity, and it is clearly impossible to discuss them adequately in a short compass.
I am bound, in fairness, to say that I doubt the practicability of some of your proposals but I am sure you will not expect me to comment on them in detail at this stage, though I want you to know that I have read the Memorandum carefully and with great interest.

Cripps did not rest content with this reply. He saw Halifax and said:

I asked him if he would object if I telephoned to Felix Frankfurter to ask him to get the President of the U. S. A. to approach the British Government on the basis that if Hitler really meant what he said about the ethnographic division of Europe, then there did not seem any reason why a conference should not take place. After some discussion he said that if the U. S. A. did make such an approach I could take it that the most careful consideration would be given to it and that it would not embarrass the Government. He had no objection therefore to my telephoning on my own responsibility if I wished. This was the most that I could expect and the most that I wanted.

This he did. He explained to Supreme Court Justice Frankfurter that this was entirely a personal effort on his part to interest President Roosevelt, but he felt confident that any action taken by the President would receive the most serious consideration of the British Government.

In the midst of this excitement there came an echo from a time which now seemed long ago. The Labour Party Executive met after its summer recess and dealt with the letters from the five expelled members who had applied for readmission to the Labour Party on June 2. They were asked to express their regret for past actions, and to refrain from campaigns to change party policy. All of them refused these conditions. Sir Stafford replied:

I am not prepared to express regret at the action taken by me, as I am now, more than ever, convinced that the action was not only fully justified, but was the only action that I could have taken consistently with my duty to my constituents, and the best interests of the workers of this country. . . . I should have thought that such matters as are dealt with in the Executive's decision, had become irrelevant in the light of the national and international situation.

Ironically, the Government which had no use for his services when he offered them unreservedly at the outbreak of war, suddenly asked his aid. Would he help in the drafting of anti-profiteering legislation? He made a draft and Gwilym Lloyd George and Oliver Stanley accepted it. He advised them on the procedure to be adopted.

After the legislation was carried through, G. Lloyd George and Stanley wanted him to take on the job of administering the legislation he had drafted but were nervous about the manufacturers' reaction if he were appointed. One day he saw Stanley, who apologized for not appointing him as chairman of the Central Price Regulation Committee. As he had expected, so it had happened—the trading interests would not have him. The interests to be controlled could manage their own controlling.

These incidents he dealt with in passing. His mind was occupied with the great issues of international relations in wartime. He had learned much about India since the beginning of his friendship with Jawaharlal Nehru, whom he had first met in England in 1937. This son of India, educated at Harrow and Cambridge, second to Gandhi in the leadership of the Indian people, was a refined, cultured man who, with his record of unswerving loyalty and courageous leadership, appealed to Sir Stafford as had few other men in political leadership. Although Nehru was not a Christian, he led what Sir Stafford would describe as a Christian life in its quality of unremitting social service to his fellow men, while he regarded his political course as that of a socialist standing firmly and courageously by his principles, whether his path led to prison, as it had so often, or to the heights of power.

Cripps was equally concerned with the situation in China. He had watched from afar the course of the Chinese Revolution and the travail of the Chinese people. He knew that when Sun Yat Sen set the national revolution going in 1911, that was the great beginning of a new birth for the Chinese people. Their betrayal by the western powers, when the Japanese invaded Manchuria in 1931, had roused his indignation and played the greatest part of all in destroying his illusions about the League of Nations. No one knew better than he that, while China was putting up tenacious resistance to the continued Japanese invasion, she was also in a continuing social revolution, which had yet to reach its full consummation in a liberated China, with her people on the march toward a Socialist society.

Hence it is no surprise to find him in these days dining with the Chinese ambassador in London one day and another with Krishna Menon, who would one day be India's ambassador to Britain. On October 23 he saw Lord Halifax about his proposed journey to India, China, and Moscow. Halifax was rather wary of the proposal lest it be interpreted as some London-Moscow-Chungking diplomatic maneuver. As for India, he feared a head-on collision, but could not see what the Government could do about it, for he felt it to be impossible to go beyond the statement recently made by the Governor-General. Halifax claimed that he was not a "wicked imperialist" but he could not accept the Indian National Congress as the only spokesman for the Indian people. Cripps says,

I pointed out that if we believed in Democracy, Congress did represent the majority of British India according to the election results, and that they did distrust this Government and that the Governor-General's statement would make them more distrustful. To offer consultation only on how they could help us in the war and not on Indian affairs was really insulting them. A Consultative Committee ten years ago was one thing; it was another to offer it ad hoc in this crisis. I agreed a head-on collision was inevitable if the Government persisted in their views and pointed out that even if he were not a thoroughgoing Imperialist, others in the cabinet, such as Winston, were. . . . We got nowhere and it was clear that the Government thought they were doing the right thing and it was no good discussing the matter further.

Cripps explained that he did not want to go to India or China or Moscow as a government representative, but in a personal capacity. All he wanted from the Government was an understanding that they would give full weight to his observations on his return. He put forward the following plan:

1. That the Government should be prepared to assist in summoning a Constituent Assembly within one year of the termination of the war.
2. That the Assembly should be constituted upon the basis of the present Provincial electorates, plus a proportional representation from any States who would introduce sufficient democracy to enable representatives to be elected to the Constituent Assembly.
3. That a three-fifths vote should carry in the Assembly.
4. That if the representatives of the major parties—judged by the provincial electoral results—agreed upon a better method of representation, then that better method of representation should be adopted.
5. That the Government would accept and abide by the results of the Constituent Assembly, provided the latter would enter into a Treaty with Great Britain for a given number of years (say 15 years) during which the transition should be carried through, the method of transition and the financial, defence and other details to be settled in the Treaty, which should also contain some clauses giving protection to minorities in British India.

At last he was assured that if the Indians approved of his

plan the Government would give it their serious consideration. On November 29 he wrote in his diary:

> This is really promising progress and means that if I can get the Indians to consider my proposals, there will be a real chance of acceptance by the Government of this country. . . .
> This morning I parted from my Chambers finally and so closed a long chapter of my life at the Bar. I have no regrets except for associations.

He wrote to his constituents:

Dear Comrades,

As you know, I have always taken a very great interest in the affairs of India and the struggle of the Indian people to attain their freedom, and their own democratic Governments. Owing to the action of the British Government and the War situation, matters have taken a very serious turn in India and it looks as if there was every prospect of a real clash occurring unless something can be done immediately to bring pressure upon the British Government to take a more enlightened view.

I have been doing what I can in this country to persuade the Government and their advisers of the need for some positive action, but I have felt that I was strongly handicapped through lack of actual knowledge of the Indian situation and Indian personalities.

It is also clear that a great deal depends upon the advice sent by the Viceroy to the Government and nothing can be done in this direction unless I can see the Viceroy in India. In addition to this my very good friends in the Congress Party have expressed an urgent desire that I should go to India and I feel that this practical demonstration of sympathy with their views is very desirable at the present time.

I therefore decided to go to India entirely on my own, not of course in any sense as an agent or emissary for the Government, in order to get first-hand knowledge of the situation and do anything I can to assist in a solution.

I have a very strong conviction that the end of the war, when it comes, will present problems in which the Asiatic peoples will have to play a very large part, especially Russia, China and India. I am therefore going to take the opportunity of going on to China to investigate the situation there, and as a result I may be away from this country for some months.

I have thought very seriously over the question of whether I was justified in leaving the country at the present time and have come to the conclusion that nothing decisive is likely to occur here before the late Spring and I shall be utilising the intervening time to the best advantage by equipping myself with knowledge of the Indian and Chinese situation. I should of course be able to return in comparatively short time if any particular situation arose which demanded my presence in England.

I know I shall take with me your best wishes and I shall convey these to the Indian people and also to our Chinese comrades.

I am sure that while I am away you will all of you do your utmost to keep the flag of Socialism and freedom flying in Bristol East.

Twenty-four hours after writing this letter he took leave of England, accompanied by Geoffrey Wilson, his secretary and friend, on a journey which lay far east of Suez and Mandalay. History was to be made.

XI. A Journey of Political Exploration

W HEN Stafford Cripps and Geoffrey Wilson set forth on their journey to the Far East and beyond, they were going on no mere sight-seeing excursion. They had a purpose which would preoccupy their minds and set limits on what they could see. Yet they traveled with eyes and ears open. Their diary records what they saw and learned as well as what they did.

They left London on November 30, 1939, and reached Paris the next day. True to plan and form, Sir Stafford had arranged two interviews before lunch, one with the French Colonial Minister, Georges Mandel, and another with a Pole who had been in charge of health services in China. Cripps discussed the problems of the Far East with Mandel and later in the day had a brief discussion with the Minister of Finance, Paul Reymand. There followed a few hours when the travelers were free to wander around the Paris of the "phoney war" period. They looked inside the Cathedral of Notre Dame, crossed the Seine and inspected the famous bookstalls, snatched a little refreshment, and boarded the Simplon Orient Express. There was no time to stop in Switzerland, the oasis of peace. At Milan they changed to one of the electric super-trains of Mussolini's Italy.

For Rome and the shadows of her ancient glories there was no time allowed in their schedule. Fascist Italy, an ally of Nazi Germany and on the brink of war with Britain, was not a place for an Englishman to stay longer than necessary. They took off by airplane for Athens. Flying south-east they crossed the Gulf of Taranto toward the island of Corfu, the spot where Mussolini, soon after he came to power, had first shaken his fist at Europe. As they circled to descend near Athens, there lay the ancient Acropolis; from the air it looked amazingly insignificant. After one hour's stay they were off to Alexandria.

From the diary:

Fortunately, the aeroplane was extraordinarily comfortable with chairs that let down and had foot rests attached. A steward brought round coffee, tea, tomato juice and biscuits at all the right times, and perhaps more important of all, the plane made so little noise that it was perfectly easy to talk without ever raising the voice above normal conversational level.

Five other passengers were aboard, three English and two Dutch. The most interesting was a Mr. Baker, eighty-three years of age, making his eightieth journey to the East. He was an eminent agriculturalist, with plantations in Malaya and interests in New Zealand. Sir Stafford and he were soon involved in deep and enthusiastic conversation about compost-making and soil fertility, and oblivious to their passage through the air. Suddenly Alexandria was below. The sun was setting and before them stretched a lovely scene, the sands of Egypt with palm trees silhouetted against the bright red sky.

Hardly had they reached their hotel and gone to bed, it seemed, than the early morning was upon them.

The sun came up above the horizon as we were driving to the airport this morning, and within a few minutes we had taken off. For the first half hour we flew over the delta of the Nile, a wonderfully rich and fertile region, with so much water about everywhere that it must be mighty difficult for the people to get anywhere at all. Then over the sea for an hour to Palestine and ten minutes later we landed at Lydda, the airport of Jaffa, Tel Aviv and Jerusalem. That airport is a real work of art. It was built by a man called Price, who is architect to the Palestine Government in conjunction with Gumley, the Director of Civil Aviation. The proportion and the colours are superb and there is a lot of simple but most delightful ironwork. It is difficult to believe that a better airport could exist anywhere. . . . We headed straight for Baghdad, first over rocky hills covered with olive trees, then over the Jordan Valley with a view of the Dead Sea in one direction and the Sea of Galilee in the other, then over rising hills inhabited by the Trans-Jordan Arabs and so on to the Syrian desert. That was the most fascinating part of the whole flight so far. We were five thousand feet above the ground and kept seeing little black rectangular shapes which we identified (quite rightly) as the tents of the nomadic tribes. Often we saw tiny specks round about them which were caravans crossing the desert. It seemed quite impossible that such numbers of people and animals could keep alive on the amount of water and green stuff which we were able to see. A panubiot would have a.pretty thin time! We crossed the pipe line several times and saw encampments along it, and were able to see where the caravan trails wound their way through the sand. . . .

After about two hours, we at last saw a river which we finally identified as the Euphrates. Cultivation began to appear, and soon we were in an area intensely cultivated by means of a most elaborate system of irrigation. Then we came to the Tigris, and a few minutes later landed at Baghdad airport, some way from the town, which is reported to be entirely uninteresting.

But Baghdad had figured once in the Kaiser's dream of a railway, a highway of Empire, stretching from Berlin, the center of Europe, through Baghdad to the East.

The travelers recorded that:

We followed the course of the Tigris which winds so that we crossed it every few minutes, and at one time the pilot came down to 100 feet or less so that we might see the ruins of Ctesiphon—a huge construction built in the 13th Century entirely of brick, with an arched span which seemed impossibly large for such material.

Taking over the writing of the diary at this point, Wilson says:

I have always imagined that Mesopotamia, in which the Garden of Eden was supposed to be situated, would be a mass of luxuriant vegetation. That's what comes from looking at the map and seeing it coloured green. In fact, it is dull and uniformly brown except in patches along the banks of the rivers and elsewhere, watered entirely by means of irrigation works. It was not very interesting except in bits, and Stafford spent his time reading about China and killing flies.

A few miles above Basra the two rivers join and they celebrate the fact by flooding the entire countryside. Instead of cultivated land there is nothing but marsh, inhabited by the Marsh-Arabs, whose villages as often as not are entirely surrounded by water, and visible means of livelihood are absolutely non-existent. It was about the most dreary and desolate place that could be imagined, and even the desert would be paradise compared with it. Just at sunset we landed at Basra airport, with which is combined the Shatt-al-Arab Hotel.

Half an hour before sunrise the next morning they took off from Basra. It was pitch dark and suddenly they were over the Abada oil field "which looked like some huge jewel with its twinkling green and yellow lights." There was no long creeping-in of the dawn with gradations of light from darkness to gray and on to the golden light. Quickly the sun was up, and they were flying toward it as it rose higher over the mountains of Persia. Along the coast line of the Persian Gulf, seven hundred miles of desolate shore:

There was scarcely a single patch of green—nothing but sand and mountains made of sand, with high mountains in the distance and an occasional tiny village which was hardly distinguishable at the height of 11,000 feet at which we were flying.

All this was disappointing. Where were the "Persian gardens" and all the fantastic places of beauty and luxury of this land? Where was that

> . . . Strip of Herbage strown
> That just divides the desert from the sown,
> Where name of Slave and Sultan scarce is known.

Omar Khayyam must have been dreaming of some other land.

It seemed quite impossible that people could find enough to live on in such a place. . . . The most extraordinary place was the Point of Man over which we passed just before we reached Jask. It is a quite fantastic collection of rocky mountains rising steeply from the sea, with occasional narrow plateaux at the top. These plateaux were the chief cultivated areas, though how anybody got to them was a mystery.

They swept along the coast of Persia and suddenly they could identify the spot where they were crossing into India. Karachi lay before them. The mayor of Karachi, the local leader of the Indian Congress Party, newspaper reporters, and many others were waiting to greet them.

After the Indian custom, the two guests were garlanded with flowers and greeted as though they were long-absent friends returning home. Although Karachi was simply a stopping place for an hour, they were in India, and work began at once. Sir Stafford wrote:

I spent the hour at Karachi having questions fired at me from all sides, wanting to know my views on every conceivable subject. . . . I also put a good many questions myself as to the possibility of a settlement of the Indian difficulty, and gathered that as a whole they thought Gandhi was being too slow and holding them back too much, but if there was any chance of the British Government giving way, then perhaps it was the right thing to do.

At Allahabad Jawaharlal Nehru and fifteen others were waiting with a beautiful garland for Sir Stafford. The two men greeted each other warmly. They were friends of some years standing and had so much in common that they felt toward each other like brothers, who could talk with frankness and understanding. They drove to Anand Bhawan, Nehru's home. Cripps submitted to Nehru a draft of the proposals which he had discussed with the leaders of the British Government, and sent a copy to Gandhi.

Nehru and his friends who were invited to meet Cripps, found it difficult to believe that the British Government would make a promise of independence and fix a date for it. They wanted to know too what was meant by the words "dominion status." If this expression really meant "independence," why did they not say so? Why did not Sir Stafford himself use the expression "independence" if it meant the same as "dominion status"? It was shorter. They knew what they meant by independence, while they were not sure what the British meant by "dominion status."

The day after his arrival Sir Stafford recorded:

The day has been so full of interest that it is only the high lights that can find a place here. It began with a visit to the Agricultural College about six miles away, of which Sam Higginbotham is the head, an American institution which now has such a reputation that students come there from all over India to study agriculture and the use of the products of the land.

On our way back to Allahabad, we passed the Central Prison where Nehru and Ranjit Pandit spent so much of their time, and also a Basic College. The latter is a part of a new educational scheme which Congress has started in all the Provinces where they have control and particularly in the United Provinces. It is on lines similar to the Montessori system, and is intended for children between the ages of five and ten. The idea is that the children should learn by doing, and by doing something useful, and although the scheme is in its infancy, it has already broken down much of the hostility which the educational officials had at first shown.

The whole place left an impression of an enormous vitality that had been released among the people by the fact that with their own government they were responsible for their own affairs, and even the resignation of the Congress Ministry is not likely to effect this particular development. The school at Naini, which we had been to earlier, was run on the same lines, and we were full of admiration at the results produced with pitifully inadequate materials—how inadequate can be partly judged from the fact that the teachers were paid only 17 rupees, or 27/- a month.

After lunch we set out by car again to visit a village. We crossed the Ganges and then turned off the metalled road on to a track composed mainly of dust. . . . The entire population of the village turned out when our car arrived and it was quite touching to see their devotion to Nehru and his simple unaffected interest in them. Some rural development had been carried out here, so the cattle were better cared for than elsewhere, and there was a tiny reading room. We went inside one of the houses—all of which are built of mud with sun-baked tile roofs, and the poverty was awful. It consisted of two rooms, the first used as a sort of kitchen, about six feet by twelve, and lit only by such light as came in through the door, and the other room opening off it, about the same size, and light of its own. The entire household goods consisted of not more than a dozen utensils and a few pieces of white cloth, but the whole place was spotlessly clean. They don't seem to mind how filthy the village is, but the house must be properly kept. . . .

Our guide this morning was Ranjit Pandit, Nehru's brother-in-law. He is one of the most cultured and delightful men that I have ever met, and is a member of the U. P. legislature. He is a mine of information for all our questions about trees and birds, agriculture, industry, religion and politics, and while he was in prison he occupied himself making an English translation of one of the Sanscrit classics. He also gave us a most interesting account of the British dealings with the Princes, about which he has written in a book which he is going to give us, and explained the political position in the Punjab.

The next day there were so many requests from societies in the University of Allahabad that there was no alternative than for Cripps to address nearly all the students of the university in its great hall—nearly twelve hundred people. Nehru also spoke and was received with that tremendous enthusiasm he evokes wherever he goes. After the meeting, Cripps and Nehru headed an impromptu procession back to Anand Bhawan.

From Allahabad they went on to Delhi. Of this journey by rail Geoffrey Wilson said:

We are travelling in a first-class carriage. We have a large box to ourselves for the moment. The box is the full width of the train and about twelve feet long, contains two beds, two chairs, two electric fans, three different kinds of covering over each of the eight windows, and has a lavatory attached in which there is a shower bath, but no towel. Fortunately, we were far-sighted. It's very spacious but rather depressing, the woodwork being dirty brown and the upholstery a drab green imitation leather, nor does it appear too clean. The whole affair looks as though it had been in the height of fashion thirty-five years ago, and had not been touched since. We carry our own bedding with us in a large roll like a holdall. We shall be spending ten of our sixteen nights in India in one of these, so we are trying hard to find out how to behave. . . .

The night journey was not altogether a success, and the carriage looked even drabber this morning than it did last night, after it had acquired a good thick layer of dust on a stretch of line which we were assured was comparatively clean!

Delhi, city of grandeur and power, is the ancient capital of Hindustan, standing midway between Bombay in the West and Calcutta in the East. The city had a population of two million people in the days of the Great Mogul Empire when Jehan was the ruler. If old Delhi, with its great Mogul palace of purpled ease, typified the grandeur of the dead empire, New Delhi in its own splendor exemplified the majesty and might of Britain's power at its zenith. Here were the Viceroy's residence and the Parliament building which, in their magnificence and spaciousness, surpass the buildings of Washington. Near them, as if taking shelter beneath the imperial power, are the palaces of the Indian princes and the luxurious private houses of the rich.

All this was interesting, but the travelers were busy paving the way from the pomp and circumstance of yesterday to the liberation of tomorrow. They were searching the minds of men and grappling with the foundations of power. They started the day with press interviews and continued until night listening to the views of leaders of organizations and prominent persons.

One such was G. D. Birla, an important mill owner and supporter of Gandhi. He favored the separation of the Moslems
and the Hindus, just as in business "you cannot carry on with
an unsatisfactory partner." Liquat Ali Khan, the Secretary of
the Moslem League, said that "it would not be possible to settle with the British unless there was first an internal settlement.
. . . Unless a constitution could be devised which would make
it impossible for one community to rule by itself, it would
never bring peace to the country."

During the night they traveled to Lahore, where they conferred with the Prime Minister of the Punjab Government, Sir
Sikander Kyat Khan, and others members of the Cabinet. Sir
Sikander was a Moslem and nominally a member of the Moslem League, but he would not permit it to function in the
province. The diary reveals that the Prime Minister held the
view that

It was time for the British Government to make a declaration of
Dominion Status. . . . Half a dozen people could settle the Communal question in principle in half an hour. The states would have
to be treated differently and would need a respite to get used to
things. There would be no need to change political boundaries. . . .
He had suggested to Jinnah and Gandhi that they should put their
cards on the table, but nobody would do it. . . . India was not prepared for violence and would not be for another fifty years. It
would soon be suppressed by the help of various sections in India.
He agreed with Gandhi that there must be an agreed settlement,
and a Constituent Assembly would do more harm than good from
a communal point of view.

From Lahore the travelers returned to Delhi for another day
of interviews and discussion and then took a train for Bombay.
For hours they gazed at the countryside as they rolled along.
Now they saw a fertile land very different from anything they
had yet seen, passed through rich woodland, crossed many
rivers, saw large herds of cattle, and were especially struck by
the gay colors worn by male and female alike, "in so far as they
wore anything." Incidentally, it had dawned on the railway
authorities that there "was a war on." In the cars were notices
announcing "Precautions against possible Air Raids. Please in
your own interests keep the window shutters of your carriage

closed between Bombay Central Station and Bassein Road after darkness has set in."

Bombay is to India what New York is to the United States. As a port, it is one of the best in the world. It is the western terminal of the Indian railways and its Victorian station is regarded as one of the finest structures of its kind. Set amidst bold and striking scenery, with more than a million population, it is at one and the same time a great city of immense wealth and a cesspool of poverty, misery, disease, and filth.

Here Cripps had one of the most important of his conferences. He went to see Jinnah, the leader of the Moslem League, at his home on Malabar Hill. This tall, thin, dark figure gave him the impression of a man in everlasting conflict with himself. The most powerful figure in the Moslem League, he was neither admired nor loved by his followers. But he held a key position for the future of India.

He opened the conversation by suggesting that, as Sir Stafford was "being shepherded around the country by the Congress," his mind was already made up. After Sir Stafford had put him at ease in this respect, he proceeded to state his views with ability and clarity. There was no doubt about his detestation of the Hindus. He said he would consider Sir Stafford's memorandum on its merits. Perhaps it was the last chance to secure co-operation.

Cripps went to the trade-union headquarters for a talk with Joshi, the trade-union leader. There emerged from this conversation an important observation to which none of the political leaders had referred. Joshi said that in all their history the unions had had no communal troubles in their own ranks, although twenty-five per cent of their members were Moslems and untouchables also were included. In their view, the best cure for the communal disease was working together on an economic basis rather than a political one.

From Bombay, Cripps and Wilson journeyed to Hyderabad to see the head of the greatest feudal state of India. Waiting at the station to receive them was a very smart A. D. C. who got into great difficulty. Sir Stafford and Wilson were traveling second class. This led to a case of mistaken identity, for as they stepped to the platform they were ignored while the A. D. C. sought to persuade a good-looking solitary Englishman, who was traveling first class, that he was really Sir Stafford Cripps. A look of horror swept across the aide's face as the second-class passenger announced himself, but jumping to attention and making all the necessary salutes, he rushed Sir Stafford into a car and swept Wilson aside into another one, provided for the person of inferior social standing. The idea of Wilson's traveling in the same car as Cripps passed his comprehension.

In due course Cripps was ushered into the presence of His Exalted Highness the Nizam. Here Sir Stafford got a shock, for as he entered the antechamber he was met by a middle-aged man in a white coat that would have looked smarter had it been sent recently to a cleaner's. He thought this must be the Nizam's secretary. But it was not. It was "H.E.H." himself.

They talked together for an hour, seated on a plush-covered sofa surrounded by chairs and knickknacks that might have been lifted from the boarding house of a retired civil servant on the Brighton sea front. Sir Stafford is not inexpert in furniture-making and is a good judge of what is good and what is bad. He was startled to find this man of immense wealth living among such fusty, second-class stuff. He was soon to find that the Nizam had a mind as fusty as his furniture. Nevertheless, he was polite and even charming and listened patiently while Sir Stafford told him that British India would certainly get its freedom after the war and the pressure on the States would be much greater if they had not themselves taken steps to make their governments more democratic. It would be no use thinking that British troops would be available to uphold the princes. The Nizam asked a few courteous questions but did not show that he was likely to do anything about anything.

Sir Akbar Hydoris, a state official, later confirmed Sir Stafford's impressions, saying: "What could one expect from a man who had never been outside his own state except on one or two occasions to Delhi, and who had had no education?" Sir Akbar himself was a cultured man, a lover of the arts, and a politician. He understood the realities of the situation, but he was no democrat. He recognized clearly that the Moslem community of Hyderabad, comprising not more than fifteen per cent of the population, was the ruling body and was completely identified with the feudal landlords. They admitted that there was no logical basis for their domination of eighty-five per cent of the population which is Hindu. Their concern, however, was not for logic but for power. This they had, and they intended to hold it as long as they could.

At Wardha the travelers were met again by Nehru, who had made arrangements for Sir Stafford to meet the redoubtable Gandhi, the little bald-headed, dark-skinned man, who was the greatest leader India had produced in its long struggle for freedom. An ascetic, somewhat of a mystic, a profound believer in the simple life, he was also a shrewd politician whom no one could divert from his course. Gandhi's influence was so great in the Indian National Congress and among the millions of its supporters that Cripps could have saved himself a great deal of time and energy by submitting his proposals to this man alone. Such was his power that if he rejected them they would be rejected by the people of India. If Cripps did not realize this at this time he would later. Indeed, the British Government would ultimately do what Gandhi said they should do from the outset—leave the Indians to settle their own future form of government.

Ever since Gandhi became the leader of Congress in 1919 his leadership had been unchallengeable. Jawaharlal Nehru says of him:

It was the utter sincerity of the man and his personality, that gripped; he gave the impression of tremendous inner reserves of power. . . . Every gesture had meaning and grace, without a false touch. There were no rough edges or sharp corners about him, no trace of vulgarity or commonness, in which, unhappily, our middle class excel. Having found an inner peace, he radiated it to others and marched through life's tortuous ways with firm and undaunted step.

Gandhi's whole life was dedicated to a purpose—Indian independence. But the means of attaining his purpose were more important to him than the end. Indeed it might be truly said that the means were ends in themselves, for they meant to him a way of life. His rejection of violence was more than a political tactic. It was a positive assertion of the human spirit against material power. It implied a supreme self-control and a superb serenity of the mind combined with a tremendous faith in his fellow man. It was this that made him the natural leader when

he first proposed non-violent passive resistance to acts of repression. Passive resistance meant turning the cheek to the
smiter, being ready to face imprisonment, beatings, death,
without violent retaliation. Through the years since then he
and scores of thousands of his followers had been imprisoned
time and again. He had never wavered. He belonged to the
mystics who walked by faith. But he was an intellectual, too,
a trained lawyer and politician with a remarkable capacity for
seeing essentials and first principles and taking the measure
of his fellow men.

When Nehru brought Cripps and Wilson to see Gandhi in
his hut in a village some five miles from Wardha they literally
filled the hut. It was a bamboo framework covered with a
mixture of mud and cow dung. Gandhi's bed was on the floor.
There were a few pieces of bamboo furniture, a packing case,
a few books and papers, and his false teeth in a box. He did not
much care about those teeth, and they were in the box more
frequently than in his mouth.

What a meeting was this! The little elderly dark man, living
a life as simple as that of any peasant, and yet one to whom
millions looked with adoration and faith, sat with crossed legs
upon his mattress bed. Beside him on the floor sat the handsome intellectual Nehru. Both faced the tall bespectacled cultured lawyer politician, the son of an English baron, Sir
Stafford Cripps K.C. M.P. sitting on a stool in his socks, charming, free, and easy. Over a simple meal of bread and fruit they
talked of how to take "the brightest jewel" from the British
Crown and to set four hundred million people free from
imperial control. As they talked and Cripps explained his
document, they took the measure of one another. Gandhi
thought Cripps "lacked humility." Cripps thought Gandhi
"shrewd and clever."

The next day they met again. Cripps said afterward:

One cannot but be impressed with the vigour with which Gandhi
holds to his creed, and the calmness with which he is prepared for
any sacrifice in order to attain it. His whole way of life, with its
extreme simplicity and selflessness, is part of his creed and demon-
strates his sincerity. . . . I feel there is a much better chance of the
solution of the problem while he is still alive and in control, than
there will be if and when he goes. . . . Nehru is the next in im-

portance to Gandhi and then Rajagopalachari of Madras and Vallabhbhai Patel of Bombay.

And now for Calcutta and the Viceroy, Lord Linlithgow. For an hour Stafford talked to this sphinxlike person of the political situation in India, of his discussions with the Government at home, his memorandum, and the next steps to be taken. He summarized his impressions of all the conversations and conferences he had in the journey across India:

I told him that in my view, negotiations between the Moslem League and the Congress were out of the question at present unless a third party brought them together and that *he* was the only possible third party; also that they should be asked to put down in writing, Congress, how far it was prepared to go in meeting the Moslem demands, and the Moslem League, exactly what demands it made, so that he might compare the two statements and attempt to bridge the difference by negotiation. . . . I further told him that in my view, unfortunately Zetland had little power or authority in England and that owing to the preoccupation of other members of the Cabinet with war questions, he as Viceroy, was in fact the most important determining factor on the question of Indian policy. . . . I left him with a copy of the memorandum which I prepared in London and told him of Gandhi's reaction to it, also the large sheet of results of the last elections.

The end of his Indian mission was at hand. He felt that his journey had been worth while. He now knew from first-hand acquaintance and free discussion with all the most important people controlling the affairs of India what they thought should be done. Convinced that all he had seen and heard supported the course he had taken, he hastened on his way. But before leaving India there was one man he must see—the poet Rabindranath Tagore who lived in an old-fashioned mansion on the outskirts of Calcutta. Of this visit Cripps wrote:

There must have been five vast courtyards with buildings all round. We were left by the secretary to wait in an extremely pleasant, simply furnished and restful room and then we were taken to see the poet. He was in his chair in his bedroom, dressed in a black sort of gown that set off his magnificent white beard. The room itself was as simple as could be imagined—a small bed, two tables, four chairs, some perfectly lovely red roses, and that was all. He talked with us for nearly an hour, of the Chinese, of the situation in India and the British in India. He was very philosophical in his manner and very gentle and we considered it a great privilege to have that time with him, though we should very much like to have gone to Santiniketan and seen the work he is doing there.

That was Christmas Day, 1939. The next morning the travelers went to the Dum Dum airport, climbed into a plane, and soared high over the mouth of the great and sacred river Ganges as they swept eastward to Burma.

XII. In Time for the Showdown

CRIPPS AND WILSON dropped from the skies into the airport at Rangoon from the French aeroplane which had brought them from Calcutta. After one night in the expensive Strand Hotel, they went to stay with U Tin Tut, "a civil servant with a very nice and comfortable house and three charming small daughters."

On that day there arrived a deputation from Generalissimo Chiang Kai-shek, led by W. H. Donald, the Australian adviser to Chiang, who brought a message welcoming Sir Stafford and his friend to China. There was very little time to take stock of the situation in Burma. But Cripps met various groups of people, workers' organizations and political representatives. His most important interview was with the Governor.

The British Governor of Burma lived at Government House, Mandalay, an extraordinary place. Surrounded by a moat about a hundred feet wide, it stood on the wall of a fort in an enclosure two and a half miles square. The wall was of lovely red brick. The house itself, constructed entirely of wood, was as wide as the wall and stretched along it for a great length. All the rooms opened out of a long passage running the entire length of the building. The isolation by moat and the old-fashioned wall of the middle ages symbolized the remoteness of contact and outlook of the governing elements from the people.

Of his talk with the Governor, Cripps wrote:

I had a talk about the Chinese position and found him very sympathetic to China and quite confident that China would be victorious. He said he always saw as many of the Chinese Ministers as possible when they came to Burma and expressed his desire to see Donald who had not yet turned up in Mandalay. He told me that it was due to him persuading the ministers after a long effort that the Burma Road was opened up, but he was not in favour of a railway being constructed as, from the point of view of Burma, it could not be remunerative. . . . From that point of view he regarded it as a strategic danger as he thought the frontier could now be defended against China by Burma, but if the railway went through it could not be, except by posting large forces on the border, which would be very expensive.

Now the journey into China began. The railway ends at Mandalay. From there they had to proceed by car to Lashio and the famous Burma Road. Their way lay through enchanting country. Sir Stafford wrote:

Wherever we were there were the most glorious views of mountains and valleys, not fierce or wild, although much of the country was quite uninhabited, but with a certain softness which made it the most beautiful country I have ever seen. The first half was through densely wooded country but gradually it became barer, until towards sunset we dropped into the valley of the Schweli River which was a mass of paddy fields, and we watched the sun go down behind the mountains at the head of the valley in a glorious light of red and blue and green.

The people and their clothing were as varied as the scenery and we wished we had someone with us who could tell us all about them. Mostly they were Shans and Karens, sometimes with caravans or bullocks or ponies, sometimes in a procession by themselves carrying their wares over their shoulders. These they invariably carried in bundles or baskets on either end of a stick over the shoulder so that the weight was balanced. Some carried bows though there were no visible signs of arrows, and nearly all had long knives which they carried in wooden sheaths, and many had slung over their shoulders gaily coloured bags with tassels hanging from the bottom. The most attractive were worn by some of the women, who had dark-coloured trousers, often embroidered with a deep red, and black or dark blue embroidered skirts down to their knees with dark blue and red turbans, and they, like the men, always had their bundles balanced at the end of a pole. There was definitely an autumn look about the country so that the flowers were in any case not at their best, but they were so covered with dust along the whole road that it was difficult to see much except bright yellow Korean chrysanthemums, and yellow rock roses. There was also in blossom a tree which had every appearance of being some sort of cherry.

Whether it was a Chinese with a sense of humor, or the Australian Donald, who was responsible for diverting the travelers from the main Burma Road to cross the frontier over the bamboo bridge, is not known. But it certainly gave them an un-Chinese reception, for they landed in the center of a most modern aircraft factory under American supervision. They were housed in a brand new spacious wooden building and dined in a fair-sized ballroom complete with Christmas tree, soft lights, and ping-pong tables. Sir Stafford says:

It belonged to the Curtiss-Wright Corporation and the superintendent M. D. Walsh is a very fine type of man, quiet but obviously most efficient. The works manager, Hunter, and the chief engineer, Green, are both excellent fellows, and the former in particular impressed me greatly in his attitude of care for all the staff and employees. . . . Some 2,000 people are living on the site, which occupies a square mile, and a large number of coolies live outside in their own huts. . . . The factory originally started in Hangchow and then the Japanese made that unsafe so they moved to Hankow, and they had just started to build at Kunming when that was bombed, and finally they came to their present site. A year ago it was virgin land, and in spite of the fact that all the building material and machinery has to come up through Rangoon and Bhamo and thence 70 miles by a very poor road, they had already started producing aeroplanes, and hope within six months to be turning out one a day.

Before we left the staff assembled, both Chinese and American, and Col. Hain made a short speech in English, introducing me as the leader of the English Liberals!

After this surprising introduction, the travelers were switched back to the main Burma Road to continue their journey. On they rolled through open country, passing here and there the local Shans dressed in their dark blue costumes and turbans. Here the people were few and wild life was more abundant—an eagle soaring in the sky, the birds in the paddy fields, and wild ducks.

As they began the ascent of mountains, the country became bleaker and barer. Bamboo disappeared and fir trees, scrub, and long grass marked the landscape. Up they drove to six thousand seven hundred feet, and then down the Salween gorge. All the sides were steep, deep red in color, and terraced fantastic patterns by the paddy fields. From the height as they descended, the view was as from an airplane. Mountain ranges stretched as far as the eye could see.

At last they reached Paoshan, the first Chinese town they had seen. It was a fair-sized market town once used as a place of banishment from Peking of officials who had fallen into disfavor. They passed through several gates and narrow streets packed with people to a Rest House which was once a Taoist temple, a jumbled mass of tiled buildings decorated with a variety of animal figures, in stone, disporting themselves in many positions. The Rest House was high above the town amid ancient courtyards connected by circular doorways. Here the travelers stayed for a day and, as usual, spent it in seeing all they could and interviewing all who could give them such information as they were after: of the thirty thousand people in and around the town; of the magistrate and his powers, his revenue, his budget; of the council of elected persons and who elected them.

On they went into the Mekong Valley, traveled along twenty miles of gorge, crossed a suspension bridge made of steep ropes and wood, climbed three thousand feet up the mountain side, and reached the Guest House of Yung Ping, having taken four and a half hours to cover ninety miles. And then on again, climbing to 8,000 feet through thick pine forests. From the mountain top, besides the valley of the Yang river stretching out before them, they could see beyond a huge range of snow-covered mountains. Down into the valley they went and across the river, and up through gorge after gorge of great splendor until they were startled to find soldiers standing with fixed bayonets. It was a guard of honor for Sir Stafford. The manager of the Highway Company was their host for two days. He told them that life here was almost the same as it had been a thousand years ago, and truly they saw little that was modern. They were surprised to learn that:

The inhabitants include a number of Moslems and also Chinese Jews, who came to China 2,000 years ago, and settled in Hunan, whence the Jews in Tali Fu are come. They still retain the Hebrew language and religion, and are chiefly engaged in the merchant and distributing trades. Once a year, in May, there is a great market

and at this time Tali Fu presents the most marvellous medley of
costumes of every kind.

At a little place called Unnan, they were stopped by a soldier with a red flag. Generalissimo Chiang Kai-shek had sent
a messenger with a note to Sir Stafford saying that his private
airplane had come there to take him and his friend the rest
of the way by air.

In a fine four-seater Beechcraft plane they swept over a
jumble of mountains twelve thousand feet high, saw in perspective the road they had been traveling, and within little
more than half an hour topped the last range of mountains.
Below them lay a great lake with Kunming at its northwestern
end. On an island in the middle of the lake was a modern
hotel with all European sanitary conveniences and service.
Here the Australian, Donald, was waiting for them and became their guide and informer.

From him they learned much of the background of China,
old and new. Again they began the rounds—medical college,
local government administration, the railways, the banks,
industries, machine tool factory, learning of the mineralogy of
the province, its transport developments, its social services,
the economic and political structure. Cripps made this note
in his diary:

The two impressions one carried away were first, the amazingly
diverse and accurate work which was being done under improvised
conditions inspired by the determination to preserve China, and
secondly, the fact that Great Britain is being completely left out as
a supplier owing to the foolish policies of the past. The whole
impression today is that the connection between China on the one
hand and America, Switzerland, Germany and Russia on the
mechanical side, which will form the basis of the reconstruction of
China, is growing closer and closer. The latter four countries are
taking the fullest advantage of their opportunities, whereas apparently Great Britain is allowing her chance to go by default. . . .
British stock in China is very low indeed.

In those five days in Kunming there was not a factory, a
school, a power house, an institution, a man or woman from
whom he could learn of the life of the region and country,
that Cripps did not visit. Nor was it a one-way affair. On the

evening before he left he was taken to the Yunnan University to address what he thought would be "a select party of about twenty professors and persons of literary eminence." An old temple was the assembly room. When Sir Stafford arrived, there were twelve hundred people in the room and an overflow outside. He held forth for an hour and a half.

The next day they arrived in Chungking, the temporary capital of China, situated in west China, some nine hundred miles from Shanghai. It had about a million inhabitants. Its remoteness from the great ports is an indication of the extent of the Japanese penetration into China, although most of the occupation lay along the railways, and great stretches of the so-called occupied regions were controlled by the Chinese. At this time, January, 1940, there was a truce in the Civil War between the Nationalist Government and the Communists in order to fight the Japanese. It was an uneasy truce in which all the problems which had given rise to the Civil War remained. Both sides were without confidence in the truce and in their mutual concentration on the external enemy.

No sooner had Sir Stafford arrived in Chungking than he "unpacked hurriedly and was taken to call on Foreign Minister Wang," then to the British Ambassador, Sir Archibald Clark Kerr. Sir Stafford found that the Ambassador agreed with his criticisms of the British Government's policy of appeasement of the Japanese. Clark Kerr was keen that Sir Stafford should return by way of the United States, in the hope of being able to influence America in the direction of a better co-ordinated policy of England, France, and America toward aid for China.

Cripps discussed the internal situation with Sun Fo, son of Sun Yat Sen, "father" of the Chinese Republic. He learned of the existing methods of government and as much as he could of the Kuomintang Party which controlled the government. After his talk with Sun Fo he had his first interview with the Generalissimo. Of the latter he said:

He is a fine clean-looking man and is very impressive with his modesty and sincerity. He hardly spoke at all except to elucidate some point or to express approval of some idea. I gave him a long sketch of Foreign policy of Great Britain as frankly as I could and I found that he had said to the British Ambassador very much what I had said to the Cabinet as to the danger of the German pact last summer. He is obviously of the opinion that communism is unsuitable for China at this stage and I agree with him. And I do not think that he is anxious to be too close to Russia, but he did not say anything directly on this point. He asked me about the Burma Road and whether I had any suggestions, and I then developed my ideas about a closer rapprochement with both Burma and India, especially the latter so far as immediate help was concerned.

Then came his first meeting with the Soviet Ambassador:

I thought the Ambassador was an attractive young man, and just occasionally he smiled and then he looked very sociable and friendly. He told me that he had had a telegram from Maisky about me and that he was therefore dealing with me very frankly as a friend of the U. S. S. R. I told him about the relations between Great Britain and Soviet Russia and the part that I had played and stressed my anxiety for the improvement of those relations. He was anxious to know whether I thought that there was any likelihood of a combination of Germany and England against Russia. I thought this a rather odd question, but perhaps it was part of his frankness. I told him that the British Cabinet would probably like it once they could get rid of Hitler, but that I did not think it would come off. He made enquiries of the views of all the various members of the Cabinet as to their feelings about Russia and I expect a long report will go to Moscow. To me much the most interesting part of the conversation was about Finland. I told him that many friends of Russia thought that she should have waited to get the readjustments that she wanted without copying the Nazi methods of aggression, and that I should like to know what he thought was the answer that should be given to those who accused the Russians of imperialism. However, when I asked him if he would tell me definitely what was the aim of the Russian Government as to this war he replied that they would under no circumstances annex or occupy any Finnish territory as they did not believe in that, but they would, when the Finns had a Government which really represented the interest of the people, enter into diplomatic negotiations with it and then they were quite certain that all the matters could be very quickly settled. I told him that if such a categorical statement were made publicly it would comfort a lot of people in England, China and India whom I had met, and who had been friends of the U. S. S. R. but who were more than puzzled by the Finnish war.

Sir Stafford sounded out the Soviet Ambassador about his proposed visit to Sinkiang and the possibility of a talk with some of the Russians at the frontier. The Ambassador thought it a good idea. A wire would be sent. This was to lead to big things.

On January 20 came the news that the Soviet Government had no objections to Cripps' visit to Sinkiang. Again he talked with the Generalissimo, who wanted to hear of his visits to Chinese institutions and his opinions of their economy, the economic, industrial, and agricultural developments which he had witnessed. The Generalissimo asked him to stay for some months, make a complete tour of all the industries, and then help him in planning their future! Or could he recommend anyone like himself for the job? Sir Stafford said he would think about it.

Before leaving for Sinkiang he went to Chengtu, and from this center made visits into the surrounding country. Chengtu is in the middle of a huge plain spreading out fanwise and covering an area of some 2,000 square miles. Of it he says:

Chengtu is one of the most ideal spots on earth. The climate is never very cold, even in the severest times there is no frost, and in the hottest summer it is always cool at night so that blankets are necessary. The soil is so fertile that they grow as many as three crops in the year and sometimes four. In about a fortnight's time the whole place is a mass of blossom and already (January) there are lots of Kai Wah out everywhere and on sale in the streets. Every kind of fruit can be grown including strawberries and the most wonderful peaches. There is practically no trouble from malaria. Add to all this that Chengtu is a real centre of culture and activity of all kinds and I don't see what anyone could want better.

Back in Chungking he saw the Soviet Ambassador once more. He said of this interview:

I told him of the anti-Red scares circulating in America regarding the Russian control of China and my desire to counteract these by being able to describe, from first-hand knowledge, the complete Chinese control of Sinkiang, which he assured me existed and as to which he seemed quite anxious that I should make enquiries. He said that the Russians had absolutely no territorial ambitions in this direction. I then asked him about the rumours as to a Russo-Japanese Pact for the division of spheres of influence in China and he similarly assured me that this was nothing but Japanese propaganda and had no substance. He was very enquiring as to my views on the likelihood of British and American action towards Japan and also towards China. I raised the question of whether the Moscow people would care to meet me to discuss British Foreign policy and he said he had not had any reply yet to his earlier query on this subject but would again telegraph Moscow, making the suggestion that I could either fly by special plane to Moscow for a few hours talk or that they could come to Alma Ata and meet me there.

He went to the Generalissimo again and there were Clark Kerr, Madame Chiang, and Donald:

The G. asked me about my Chengtu experiences, about which I told him. . . . He also said he had read my memo on gasoline and he had passed it forward with instructions for it to be put into operation. I gave him the one on Haiphong railway transport, and also promised him one on road transport by handcart. I also dealt with the question of the co-ordination of agricultural research and the need for some organisation to put into operation the results of that research.

The Generalissimo again renewed his appeal to Sir Stafford to return, after he had been home to England to influence British foreign policy, and to bring a team of young people with him. But Sir Stafford would promise nothing more than that "he would think about it." Sinkiang was calling. The Generalissimo and his wife thought he would be very cold and called in a tailor from the Industrial Co-operatives and had the two travelers measured for trousers and short coats thickly lined with silk waste.

Within a few days the tailor fitted them up with "two most lovely blue silk-padded suits." On Sunday, February 4, Sir Stafford received a message from the Soviet Embassy to the effect that a special plane would be waiting for him at Alma Ata, just over the Soviet-Sinkiang border, to fly him direct to Moscow (3,000 miles) and then back to Urumchi. That meant about 8,000 miles of travel in seven days. So at last his long and persistent efforts to meet the Soviet leaders were to be rewarded.

Geoffrey Wilson writes that on February 6, Cripps

stepped into a German aeroplane wearing Madame's suit of rompers, his furlined Chinese gown, felt boots, a fur cap, and Don's scarf and walking stick. My garb was a little more assorted—Madame's rompers, my own socks, stockings and shoes, the Vice-Consul's heavy overcoat, the Consul's golf jacket, and no hat at all as I proposed to buy a fur one.

The first hop was to Chengtu. The second morning when they soared aloft, they could see far in the west before them, a huge range of snow-covered mountains and nearer still a lower range sprinkled with snow, its peaks jutting through the clouds. Suddenly the clouds broke, and they found themselves flying over fantastic country, narrow waterless valleys or river valleys, and hills and dales. Before they realized it, they were circling a walled town and came down to an airdrome on the bank of the Yellow river, in the midst of magnificent hills. The town was Suchow. On the left were the high mountains bordering Tibet, on the right the seemingly endless sand of the Gobi desert.

Here they had to stay the night. The Chinese Consul and his wife and son were on the same plane. All having dropped in unexpectedly, they had to make the best of improvised airport accommodation. So in a room twenty feet square, warmed by an iron stove with an iron pipe running along the ceiling, and four beds down each side of the room, they looked around to see how best to arrange themselves for the night. All was beautifully clean, with a large rush mat on the floor, one table, one window, a map of the world in Russian on the wall, and three colored prints representing Chinese rural life. The outlook from the window was magnificent. While they gazed in admiration on the Tibetan mountains, they must think how the Consul and his family could share the room with them. The problem was solved after much meditation by the woman and the boy going elsewhere, while the men shared the room to the tuneful accompaniment of the champion snorer of the party—the Chinese Consul.

Now began the journey over Sinkiang, the great highway province, a thousand miles from east to west, connecting China and the Soviet Union. Across it runs the most romantic road in the world, through "incredibly beautiful mountains and desert,"—the famous Silk Road, the oldest of caravan tracks, which had been in use when Columbus discovered

America. Cripps and Wilson were the first Englishmen, indeed the first white foreigners, to pass through this land since 1934.

It was of special importance to Sir Stafford that he should become acquainted with Sinkiang. There were so many rumors about it in Britain and America, especially with regard to its relations with the Soviet Union, that he was anxious to see the situation for himself. The province, nearly twice the size of Germany, has a population of only four and a half million people. Was it an independent state? Was it controlled by Russia or by Chungking?

Of the journey by plane on that early February day of 1940, he wrote:

It was a most marvellous trip, with the high range of mountains first of all on our right to the north until we crossed them half way, when we skirted them on our left, flying quite close to the side of them, having the most wonderful view into and across them, while on the other side was a huge snow-covered plain bordered by another range that was just visible in the distance. As we approached Urumchi, fir trees began to appear on the northern slopes of the mountains, and in some places were thick enough to form forests. One range of mountains was almost a deep purple in colour on its northern slopes where it was not covered with snow, and the effect of this with the snow in the brilliant sunlight was indescribably beautiful. . . . I think it was the best piece of mountain scenery I have ever seen, and the whole journey through from Suchow made one feel that the desert space that separates Sinkiang from China is a very good reason for the lack of close contact of Sinkiang with the rest of China. Indeed it is a little difficult to see how until the coming of aeroplanes it can ever have been organically connected with China.

But soon they were down from the contemplation of sublime scenery to the ridiculous acts of man. At Urumchi they were told that they would have to stay a day or two because of bad weather ahead. Then the fun started. They sent their cards to the Governor and the Civil Governor and suggested that their luggage need not be examined. But the police were on the job, and while they sat in the dining room of the airport, drinking tea and eating fruit and youghourt, the equivalent of the "gentlemen in blue" went through their luggage piece by piece. Every letter was unfolded, every piece of paper examined, and some were taken away to be translated. The Governor sent word that he was too ill to meet them, but he had made arrangements for their accommodation and sent all the appropriate messages. Now, says the diary:

The personnel of the airports is almost entirely Russian. This naturally gives the impression to the visitor that the Russians are very much in control of the situation, which is not the correct impression so far as other things are concerned. We had some talk while we were waiting to get into our hostel about affairs in Sinkiang, and were told that they were doing quite a lot in Chinese education with Russian as a second language, that they had a number of middle schools, a big normal school for which they are erecting a fine new building which we saw, and a university college with departments of all kinds, especially in the sciences, and an agricultural research institute. We were also informed that there were a great many mineral resources in the province, but not yet developed for want of capital. . . . There is as yet very little industrialisation and the chief products are wool, hides and skins, with raisins from Tulufan, saltpetre which has not yet been properly exploited, and silks, especially carpets from the south as well as wheat. Jade and gold are also found in the provinces. . . . There were foreigners in many but not all of the departments in the province. All these are, of course, Russian. One appreciates the difficulties of approach from the Chinese side when one realises that it is impossible to get goods from the Russian border to Lanchow by road because a lorry would require to carry a full load of petrol to complete the journey and would have no space for any goods. It is, therefore, a geographical necessity for any technical development to take place from the Russian side, and this is in fact what is happening. . . . All the inhabitants here have fur caps, knee boots, sometimes of leather, but more often of felt, and sheepskin coats. There were few Chinese types, most of the people being considerably larger and of a more Mongol or Tartar appearance, though Madarin Chinese is the generally spoken language. This place has the appearance of a town of nomads. We often see loaded camels going through the streets and a great number of pack ponies and donkeys. In fact, one of the great differences from the Chinese towns we have seen is the small amount of human transport and the use of animals instead.

At last, after days of waiting until the weather cleared, their plane took off for Alma Ata. Beyond Tashkent they were in a region of deep snow, and so it was all the way to Moscow.

Michael Tichomirov, assistant head of the press department of the Foreign Office, was waiting at the airdrome with a car to rush them to an hotel.

At last Stafford Cripps was in the place where he had wanted to be for so long—in Moscow, the Mecca of revolutionaries from the ends of the earth, the capital of the Soviet Union, with the many-colored onion-shaped domes of its hundreds of churches, its towers and minarets, its buildings old and new, and its high-standing walled city of ancient palaces within the larger city, all deep in snow. But he was preoccupied with the purpose of his mission. From the outset he was talking with Tichomirov, going over the ground he had already covered with the Soviet Ambassador in Chungking. He told what he wished to discuss with Molotov, of his thoughts about the invasion of Finland, about relations with Germany. But above all, he wanted to discuss with Molotov the possibility of concerted action among Russia, Great Britain, the United States, and France.

The next day he crowded in visits to the Moscow Underground Railway and an exhibition of Chinese and western pictures. But all this was overshadowed by the fact that in the early evening he was to meet Molotov in the Kremlin. Right on time, he arrived at the Kremlin gates and was ushered into the Foreign Office. Of this visit he says:

These are magnificent offices, very up-to-date and most beautifully furnished and decorated, the best government offices I have seen anywhere in the world. I was not kept waiting any time at all and was shown into Molotov's magnificent room where he and the interpreter were waiting. Unfortunately, the latter was a very bad interpreter and although he translated the general sense of our remarks, one lost all the fine points of personal expression. My general impression of Molotov was of an intelligent and extremely careful man who was not going to commit himself on anything until he had ample time to consider it in all its aspects. It was, in consequence, a very considerable job to get out of him any expression of opinion at all, especially on any point as to which he had not been fully prepared beforehand. . . .

It was quite clear that Molotov took the view that the British Government's policy towards Russia had never changed and had been throughout a hostile one and the Russian Government did not consider it worth while to enter into trade negotiations in that hostile atmosphere. He gave instances dating from last spring down to the present time as if they were all indistinguishable. . . . He gave me an explanation as to the Russo-German pact, saying that they felt themselves obliged to enter into some agreement on the west in order to avoid the danger of being drawn into the war, and that the French and British missions quite clearly did not intend to make any reasonable arrangement. At the same time the Germans changed their anti-Russian policy, Russia felt herself obliged for her own safety to enter into an agreement with Germany. I rather gathered from this part of his explanation that he intended to point out that the German agreement was not in any way an act hostile to Great Britain. I then asked him about the chances of some agreement either of a trade or a political nature being arrived at between Great Britain and Russia. He said that if at any time the British Government would adopt a friendly attitude towards Russia there would be no difficulty in coming to an arrangement, either on trade or political lines, but without this it would be impossible. . . . I then told him about the disillusionment and misunderstanding among Russian sympathisers on the Finnish situation and gave him the suggested draft of a statement which might be put out explaining the Russian attitude. His immediate reaction was that it was quite unnecessary, but after some discussion and explanation, he said he would have the document translated and would consider it. . . . As regards general Far Eastern policy, I asked him whether in his view it would be possible for Russia, Great Britain and America to concert a pro-Chinese policy, and it was to this that he replied that the question was one of which he had not been forewarned. I persisted in the question, however, and he then asked me what British policy was as regards China, to which I replied that it was to help China as far as possible without raising too much hostility from Japan. To this he replied that Russia's attitude was well known, to help China defeat Japanese aggression, and he did not seem at all averse to the idea of some concerted policy between the three countries. . . . I ended up with two final questions on the attitude of Russia, first towards India, and secondly towards Japan. As regards the first I asked if there was any possibility of what some people in England feared, i.e. intervention in India through Kashmir. At this he laughed and said it was obviously merely the ridiculous suggestion of some anti-Russian person and there was not the slightest possibility of any such thing happening. As regards Japan, I told him that a number of people in England were talking of the possibility of an agreement between Russia and Japan on the lines of dividing China into spheres of influence, an inner one for

Russia and an outer one for Japan. He said that this suggestion was equally ridiculous and that there was no possibility of any such arrangement being made by Russia. After a few polite exchanges, the interview which had lasted nearly two hours was ended. The only thing he asked me to do was to try to make clear to people in England the real basis of Russian policy. He assured me that Russia was not at all unmindful of its friends and supporters in other countries and was most anxious to preserve their goodwill.

Cripps thought the visit well worth while. It had confirmed his views on some things, enlightened him on others, put him in good relation with the Soviet Government, and strengthened his hand with regard to the policy he had been pursuing in England. And now for Chungking, Tokyo, America, and home.

Early next morning Cripps and Wilson were on the way to Kuibeshev. The weather was bad. Snow covered the earth. Visibility was poor and the plane had to fly low, rocking, swaying, bumping. After four and a half hours they came down at Kuibeshev into deep snow, so deep that the plane could not taxi. They were stuck, and there they stayed for two and a half hours. They had been forced down by snow piling on the cockpit window so that the pilot was unable to see where he was going. At last, with the aid of skis, passengers and pilot plodded their way to the hostel on the airfield. They learned another Russian expression which they promised never to forget—*plokay pogada* (bad weather). They watched a tractor plowing the runway clear of snow. There was a biting wind and the temperature was far below zero. So the day and night went by.

The next morning they heard the airplane engine turning over and hope rose. Into the airplane they went again. At ten o'clock they were being towed ignominiously back to the starting point. On the second morning, after cocoa, bread, and three fried eggs each, they got off in bright sunshine in a plane whose inside temperature fluctuated between 22 degrees of frost and 80 degrees F. They flew over the frozen Sea of Aral and an endless plane of snow to Tashkent and on to Ile. Here bad weather held them again. This time it was not the snow but the thaw. The landing ground had become a sea of mud and the plane could not take off. At last they decided to travel the next stage by road.

So Sir Stafford sat in the front of a twelve horsepower car with a tin of petrol between his legs, a dispatch case on his knees, and behind him Wilson and another traveler, three suit cases, two boxes of food, two bottles of water, a typewriter, a large tin of petrol, and other odds and ends, beginning a drive of twenty-five hours, suspicious of their luck but hopeful. Their driver was a swarthy Mongol dressed in a huge sheepskin coat. The road was a mass of mud and slush. The car looked all right from the outside. Its main defects were that it had no brakes, the accelerator stayed either all on or all off, the radiator boiled ceaselessly, the spare wheel was flat, and there were no chains on the tires. The driver knew little about driving and nothing about the mechanism of the car. Other defects were comparatively insignificant. Anticipating trouble from the boiling radiator, the driver had equipped himself with a sardine tin and whenever the travelers came within sight of water he would stop the car and rush off, fill it and bring it back to empty into the radiator. Naturally that did not lend speed to their progress.

Plunging into a beautiful gorge, everyone was too preoccupied with the condition of the car, the driver, and their position on a steep slippery hill, to admire the glories that were around them. At last Sir Stafford took over the driving.

The adventurous party reached a village where a Russian mechanic accomplished a little repair work. They climbed over mountains and down into valleys piled with snow. The moon rose and lit up the lovely scene. Snow was falling and for hours they were alternately digging the car out of snow drifts and pushing it along the road. Once when they were stuck a train of pony carts loomed up in the moonlight. It was going in the opposite direction along the old caravan track and no help came in response to loud appeals. The people of the caravan were too busy with their own troubles to think about the moderns and their difficulties.

The moderns struggled on and at last started to run downhill along a good surface. On their left reared up what looked like a great embankment of snow. But as they neared it and the moon came out and shed its light upon the scene, they stopped and gazed. Before them lay a wide lake, frozen solid. The pale green surface of the ice stretched out in an irregular pattern to the ranges of snow-covered mountains in the distance. With the soft moonlight on the mountains, the shadows in the valleys, the translucent atmosphere along the lake, the whole scene was indescribably beautiful and held them spellbound.

At last came Urumchi, thirteen days after they had left it, expecting to return in six. The next stage of the journey was uneventful. The car behaved itself and the road became easier to negotiate.

At Hami they found that an airplane had been waiting a week for them. After two days' wait for their luggage to catch up with them, they flew to Chungking.

The next day was one of interviews with the important people in the capital, beginning with the British Ambassador and ending in the evening with the Generalissimo, who, like all the others, was anxious to hear all that Cripps had to tell him of his mission. They covered familiar ground with the added information that the long journey had yielded.

Flying to Hong Kong, the travelers had lunch and a long talk with Madame Sun Yat Sen, T. V. Soong, and others. Then they boarded a steamer bound for Shanghai. On the way they called at Amoy, which was under the control of the Japanese. Its population since the Japanese came had dropped from 170,000 to 15,000. Cripps' diary notes:

The town this afternoon looked like the city of the dead. This ship last year called between air-raids and took on board some 2,000 refugees. It is some indication of the terror inspired in these people by the loathsome bestiality and senseless cruelty of the Japs of which the American Consul gave us some examples.

At Shanghai they boarded an airplane without delay and flew to Tokyo. Sir Stafford recorded in his diary:

The next day I had a talk with the Ambassador. He is very pro-Japanese and takes the view that nothing should be done to antagonise Japan until we know for certain whether we are going to fight Russia, as in such an event we should need to make an alliance with Japan.

At the home of a Japanese gentleman whom they met at the British Embassy they were entertained at lunch in proper Japanese style:

At the front door we removed our shoes and put on felt slippers. All the floors are made of very smoothly polished wood and are covered with fine matting, and the first room we were shown into for a cup of pre-lunch tea had in it no furniture at all with the exception of a table about 12 inches high with six cushions around it. The only decoration was one picture, one ornament, and a bowl of flowers and I understand that this type of furnishing is typical of a Japanese house. From that room we moved on into the dining room, similarly furnished but, as one is supposed to kneel at a Japanese table, and as our host has many foreign visitors, he had made the table slightly higher than normal so that they can get their legs underneath it if they want—and after a short time on our knees we did want!

They visited the Parliament House, or the Diet, where Sir Stafford talked with the Speaker and the oldest member of the Social Mass Party. This party, he learned, was similar to the Labour Party in England, but had only thirty-four members in the Diet. It was mostly drawn from the working class and concentrated on domestic policy only. The Tokyo schedule ended with a visit to the American Ambassador. Quickly they flew away to Formosa and then on to Canton.

Since the Japanese occupation of Canton, the wealthy Chinese had left. Huge areas were nothing more than masses of ruins with no complete house left standing in what used to be the busiest part of the city. One fifth of the area of the city had been bombed or burned out and no attempt had been made to clear up the debris. Of the million inhabitants, nearly half had fled when the Japanese came. Now they were trickling back, but the wealthy stayed away.

From Canton the travelers returned to Hong Kong, where they took off by clipper for America. The Philippines, Guam, Wake Island, Midway. They crossed the international date line and gained a whole day to make up for lost time. Onward they flew to Honolulu, landing at Pearl Harbor.

Pearl Harbor! How ominous and tragic the name sounds today! On the day they arrived, American warships lay quietly in dock. The waters were still and the sun shone warm. Here even the rain is known as "liquid sunshine." The whole island lay before them like an island of the blessed. The flowering shrubs and trees were a blaze of color. The African tulip tree was in full bloom. The bougainvillaeas and hibiscus were of every range from pale pink to orange and scarlet. There were blue moonflowers and wild roses in abundance. The gardens were filled with orange and yellow lilies, and how green were the trees and the grass! Here was a place to stay and let the mad world go ringing down its disastrous way. But they could not stay. They must fly on.

At Los Angeles they dined with Charlie Chaplin and Mr. and Mrs. King Vidor. Of Chaplin, then completing his first talking film, "The Dictator," Cripps wrote:

> At heart he is an anarchist and does not believe in any form of government and is very afraid of collectivisation. He is very doubtful of the benefits of machinery since the mechanisation of industry has destroyed craftsmanship which he believes lies at the root of man's self expression. He does not think there is any substitute for earning one's living by the sweat of one's brow and he envisages the decline of civilisation with the increase of mechanisation. He dislikes the pretentiousness of wealth, especially in America, and believes that the increase of facilities of all kinds is sapping the virility of the people and making them less fit to develop a decent civilisation. . . . His criterion of civilisation is that there should be plenty of "fun" (he insists on this word rather than happiness) for all people. . . . I thought him a very nice, simple, charming man and hope to see more of him.

The next day they were off by plane to Washington. Every waking hour of the succeeding days was filled with interviews, meetings, conferences. Cripps was spreading light about the realities of the situation in the Far East, and urging action. He talked with Benjamin Cohen about his views on what American action in China ought to be; he met Stanley Hornbeck, political adviser to the Secretary of State, whose analysis of British foreign policy in the Far East he found to be very like his own.

After the talk with Hornbeck he went to see Cordell Hull, a "tired old man." Next came talks with Jack Fisher and Gardner Jackson about the affairs of the American Federation of Labor and the Congress of Industrial Organizations. Then on to the Chinese Ambassador, and from him to John L. Lewis, boss of the American miners.

Another day Cripps met Miss Frances Perkins of the Labor

Department and Henry Wallace, and urged them to action on behalf of China. Then came a talk with Constantine Oumansky, the Soviet Ambassador. From him he went to Dexter White of the Treasury Department, who spoke "about the ineptness of the British approach to America on financial matters" and informed him that "the Americans did not like to be treated either as fools or children. They knew perfectly well what were the resources of Great Britain, and although they would probably be prepared to give financial assistance, they certainly would not do it until Great Britain had sold her foreign investments and realized their value."

After that bit of "real politics" about the money bags, came a long discussion with Lord Lothian, the British Ambassador.

On April 8 Cripps and Wilson flew to New York and were rushed off to a press conference sponsored by the Chinese Industrial Co-operatives. There were scores of journalists, some looking for "Crippsian indiscretions," some for information, and some there to shoot off their own fireworks.

"What about India?" one asked. The answer came straight:

The Congress Party is determined to have self-government for India. The Congress is quite prepared to sign a treaty with Britain providing stages of progress to that end, but Gandhi cannot hold the Congress in check indefinitely.

"Is violence a possibility?"

Gandhi says he will not start the non-co-operation program until he can be sure it will be non-violent . . . but it is doubtful that he can be sure under the circumstances.

"How long can Gandhi hold his crowd back?"
"Perhaps till the Autumn," Cripps answered.
"Much Russian influence?"
"No. This agitation is purely national."
"Has the British Government enough force to suppress violence?"
"Yes, at present."
"German influence there?"
"There is no room for it," answered Sir Stafford. "Indian Nationalism is too strong."
"How's Mr. Stalin?"

"I understand he's not well. But I have no real information. I was in Russia only 36 hours."

"Isn't that long enough for an Englishman to form an impression of anything?"

"That depends on circumstances," was the quiet reply.

So question and answer went on until they had covered almost every political and economic issue with which he had dealt in the course of his great journey.

The next day Cripps visited Sidney Hillman of the Garment Workers' Union and Quill of the Transport Workers and spoke before the Foreign Policy Association on India. With Pearl Buck, he addressed a meeting urging support of the Chinese Industrial Co-operatives. On that day came the news of the German invasion of Norway. The "phoney war" was ended. And the last lap of Cripps' long journey was at hand.

On April 12, 1940, Cripps and Wilson watched the skyline of New York fade into the distance from the deck of the Italian ship *Rex*. Soon America and all its busy life was lost to view. For the first time in months, they could relax and rest, assimilate their experiences, prepare for tomorrow. There was no place of call until they came to the "Pillars of Hercules" and turned into the harbor of Gibraltar. Here, under the towering fortified rock, standing as Britain's sentinel at the doorway of the Mediterranean, they stayed a while, but as the sun set behind the Sierras, the *Rex* sailed away toward Italy.

Sir Stafford returned to London by way of Paris. On April 23, 1940, there was a family gathering in London to celebrate the fact that in 145 days he had covered 45,107 miles by air, sea, rail, and car, had visited fourteen countries, and had seen the rulers of 1,300,000,000 of the world's population.

On the day of his arrival in London, the triumphant invasion of Norway by the Nazis reached its completion. The Nazi forces were poised ready for their overwhelming onslaught on Belgium, Holland, France. The days of smug satisfaction and soporific utterances were at an end. No longer could Chamberlain lull the people with "time is on our side" or with assurances that "Hitler had missed the bus." There was alarm even in Parliament, for the enemy was at the door, and the Government seemed not to know what to do about it.

Such was the situation when Sir Stafford, the man without a party, resumed his place in the House of Commons. Hence, on the memorable day of May 7, 1940, he was in his place to take a principal part in finishing the job to which he had set his hand when he launched his campaign for a "Popular Front Government." On that day the Opposition, in a crowded House of Commons, opened the attack on Chamberlain in a two-day debate on the disaster of Norway. In his prim, school-masterly, quiet way, the slim, bald-headed Clement Attlee began:

It is not Norway alone. Norway comes as the culmination of many other discontents. People are saying that those responsible for the conduct of affairs are men who have an almost uninterrupted career of failure. . . . To win the war, we want different people at the helm from those who have led us into it.

And then the storm raged from all sides of the House. L. S. Amery, an old friend of Chamberlain and a leader of the Tory Party, in a voice of passion, quoted the famous utterance Cromwell used on another fateful occasion: "You have sat too long here for any good you have been doing. Depart, I say, and let us have done with you. In the name of God, go!"

Here was drama of the first order! It went into the next day when Herbert Morrison announced to a House packed to its capacity that the Labour Party would divide the House on the question of confidence in the Government. Chamberlain, enraged by the turn of events, called on his friends "to support us in the lobby tonight."

Winston Churchill, out of Cabinet loyalty, stormed to the defense of Chamberlain. Lloyd George in a devastating speech told Churchill not to turn himself into an air-raid shelter for Chamberlain and ended his speech with these words: "There is nothing which can contribute more to victory in this war than that he [Chamberlain] should sacrifice the seals of office."

Now Stafford Cripps rose from the back benches. He began:

This debate is the most momentous in the history of Parliament. . . . It is constantly said that "you must not attack the Government because it will endanger the country." There are times when the only safety of the country is attack upon the Government, and it will be a grave dereliction of duty on the part of members of this

House if, being honestly convinced that it is necessary to challenge the issue, they take no steps to do it. . . .

It is a perfectly trite and true saying that the onlookers often see most of the game, and there have been, especially in America, but in all neutral countries, many very keen observers of the war in Europe. They are perhaps not so oppressed or encouraged by immediate events as are those who are here intimately taking part in day-to-day affairs.

Upon certain points, I found, in contact with Americans of every sort and kind, almost unanimous agreement. Uniformly, they take the view that the efforts of this country have been ill-organised and have been permeated with the spirit of indecision and lack of boldness that would seem to rise out of the failure to appreciate the extreme seriousness of the war situation. Of the Prime Minister and the Chancellor of the Exchequer, they were scathing in their criticism, and the question that was put to me more than any other while I was in America was, Why was it that the British people, if they desired to win this war, did not bring about a change of Government? Certainly they regard such a change as essential, and measure the necessity in weeks and in months.

Sir William Davidson, a very good friend of Mr. Chamberlain, interrupted with the question, "What reasons did they give?" That called forth the retort:

If you will apply to Mr. Stimson he will give you the reason as regards the Chancellor of the Exchequer, and if you apply to many others they will give you the history from the time of Munich onward about the Prime Minister, and these are full and sufficient reasons. . . .

I am trying to inform the Hon. Gentleman and others what American opinion really is. They are certainly of the view, and this was made clear by the American Press, that the prestige of this Government has suffered another serious blow by the events which have taken place in Norway. These criticisms were so markedly universal in America, that it was absolutely impossible for anybody to overlook them. When one returns to this country after an absence of months, trying in the meantime to observe from a distance the development of events, one is struck by the depressing atmosphere which prevails in this country. In the Far East, for instance, in such a place as China, however difficult material matters may be for these people, one senses an intense feeling of hope and of life. In this country there seems to be no conviction. There is doubt and despondency widely expressed on all sides.

No one will convince me that the spirit has gone out of the British people, but it is obvious that undecided and half-hearted leadership has created a sense of frustration in the people where bold leadership would give confidence and courage. In almost every department of Government the same fatal indecision and lack of realisation of the urgency of the situation seem to rule. Indeed, it is hardly possible to detect in some cases where the Government have yet made up their mind that this country must be organised for victory, regardless of all costs. . . .

Every Honourable Member today has a duty which I believe far transcends any party loyalty; it is a duty to the people of the country as a whole. I never thought that I should be present in this House of Commons when in a moment so grave a Prime Minister would appeal upon personal grounds and personal friendship to the loyalty of the House of Commons. I trust those revealing sentences which he spoke, will show that he is unfit to carry on the Government of this country.

Chamberlain's course as Prime Minister was run. Two days later Winston Churchill became Prime Minister in his stead, and Cripps, the man without a party, was called to go forth and complete an international task to which he had set his hand in the days when the shadow of Hitler first fell across the shores of England.

XIII. An Interlude

A T THIS point it is necessary to pause and take stock of the circumstances in which Stafford Cripps found himself in the dramatic days that followed. From the moment he reached London on April 23, the days and nights were crowded with incidents, reports, interviews, discussions. Friend and foe alike were asking, "What will Cripps do now?"

The day after his return he saw Maisky, the Soviet Ambassador, and learned that he had not seen Halifax at all for three and a half months. There was intense anti-Russian feeling in all quarters. After Sir Stafford's interview with Molotov, in which he had told the Russian Foreign Minister that nothing could be done to improve Anglo-Russian relations until the Finnish affair was settled, Maisky had received telegraphic instructions from Moscow to approach the British Government with terms for a Russo-Finnish settlement. These terms were more favorable to Finland than those eventually agreed upon. But the British Government would have nothing to do with them. A little later Maisky was instructed to make an approach about a trade agreement. It took three weeks to get an answer to this from the Government.

On the second day after Sir Stafford's return, the National Executive of the Labour Party turned down a resolution in favor of negotiations with Russia by 13 to 2, Harold Laski and Ellen Wilkinson being the only two supporters. Cripps found that while consummation of his policy in relation to the Soviet Union was needed more than ever, the forces arrayed against it were more formidable than when he had left the previous November. Only when Hitler's forces came crashing to the threshold of England did the Government come to the view that something must be done along the line that Cripps had urged.

With regard to India, he quickly discovered that all he had feared had taken place. Instead of the Government making a declaration definitely committing them to grant India dominion status at the end of the war, they had left it to the Viceroy, in accordance with the "man on the spot" theory. Lord Linlithgow was taking a violently suppressive attitude. No one in the Cabinet was giving any consideration to the matter, "and as a consequence," said Sir Stafford, "Winston, who supports the Viceroy, gets away with it." He at once began urging that the line of action he had advocated be taken lest Britain precipitate an upheaval in India while her hands were full with the war against Hitler. On May 1, he spent nearly two hours at the India Office and came away extremely depressed.

Still, [he wrote] the crucial decision to be taken by the Cabinet, was whether they were going to try and hold India by methods of suppression or, by granting self-government, to attempt to arrive at a favourable treaty which would regulate the future relations of both countries.

When the fall of Chamberlain from the post of Prime Minister became certain, Cripps urged the India conciliation group to cable Gandhi and advise him to hold his hand until the Government was reconstructed and Cripps could press his views upon the new ministers.

He also visited the Chinese Ambassador and told him of his talks with the Generalissimo. That began his campaign to secure co-operation between Britain, America, France, and Russia with regard to aid for China, and especially to urge action by the British Government for the extension of the Burma-Yunnan Railway. He gave to the Foreign Office a long and detailed report, with his recommendations. This report profoundly influenced the Government and it is probable that the decision to support the extension of the Burma-Yunnan Railway was a direct sequel.

In a long speech to the National Peace Council on May 9, he reported on his journey through West China, Sinkiang, and Japan. The most important part of this speech was that which revealed his outlook on the relation of the powers in the Far East. He said:

The people who today are helping China are Russia, the United

States and Great Britain. Russia has made no political demands upon China, very much to some people's surprise, and she has refused to give the Chinese Communists support of any kind against the National Government. The Generalissimo is extremely anxious lest at some future date, if the economic assistance becomes monopolised by Russia, political demands may follow. He is therefore anxious to substitute it as far as possible with help from the democracies of Great Britain and the United States. If we want to see a democracy emerge we should maximise our assistance to China and make up our minds whether we want China to survive or not. Saying nice things is not going to assist China.

There are two factors as regards the external position. The first is one which might result from an internal collapse, and then I think Russia would be tempted to step into Western China simply for the sake of creating order on her frontiers. There would be a temptation to create spheres of influence for Russia. The greatest danger is that of hostilities breaking out between Great Britain and Russia. If that were to happen, then inevitably there will be an Anglo-Japanese alliance. Either of these alliances will mean that China will be sacrificed. An Anglo-Japanese alliance would have very serious repercussions. I was given to understand by the State Department in Washington that if Great Britain double-crossed America in the Far East, the probability was that America would withdraw to Hawaii and come out of the Far East. The withdrawal of America would, of course, add another difficulty to the difficulties of the Chinese, who at the present time are getting great assistance from the United States. If Russia were to make an alliance with Japan, then I think it would inevitably be a part of that alliance that China would be divided between the two nations. So far as Japan is concerned, the United States today is holding a sword of Damocles over the Japanese to prevent them from doing anything which is more objectionable. The sword is in two parts: the first is the embargo, and the second is the American Navy. They are undoubtedly powerful weapons, but even their effect will be largely diminished if there is no concerted action on the part of Great Britain and the United States. But the United States profoundly distrusts the policy of this country in the Far East, and a frank show-down ought to be made on the part of this country.

From this speech it is perfectly clear that Cripps' outlook on international affairs had little to do with his Socialism. It is the outlook of a British liberal-nationalist whose whole concern turns not upon the evolution of world society toward

Socialism, but upon the relationship of Britain and British national interests to other national interests. He was convinced that Britain's interests were challenged at this stage of history by Nazi Germany and Japan, and not by Russia. Indeed, he was convinced that British and Russian interests coincided and were complementary. His method of analysis has not changed since he analyzed his first case at the Bar. It remains empirical, legalistic, concerned with political form and ideology and not with the social content.

Now that he was in England again, a leader without a party, how did he stand in relation to the organized forces around him? In what direction should he steer? Certainly he felt no great stirrings among the people, or the leaders, in Parliament or out. Chamberlain described the war as "the strangest of all wars." Churchill had the idea that this war would be like the last, had a high opinion of the Maginot Line, (not for purposes of frozen defense, but to enable counter-attacks) and in anticipation of long trench warfare had conceived a trench-digging machine—"White Rabbit No. 6." "This mammoth mole," Churchill wrote, "could cut in loam a trench five feet deep and seven and a half feet wide at half a mile an hour, involving the movement of eight thousand tons of soil."

But a very different form of warfare was soon to descend upon Britain. Deeply-rooted conservatism, combined with an insularity of outlook that was appalling, was supreme in every institution and every party. All the leaders were taking pride in "standing alone" when an enlightened and politically awakened people would have seen them legally tried for landing the country in so dangerous a predicament. The Commander-in-Chief stood like a brave pugilistic nude, bidding one and all, Germany and Russia too, to "come on." The Tory Party thought it could run the war without the co-operation of the Labour Party, and the Labour Party was criticizing the Government and keeping its "Socialism" pure. In the mines and factories there were mutterings of discontent and suspicion that something was wrong in high places—but nothing more than mutterings. Profit-makers feathered their nests and war industries produced cigarette lighters galore. None appeared conscious of the imminence of disaster, or of the character of the war which was about to shake the British Empire to its foundations. The Parliamentary parties suspended their differences until after the war, and the Labour Party thought it would be unfair "to take advantage of the national crisis to fight for a Socialist method of prosecuting the war." The Communist Party said the war was a nasty imperialist business and they would try to persuade the workers to stop it. Some members even whispered that they "should transform the imperialist war into civil war."

Such was the state of the nation and of the parties when Sir Stafford arrived, just as the armies of Hitler were crashing through Denmark and Norway and mightier forces were poised to sweep across Holland, Belgium, France, and to drive Britain's small expeditionary force on to the beaches of Dunkirk. When he discussed the situation with "Nye" Bevan and George Strauss, the two M.P.'s who had been expelled from the Labour Party at the same time as he but were now reinstated, they thought he should continue his independent way and "agreed that it was impossible for left-wing Socialists to formulate any policy at the present time."

He at once renewed his efforts to mobilize opinion for an alternative Government. He met Lloyd George, the old maker and unmaker of governments, and found him

most pessimistic and disturbed and generally disgruntled. I told him of my idea to publicise a draft alternative cabinet somehow so as to get rid of the argument that there was no alternative. He agreed to this view and we discussed personnel. Rather to my surprise . . . Winston could not be P.M. and it would have to be Halifax. I promised to let him see the list when I had completed it.

For two days he tried to get the big daily newspapers to publish his list for a new cabinet, but none would publish it unless over his signature, which he thought would militate against fair consideration of the proposal. Finally, he went to breakfast with Rothermere and persuaded him to publish it in the *Daily Mail*. It had a profound effect, dispelled the idea of "no alternative," and contributed largely to the final result of the debate in the House.

On May 11 he wrote,

During the week-end of May 10th, the first announcement of the new war Cabinet came out and it was clear immediately Chamberlain made his farewell speech that he and Churchill were trying to force the Labour Party into a Cabinet which would retain all the reactionary elements. This was what I had prophesied for some years and had since become the accomplished fact, Churchill having chosen the leaders of various power groups in the House, irrespective of their qualifications for a War Cabinet.

Here was a dilemma. The new Churchill Government still had Chamberlain and the "men of Munich" entrenched within it. The Labour Party had made no fight about the composition of the Government, its concern for the "purity" of its Socialism notwithstanding.

The entrance of the Labour Party into the Government created a novel position in the House of Commons. Where was the Opposition? The Labour Party itself was conscious of the position and proposed to be in the Government and out of it, to be in the Coalition Government, and to play the role of "devil's advocate" by appearing to lead opposition to the Government. This was too much for Sir Stafford. He began his efforts to organize a real Opposition in place of the sham one.

About the composition of the new Government he was most outspoken. He said:

The first shock was the inclusion of Mr. Neville Chamberlain. What led the leaders of the Party to agree to his retention? . . . Why burden the new start with this sombre legacy? Why carry the symbols of defeat into what we all hope will be a victory government? This is not the clean break we all longed for. . . . The removal of Sir John Simon to the Woolsack and the House of Lords reduces to comparative impotency a personality identified with a deplorable episode in the destruction of the system of collective security; but the mass of the people will not appreciate the remoteness of the Woolsack and will think only of the fact that Sir John Simon is the chief spokesman of the Government in the House of Lords. . . .

Mr. Kingsley Wood, having failed with dire consequences to provide sufficient aircraft, is made Chancellor of the Exchequer, as though to emphasise the moral that outstanding failure in one important office is good ground for appointment to another.

When we come to the new appointments our disappointment amounts to dismay. What conceivable reason was there for giving Mr. Duff-Cooper the Ministry of Information? Do we want to convince the world that we are determined to defend the worst aspects of Conservative reaction? As though to give point to this fear we found that Lord Lloyd had been chosen to be secretary for the Colonies. Lord Lloyd is legitimately suspected of Fascist sympathies. . . .

As though to complete the tale the news then came through that Mr. Amery had been appointed Secretary of State for India. This was surely the last post we wanted Mr. Amery to be given. . . . What impression does Mr. Churchill expect his Government to make upon the world and especially neutral opinion?

But there were no forces in the House of Commons that he could muster without the members having to face a break with the Labour Party. He was in an extraordinary and difficult position.

His independent position had its advantages. It enabled him to exercise influence on individuals by personal contact and it left him free to undertake any specific task which could implement his policy in international affairs especially. But he had no following with which to wage the struggle for his ideas publicly and in Parliament. The Labour Party had been thrust into a Coalition Government, with *the Tory Party as the leader,* and with its "Socialism" relegated to the domestic refrigerator to keep it "pure" for discussion in a more convenient season. Cripps had wanted a coalition government free of Chamberlain and the "men of Munich." The Coalition Government contained effete politicians who were not only enemies of Socialism but responsible for the extraordinary, isolated, and precarious position of the country. Nevertheless, the Labour Party had millions of people behind it and all attempts to set up rival Socialist parties had proved unavailing.

Cripps had no doubt about what he wanted to do, nor was he unclear in his estimate of the forces in conflict. Indeed, only a few weeks ago when he was on the other side of the world he had set out his views to a gathering of leaders and intellectuals in Chungking. He had spoken with a frankness and boldness that had startled his hearers. Back in England, he saw no reason to modify what he had then said.

I include here the speech which he delivered at Chungking in February, 1940, for it may well be appraised as the greatest of his career:

There is an experiment familiar to every student who has studied the most elementary electricity, wherein a magnet or a metal wire through which a current is passed is covered with a thin glass sheet upon which are sprinkled iron filings. When so placed on the glass each particle lies as it falls and there is no pattern or design in their position; they are a mass of unco-ordinated particles. If, however, the glass sheet is lightly tapped the particles will each take up an ordered position and in their totality they will display the pattern of the invisible lines of magnetic force, which are the true source of power in the magnet. I want to try and tap the glass plate of European politics so that you may see—not a series of unco-ordinated events—but the emergence of those lines of force which have in fact controlled the actions and happenings of the last nine years.

I do not hold the view that the political development of the world is determined by the malevolence of the benevolence of a few individuals. Those individuals who often appear as powerful and decisive figures in history are in my view the creation and personification of certain trends in the social, political and economic life of the different nations in which they occur. Naturally in times of transition when one class in a nation is taking over power from another class or is making the attempt to do so great opportunities occur for the uprising of prominent figures either personifying the losing struggle of the old ruling class or the winning struggle of the new ruling class.

Let me in fairness to the present British Government remind you that I have, ever since 1931, been a bitter opponent of their policies and of their European foreign policy in particular. I must go back to that, 1931, if I am to attempt to explain the present British and European policies.

During the early part of 1931 when Arthur Henderson was the British Foreign Secretary a very genuine attempt had been made by Great Britain to do three things. First, to revive and reinforce the League of Nations and the idea of collective security in association with an active movement for world disarmament; second, to attain a better understanding with Russia, the Government of which country at that time had the almost unanimous support of the British working class movements; and third, to moderate the harshness of the revenge which France and Great Britain had exacted from Germany after the last war. The general temper of politics in Europe and probably the rest of the world was then better than at any time since 1919 and there seemed to be some prospect of a measure of disarmament and of a future free from major wars.

This, however, I must add as regards the imperialist aspect of British policy during the time of the Labour Government. That Government never faced up to the implications of an imperialist policy in its effect upon foreign policy. They were content to continue the old imperialist policy of Great Britain except that they attempted to administer imperialism in a more liberal and humanitarian way. . . .

When the change of Government came in Great Britain in 1931 a new train of very important international events began.

The new National Government though ostensibly representing all elements in the country was in fact overwhelmingly controlled by conservative and imperialist forces. The leaders were known to be extremely hostile to Russia and to be unsympathetic to the tendency towards socialism and communism in Germany and other European countries. The Conservatives for some years after 1917 had regarded the Russian Revolution as something unstable and which must inevitably fall within a few years; but when it had stood through years of difficulties and was obviously becoming more and more stable they became extremely alarmed at the prospect of the spread of the ideology of communism through Germany and France to Great Britain itself. They were therefore prepared to do almost anything to build up protection for British capitalism and imperialism against the spread of this, to them, dangerous disease, which had already gained a considerable hold amongst the British working class. That basic attitude has been the determining factor in all British foreign policy since 1931 and up to September last year, and even to a large extent since that date. . . .

In the confident old days before 1914 there had really never been any doubt as to the direction of British Foreign policy. First, foremost and always was the purpose of increasing the power and territory of Great Britain as the dominant nation in the world. It was also confident in its ability to appease its own working class by gradually rising standards earned by the exploitation of subject peoples all over the Empire and of backward or developing countries all over the world. . . .

After 1919 it had become apparent that revolution was again in the air in a very serious form; it was cropping up everywhere in the world. It had, moreover, become impossible in the post-war period to appease the British working class which then numbered as unemployed over 3,000,000 of its members and standards were falling fast instead of rising. Furthermore the colonial and Indian peoples had been re-awakened during the war to make very real demands for their rights and had turned the hitherto passive Empire into a continual source of trouble and embarrassment. The economic situation, too, had entirely changed. The intensive economic development throughout the world during the war had finally disposed of the theory that Great Britain was the work-shop of the world. The advantage gained by the early invention and use of the steam engine in England had finally and forever disappeared and competitors—very keen competitors—had arisen in every market. . . .

The greatest enemy to British capitalism was thus the ideology of the Russian revolution permanently embodied in the successful Government of Soviet Russia. To fight this ideology must mean hostility to Russia, even though such hostility might endanger British imperial connections in other parts of the world. The balance of power policy which had operated with comparative ease amongst States all of which were capitalist was found to have difficulties and dangers where one factor, and that a powerful one like Russia, had definitely to be ruled out as an ally owing to the danger that such an alliance would bring from the ideological point of view. . . .

One further point must be added and that is that the natural development of that very curious conception, the British Empire, had led to the passing of the Statute of Westminster shortly after the war by which the Dominions had been formally given an independent status and Southern Ireland had finally been freed from British control. . . .

For a time after the last war it was thought by many British imperialists that the interests of British imperialism might be well served by using the League of Nations as a defence for the post-war status quo both so far as France and England were concerned and a long drawn out attempt was made so to use it, which led to the destruction of the League as a factor of political power or importance in the world. . . .

Foreign policy became more and more opportunist, always hovering between a desire to destroy, or to protect themselves from the Russian revolution and a desire to maintain the integrity of the British Empire. . . .

There is little doubt but that the Japanese appreciated this situation in 1931; knowing that they could utilise the anti-Russian feelings of the new British Government they chose the time of its accession to power for their first attack on Manchuria.

As is now well known the British Government delayed any kind of action against Japan and refused to co-operate with the United States of America in any practical policy to hold up the Japanese invasion of China. This was not because of their pro-Japanese feelings but because of their anti-Russian obsession. . . .

Their behaviour towards Germany after the accession to power of Hitler was just as remarkable. Every kind of concession that had been refused to social-democratic, or even liberal Germany was granted to the Nazis, not because the British Government feared Nazism or even because they liked it or approved its methods or policies but because they saw in it a real barrier against Bolshevism on the west.

The same policy was followed towards Italy in the Abyssinian war in spite of the obvious threat to British possessions in North Africa and to the vital sea route through the Mediterranean and the Suez Canal. . . .

The Spanish Civil War demonstrated exactly the same policy. The blatant intervention of Germany and Italy on the side of Fascism was not observed by the British Government who, contrary to every principle of international law, prevented the Spanish Government from equipping itself with defences against the Spanish rebels. . . .

France had appreciated the growing danger of Germany and had concluded but not ratified the Franco-Russian pact in which Czechoslovakia was the vital link between the two countries. The Laval Government which was substantially Fascist in outlook had far more sympathy for German Nazism and Italian Fascism than for Russian Communism. The Communist Party of France was very rapidly gaining strength and was well on the way to becoming the most powerful political party in the country. It was largely due to the influence of Great Britain that France refused for so long to ratify the pact and then when ratified did nothing to carry it into effect; as too it was almost entirely due to the attitude of Great Britain that the subsequent Popular Front Government in France under M. Blum refused to help the Spanish Government against its rebels, and thereby destroyed the possibility of that Government surviving for any length of time. . . .

It will thus be seen that throughout this period the major factor in European politics was the successive utilisation by Great Britain and to some extent by France as well, though largely as the result of Great Britain's lead, of various Fascist Governments to check the power and danger of the rise of Communism or Socialism through Russian or other influence in any other country. Japan was tacitly encouraged in the East, Germany on the west of Russia and Fascism was reinforced in Italy and Spain while the Popular Front Government was destroyed in France. All this despite the evident and growing danger to British Imperialism. . . .

I must for a few moments retrace my steps to deal with the position of Russia and Germany. Little need be said as to the latter since the whole German plan was exposed in Hitler's book, "Mein

Kampf" which I don't believe any Conservative leader discovered or read until 1939, any more than they did the stories of the atrocities in the German concentration camps.

Hitler has steadily pursued his policy and he has been permitted to pursue it because he managed to persuade British conservative statesmen that he was providing a bulwark against Bolshevism, exactly as he managed to delude the Conservative Austrians to the same effect. Now both have discovered that he is an undesirable kind of bulwark.

The agreement at Munich forced upon an unwilling Czechoslovakia marked the final success of Hitler's anti-Red Propaganda. It had enabled him to rearm with the tacit consent and active assistance of Great Britain; it had allowed him to annex Austria and so break his way into Southern Europe; it had destroyed Spain and the Popular Front Government of France; it has weakened and embarrassed Great Britain in the Mediterranean and the Far East; and finally at Munich it broke down the resistance to the wiping out of the strong salient of Czechoslovakia which was such a strategic menace to Germany.

This disastrous history ought to be a lesson to liberal democrats not to be fooled in the future by anti-Red propaganda put forward by interested parties—fascists and militarists in particular. There may be a lesson to be learnt from it in Far Eastern affairs.

Munich and what followed had a vitally important, indeed, a decisive effect upon the turn of events in Europe. And here I must introduce Russia in more detail onto the stage. After Russian policy had turned from the idea of international revolution with the disappearance of Trotsky, the policy that was adopted was that of dealing with capitalist countries as unavoidable neighbours and attempting to use their differences to the advantage of Russia and the proletarian revolution wherever it might spring up.

The policy of non-interference in the internal affairs of other countries slowly developed though it never became quite complete or rigid. At the same time Russia, to whom peace was essential for her own industrial and social development, came round to the idea that the League of Nations might possibly be utilised to her advantage, as a keeper of the peace.

The trouble was that France and Great Britain refused to play the peace game because by so doing they would have been forced into a most unwilling partnership with Russia.

The complete and ignominious neglect of Russia at Munich in the vital matter of the integrity of Czechoslovakia severely shook the Russian belief in the possibility of allying themselves with the

Western powers against the Nazi aggressors. Prague fell and with it
Litvinov and his policy. Stalin and Molotov then took over and
with a great deal of doubt and hesitation made one last effort to
concert an anti-Nazi front. But by this time they had become so
distrustful of the Governments of Great Britain and France that
their conditions for such an alliance were amplified. They were no
longer prepared to leave the matter to a mere gentlemen's agreement, especially upon the terms offered by Great Britain, namely
that Great Britain and France should decide if and whether Russia
were to come in to defend Poland.

Anyone with a grain of sense must have known that without
Russia it was impossible for Poland to survive the onslaught of the
German mechanised army and air force. However, this was disre-
garded and the guarantee was given.

It is perhaps necessary to say a word about the Polish attitude to
Russia. This of course, is traditionally hostile and after the Polish
attack on Russia in 1920 and the taking then of Russian territory
by Poland against the advice of all the allied statesmen the Poles
became more frightened as the Russian strength grew.

Colonel Beck and the Polish Government represented the big
landowners of Poland and they feared Germany far less than Russia.
Indeed no one was ever certain whether Colonel Beck had entered
into a secret agreement with Germany or not! In spite of this there
is little doubt that if Great Britain had made the inclusion of Russia a term of the guarantee of Poland, Poland would have been
obliged to consent or else to have settled her difference with Germany by a surrender of Danzig and the corridor territory.

This then was the condition in July of 1939. I spare you any
examination into the situation of the Balkan countries which were
the centre of every kind of pressure and intrigue from Italy, Germany, Russia and Great Britain and France.

It was then the failure of Britain to conclude a pact with Russia
that made the Russo-German pact and war inevitable.

It naturally followed that when Germany overran Poland and the
Polish Government ran away to Rumania, Russia entered up to the
Curzon line and a little beyond and occupied the centre Rumanian
frontier thus blocking Hitler from any expansion in that direction.

In spite, however, of the uneasy partnership of non-aggression
and industrial assistance between Russia and Germany, Russia was
not in the least content to consider her relations with Germany so
stabilised as to negate any future danger of attack from that
quarter, particularly if Germany were to be victorious in the war.

She therefore proceeded immediately to consolidate her position at the eastern end of the Baltic, where the protection of her naval base at Kronstadt and of Leningrad were the primary considerations. For this purpose she needed to hold the approaches into the Gulf of Finland, as anyone can see from an examination of the map.

With the smaller states she managed to make satisfactory agreements which may well be greatly to their benefit, but Finland was not prepared to enter into an arrangement which in my own view under all the circumstances was not unreasonable.

The demands were to exchange territory in Karelia—a very favourable exchange for Finland—which would set the Finnish frontier 50 miles instead of 20 from Leningrad, and the cession of naval bases in the Gulf of Finland with a large payment in cash by Russia as a compensation to Finland. As Finland could never be a naval power, but might be a base for a foreign naval force such as the German, these demands seem reasonable to me as a basis for negotiations. They were, however, refused and Russia then, to my mind, committed the extreme folly of attacking Finland and pretending she was doing so at the request of the Finnish people.

In this relationship it is worth while remarking the swiftness with which all the anti-Red Governments of Europe have come to the assistance of Finland in one way or another. England, France and Italy have all offered or given them assistance. One would have been more impressed with the profession of their desire to save democracy and freedom—in Finland—if they had taken as rapid action and as favourable in the case of Austria, Czechoslovakia, Abyssinia, Albania, Spain, or even China, when these countries were attacked by fascist aggression. . . .

It only remains to say one word as to the curious war that is no war between Germany and the western democracies. I am certain the people of none of the countries want to fight, and they don't know what they are fighting about or what good can possibly come out of it.

Unfortunately, to my mind, the view is now growing in England that the fault of the Treaty of Versailles is that it did not sufficiently smash up the old Germany and that this time Germany must be dismembered and destroyed. A more fatal and fatuous policy could hardly be conceived. So far as the British Government is concerned I have been unable to discover any clear idea whatever as to what is to come out of the war or what sort of peace with any guarantee for the future can ever be made.

It is true to say for capitalism and imperialism there is a menace in any form of progressive government whether liberal, socialist, or communist, whereas fascism and militarism offer these economic systems their protection. Indeed any form of true democracy must threaten the vested interests of any ruling class or caste, and that is why such classes are ready to throw over democracy, and adopt fascism to protect their own interests. It seems to me that it is the task of the younger generation in this as in other countries to work out forms of democracy that will enable them to play and control their economic life without depriving the common people of their individual freedom and their just rights. . . .

I believe that in the circumstances of this moment China has a great opportunity to make a distinguished advance along these lines of democratic development, and I trust that it may be the honour and pleasure, as it is the duty of every one of you here present to combine with your struggle for China's freedom a determination to win justice and liberty under democratic forms for the teeming millions of your fellow countrymen. In that task I wish you and your country a great and victorious success.

XIV. The Ambassador

ON MAY 20, 1940, the British Cabinet decided to invite Cripps to implement his policy in relation to Russia. He was to go to Moscow as a special envoy to explore the possibilities of reaching agreement on any political or trade matters. The circumstances of his appointment were extraordinary, and the task he was given was beset with difficulties such as few other ambassadors had had to face.

At no period since the Revolution of 1917 had there been really friendly relations between the two countries. There had been uneasy periods of diplomatic recognition and trade relations, as between enemies agreeing upon a truce until a convenient moment for the resumption of violent hostilities. It had taken seven years for a British Government to bring itself to the point of sending its first ambassador to Moscow. The very prime minister who now appointed Sir Stafford had waged an undeclared and unrelenting war of intervention in Russia for several years. Churchill never ceased to pour his contumely and hate upon the Soviet leaders until he saw that power politics in defense of British imperialism demanded an alliance against a more immediate threat.

Almost every member of the Coalition Government had run Churchill a good second in their vituperation and hatred of the Soviet regime. Even the Labour members of the Coalition had waged constant ideological warfare against the Soviet Government, and the Labour Party Executive only a few weeks earlier had opposed the sending of a mission to Moscow. The Chamberlain Government, with the support of the Labour Party, had been saved from making war on Russia by the refusal of Sweden to allow an expeditionary force to pass through her territory to aid the Finns against Russia. Not a single person within the British Government had the slightest comprehension, either of the scope and nature of the changes that had taken place in Russia, or of her power as potential ally or enemy. Not one ever dreamed of Russia's power as it proved to be when in subsequent months she "tore the guts out of the Nazi Army."

The Soviet Government viewed every action of the British with suspicion, and was skeptical of the vacillating "good will" of the British Labour movement. In the first stages of the Russian Revolution, when social revolution was developing in all the countries of Europe and not one capitalist government gave the Soviet Government recognition as a state power, it appealed to the working class everywhere to overthrow their capitalist governments. When the war of intervention was defeated and the revolution in Europe ebbed, the Soviet Union won recognition of its state power and entered into relations with all the governments that had been involved in the intervention. Deeply suspicious of all of them, it pursued a policy of coming to terms with all and preventing another wholesale combination against itself.

When the Nazis came to power, the Soviet Government recognized that two major enemies, openly declaring their intention to wage war upon the Soviet Union, stood ready to strike in the East and the West when it would become strategically and tactically convenient for them to do so. From that time Russian policy aimed at securing a collective peace and defense system of all countries threatened by the new powers. By this means a whole series of non-aggression pacts was built up, including pacts with France and Czechoslovakia. Throughout this period the British Government had refused to pursue a policy of collective security and had double-crossed France and the League of Nations by making a naval pact with Hitler in 1935, in violation of agreements with France and the League of Nations. France tore up her pact with the Soviet Union and, jointly with Britain, also tore up her pact with Czechoslovakia, thus making a gift of that country to Hitler. Britain had reduced the League of Nations to a memory of good intentions, and, by the Munich pact with Hitler, left the Soviet Government high and dry with its collective peace system in ruins. From that moment Russia resumed her pre-Hitler policy. She saw herself as surrounded by enemies with as little reason to have confidence in one as the other, and was concerned only with lengthening the breathing space before the inevitable war. She proceeded to use the new relationship between the powers to strengthen her defense in depth, advancing into Poland after the Germans had shattered the resistance of the Poles, absorbing the border states, and shattering the Finnish military preparation for co-operation in the attack from the West, be it led by Germany, Britain, or France.

Now Russia was prepared to accept the Cripps Mission. This did not mean that the Soviet leaders believed that the unrelenting class hatred, which had marked the attitude of British Governments toward them for twenty-three years, had suddenly been replaced by the spirit of friendship. They regarded the desire for improved relations to be a long-delayed recognition that in the war against Hitler the interests of the British Empire, indeed its preservation, coincided with the preservation of the Soviet Union. Here was the basis for realistic agreements between two nations in difficulties, but with little real friendship between them.

The wisdom of the choice of Stafford Cripps as envoy was obvious. His personal record in politics was one of friendship for the Russian Revolution and the Soviet Union. He would be welcomed on that account, but the Soviet leaders had no confidence in the British Government. They would act cautiously and suspiciously toward it, judging it by its deeds rather than its words. This was the background and the prevailing atmosphere of Anglo-Soviet relations when Cripps stepped into an airplane and flew to Athens en route to Moscow on May 28, 1940.

As he crossed the English Channel and flew toward Italy (which was waiting to strike at demoralized France), the armies of the Allies were being encircled and smashed on the fields of Flanders, and Belgium and Holland were being swept by the Nazi avalanche.

While he was flying, the Soviet Government informed the British that they would not negotiate with anyone who was not of ambassadorial rank. Since January, the then British Ambassador, Sir William Seeds, had been "on leave," that is, withdrawn in fact while leaving his coat tails in Moscow, to be picked up again or to be severed when expedient. He had come home in preparation for the official rupture, should Britain join with Finland in war against Russia. Such were the relations that had immediately preceded the new decision.

Sir Stafford had to wait in Athens until the British Government transformed his position from that of "special envoy" to that of ambassador. Then he flew on to Sofia. While the plane was high over the Balkan mountains, it was struck by lightning and sent hurtling down. Pilot and passengers were thrown from their seats as the plane overturned. Only the ingenuity of the pilot in scrambling back into the upturned seat and regaining control saved them all from certain death.

Cripps was met at the Moscow airdrome, on the day preceding the King's birthday, by the entire staff of the British Embassy and the Protocol Chief, Vladimir Barkoff, on behalf of the Soviet Government. The next day Premier Molotov made an unusual gesture. Sir Stafford's credentials had not yet arrived and therefore he was not yet officially the ambassador. Nevertheless Molotov remembered that it was the King's birthday and as a gesture of good will personally left his card at the British Embassy. Sir Stafford fully understood the significance of the action and appreciated it.

Here began one of the most trying experiences of Cripps' career. Accustomed to a life of intense activity, quick movement, and response to his wishes, he learned about the tedium of waiting for events to catch up with him, and what it meant to live as a foreigner in a foreign land, unable to get to grips with the work he wanted to do, and outside the main streams of life. Knowing nothing of the language of the country, he could not mix with the people. The Embassy was isolated by the very nature of the relations which had existed between Britain and Russia for so long.

The Embassy building was a huge nineteenth-century house with a grand staircase and hall, lofty rooms, great doorways and heavy doors, Persian and Chinese carpets, tapestry-covered chairs, and Louis XIV furniture. The whole place was gasping for a breath of twentieth-century aid and ideas in house equipment and decoration. Sir Stafford's study appalled him. He wrote to his wife:

My study downstairs, which has three full length life-size (or much larger) portraits of royalty, an old ugly Turkish carpet and rather decayed red-silk walls and a dark ceiling and some nonde-script furniture spotted about looks too awful and I haven't yet been able to think of anything that can be done to make it liveable in. Its only merit is that it has doors opening out onto a terrace overlooking the little garden with a tennis court (hard gravel and sand) at the bottom and behind the garages.

The front of the house, with its balcony over the porch, faced the street running parallel with the Moscow River and the Kremlin with its beautiful old red-brick towered walls standing high before him. That was a view of which he would never tire. Weathered by centuries of sun and rain and snow and wind, the Kremlin was well preserved, fit to stand for centuries. He would see it in every phase of its beauty, rich and warm in the midday sun, softening to every shade of pink and red in the evening light, and sharply silhouetted against the exciting skyline of Moscow nights. Less than six months ago he had passed within the Kremlin walls to see Premier Molotov. But then, as he made that quick call, talked for two hours, sped out again and away, it was mid-winter, the snow was deep and it was night. There was no time then to look at the ancient chapels and churches and palaces which the Czars of generations gone had left behind them.

Now he must settle within the big house and see what he could do to make it feel a little more homelike. He threw some things out, moved around the furniture he could not throw out, discovered an old radio which could at least pick up the local stations and provide some music, bought some new vases and flowers to put in them. Twenty-seven persons from England formed the technical staff of the Embassy, and fifty others were employed as servants, gardener, chauffeurs, maids, and menservants. He had to get to know them all and organize some social life. To throw a party for the staff was easy enough and it went off well. But to get to know the rest, whose language he did not speak, was more difficult. He must brush up on the French language. No sooner decided than arranged. He secured a teacher of French and, like the Potter girls and his grandmother before him, systematically "swotted" French. It would prove invaluable.

But putting the house in order was a job that he found could not be done quickly. He wrote to Isobel almost in despair,

I have dragged the three hopelessly impossible (though very beautiful) blue Chinese carpets out of the pink and white drawing room and put two of them in the dining room where they look bad but not *so* bad. . . . In the drawing room I have put the pink and white carpet (a nice one) out of the dining room and arranged all the chairs etc. around the edge leaving the carpet uncovered, except for one table uncovered in the middle of the room. . . . I must somehow try to make the place look a little presentable.

There was a dacha in the forest outside Moscow, where in the summer months it would be very pleasant. He wrote one day of his first visit there:

I drove out to my dacha in the forest about 30 mins. from here. It's a nice log house with another large one in a compound with a tennis court and a bit of garden and lots of trees. The furniture is very scratched and ugly but is quite adequate and there are 4 bedrooms and two bathrooms, a long dining room and a small sitting room and servants quarters. . . . We went for about ¾ hours walk in the forest which is flat but quite nice, mostly spruce and silver birch—smallish trees with open spaces between with grass but not many flowers of any sort! One is to get accustomed to the fact that wherever one goes two secret police are always within about ten yards. Walking, swimming, skiing, whatever it is, they are always there—silent, and one pretends they aren't there. The only thing to do is to disregard them completely. They are quite nice and most helpful if anything untowards occurs. I shall try and go to the dacha sometimes to get the sanity of nature and the exercise.

He was a stranger in a strange land. The Russians must have laughed heartily when they heard about the "secret" police who haunted him continuously; they were so "secret" that he and everybody in the locality could see them as they followed at ten yards distance or openly rode in a trailing vehicle. They did not talk with him, for they did not know English and he did not know Russian. Silence was the rule even in their "helpfulness." But he was good-tempered about it and called them his "Y.M.C.A. boys." At first he and the French Ambassador, M. Labonne, could exchange visits and talk freely, but soon that had to stop, for France went down under the Nazi hammer and his French colleague went into retirement. It was an anomalous situation, for Labonne was anti-Petain but remained technically the representative of the French Government. Cripps liked Labonne and still went to see him from time to time.

When first Sir Stafford arrived he thought that negotiations would soon get into their stride and he would be kept busy until they were completed. That was a wrong impression. In the first days he met Molotov and Lazovsky, the Vice-Commissar of Foreign Affairs. This was the first time he had met the latter and it was pleasant for him because Lazovsky spoke English well. It was he who, with Tomsky, the leader of the Russian Trade Unions, and J. T. Murphy of the English Shop Stewards, formed the committee which launched the Red International of Trade Unions. He succeeded Tomsky in the leadership of the Russian unions. He was a good linguist and had learned English in those years of the Trade Union International. He was a man who could talk if he would, but as press correspondents learned, knew how to be charming without saying one word of significance or news value.

On that memorable night in January after his arrival by air, when Sir Stafford had met Molotov, he had formed the impression that this Russian of the Russians was a man who would never answer any question impromptu or discuss anything off the record. He must "receive notice of the question," as ministers in the British Parliament say. And that was true for all occasions that were official and when he met people outside the ranks of the Communist Party. With his own people, however, Molotov is a man of wit and wisdom, cultured and erudite, a lover of the theater, of literature and the arts, and a sportsman to boot.

It was not until June 28 that Sir Stafford was able to present his credentials to the President of the Soviet Union, Michael Kalinin. After the formal general talk, the president expressed his doubts about the British Government and its real intentions. Kalinin was an old man with a remarkable record of service as a Bolshevik workman and leader. He had been in the leadership of the Bolshevik Party since before the days of the revolution. A friend of Stalin until his death,

Kalinin was possibly the most beloved man of the Soviet Union, the universal father of the people.

After the credential ceremony, Sir Stafford could begin his visits to other Ambassadors and receive them at the British Embassy. Early in July, 1940, he met Stalin for the first time. It was a formal meeting, too formal for the two men to do more than register distant impressions of each other. This was the first meeting of Stalin with a foreign plenipotentiary since he had received von Ribbentrop in 1939. Although Sir Stafford put many questions to him concerning Soviet Foreign policy, Stalin was too conscious of the existing relationship of the Soviets to the rest of the world, particularly Germany and Japan, to give the kind of answers Sir Stafford wanted. He must wait for a more convenient season and be content that their meeting had taken place at all.

He frequently met the Chinese Ambassador. He met the Japanese Ambassador formally, and they made small talk in fulfillment of the diplomatic niceties. But there was not enough work to keep him really busy, and no man hates idleness so much as Sir Stafford. One day he took five of the staff, the secretaries, and a councillor from the French Embassy to dine at an agricultural exhibition. It was the middle of July and the day of rest. He says:

It was a really marvellous evening, exactly right in temperature, a delicious gentle breeze and the most lovely sunset about nine o'clock as we sat down, in a balcony of the restaurant overlooking the exhibition, for our dinner. Gradually the place was lit up under the most velvety purple sky imaginable. . . . We hadn't time to see anything much in the exhibition. We did go round the Far Eastern pavilion which was very interesting and informative. All the products, agricultural, furs, etc. etc. were exhibited and statistics given. I want as soon as I get a chance to go and see the animals, hares, dogs, camels, cattle, pigs, sheep, etc., which are on exhibit here. There is any amount to see, the difficulty is to get the time when one can go out and to get someone to go out with.

Such days were the exception. There are around Moscow forests and fields and a wonderful countryside to be explored. But that was not what he wanted. The wonders of nature he loved, but he wanted the busy rush of the affairs of men and nations, the human associations that brought news of the world, of the war and of home, and to be in the battle.

One day he secured a new friend—"a big leggy ten-months-old Airedale" whom he named "Joe." This nearly led to diplomatic complications, for when his wife sent her "Greetings to Joe" she had to think again and write "Greetings to Joe Airedale," lest it be assumed the greetings were for "Joe" Stalin. Joe had come up from the country, had never been in a car or heard the noises of the town, and was a little nervous at first. But soon he and Sir Stafford were great friends and were rarely seen apart. Every morning they would take a turn around the garden for half an hour or so.

Writing to his youngest daughter, Peggy, Sir Stafford said,

I find my dog Joe a great companion though he is a bit of a tie and he has always to be with me or practically always. . . . He is now just behind my chair where he sits all day while I am working. If I have people here then he comes and sits on the leather sofa by me with his head on my lap! and when anyone strange comes he barks loudly (but not for long) at them so as to warn me of their approach.

As the autumn days approached he wrote again to her and described his day:

A much brighter morning with a warm sun, but now it's clouding over again. However, we had one full hour's walk this morning and it was a bright invigorating autumn morning and Joe was in very good form indeed. I think he likes the cold weather better. You notice that most of my life now seems taken up with Joe! Well, that is my only company by day and night and so I make the most of it and I think it would be quite intolerable here if it weren't for Joe!

Another day he reported the arrival of two ministers from the Baltic countries:

This gives us a little variety and company which is good for me and Joe! The latter has been very friendly. The last few days he has started to lose his fear and to walk about and back as if he were Ambassador and I were his valet!! He is most cheerful and fit. He never leaves me wherever I go (except to the Kremlin where he is not allowed, or out to dinner parties).

Joe became the confidant who seemed to understand his moods, the difficulties of his isolation, his anxieties as to what was happening in England, his nostalgia for Goodfellows which had been his home for twenty years, and his fears as he waited for news of his wife and his daughters who were making the long journey across Canada and the Pacific Ocean to come to Moscow through the back door of Asia.

One day he gave a dinner party for the two ex-ministers from the Baltic provinces, Preston from Kovno and Gallienne from Tallinin. There were about ten guests. Of this gathering he wrote in a letter,

The universal hymn of hate whenever a few Englishmen meet together against the Russians makes me rather depressed and cross. Most of them have had associations with white Russians and the whole tradition and bias of the Foreign Office and diplomatic service is violently and unreasoningly anti-Russian. There is every reason to criticize a great deal of what they do—they do it in "Asiatic" ways which are not our ways and which are often cruel and undesirable ways. Their methods very often differ hardly at all from the Tsarist methods, in fact they are Russian methods! Their lack of organisation, their way of doing things or neglecting business, is all of it quite devastating at times, but in spite of all that, one can either look upon them as people broadly groping after something which is in the right direction or as wicked and malevolent destroyers of world civilization. It is as the latter that these people regard them. The worst interpretation is put on every act they perform, the gloomiest prognostications are made as to their dishonesty and cruelty, etc, etc., and, as I say, it all makes me a bit cross and depressed. It is this atmosphere which has made it impossible ever to have any reasonable agreement between a Conservative Government in Great Britain and Russia. Acts that were overlooked in the Tsarist regime are emphasized and magnified as cruelties etc. in this one. I should not object if there had always been an equal condemnation of methods. There hasn't, and it is purely a political consideration as to whether the methods are overlooked or condemned. It is all so dishonest and so disgustingly self-righteous.

He went on to give his own impression and understanding of the developments of the Russian Revolution, both sympathetic and revealing, although derived from afar and without any attempt to understand the theories of the Bolsheviks or to make an intimate acquaintance with the inner life of the Soviet Union. He made sweeping generalizations on insufficient data, bringing to bear on the situation an outlook greatly influenced by his own idealism and social environment. But he was sympathetic and willing to be friendly. Indeed, from every point of view, the mission he had undertaken, the power relations in the world, with Britain fighting for its existence, his hopes for the future reshaping of the world, made this friendly appreciation necessary. So he continued his letter:

You can imagine that in this atmosphere I find it rather trying. I made a great effort to maintain, as I always tried to do, an objective view of the situation. This regime certainly suffers from a very great many most grave defects. Partly due to inherent characteristics of the people, partly due to external circumstances and perhaps partly inherent in every form of dictatorship.

The Russians have never been consistent plodding workers, nor have they ever been good organisers and they are not either now, though they may in the future win through to better standards in both.

The war atmosphere which has now lasted many years has compelled them to direct energy and organisation from civil to military spheres. The civil production and standards have suffered.

The means of transport are ill-organised and insufficient even for ordinary requirements; with vast military movements always going on, the transport and distribution of civilian supplies suffers greatly.

The organisation of agriculture which has so far defeated every government in the world in vast territories like these has not yet achieved success. The great experiment of collectivisation as against peasant ownership has not been determined as yet in favour of collectivisation in this country. But then transport and distribution difficulties are so great that it means great waste, and there are quite inadequate means of preserving or marketing surpluses.

If to all these difficulties you add the government of secret police and spies which is the only method for a dictatorship, then in such a country as this with a people of this kind, apt to intrigue and brought up in "underground" revolutionary activities, you get perpetual change of personnel and "liquidation" of many of the more intelligent people, creating new difficulties of organisation. . . .

Yet despite all these difficulties and drawbacks the machine turns ponderously on. There are great queues outside every shop for hours sometimes, but all the people look healthy and well-fed

(much more so here than in—say—a Lancashire industrial town).
The clothing situation is very bad and people are dressed in the
oldest things—and yet few if any suffer from cold. Transport and
production are ill-organised and yet the army, air force and navy
constantly grow in strength and effectiveness. There are shortages
all the time somewhere of some goods, sometimes grave and serious
shortages, yet a large export of commodities is carried out. . . .

It all reminds me a little of China, such excellent intentions and
plans, but just enough of the careless disregard for time and for
action to spoil them or to hinder very greatly their effect. But that
is the Russian temperament, and it's going to be a very long time
before that is overcome. . . .

. . . . So we arrive at the question. Can this Russia, somewhat
tired and exhausted after the enormous effort of the Revolution,
get over its natural propensity to sleep with the present incentives
to keep awake?

Stalin and his fellow workers, but Stalin first and foremost, is
making a tremendous effort to stimulate activity. His methods have
been very many of them excessively cruel by our standards, others
have been attempts to substitute some other form of competition or
instigation for the profit motive. He is working with about the most
difficult material possible both because of the natural characteristics
of the people, the far-flung continent over which he has to operate,
and the urgent need for concentrating on building up defences
against Germany and Japan.

Faced with a similar problem, are there any other methods?
Could any of us face them better or as well? Or should we throw in
our hand and declare it all hopeless?

This reminds me again of China. When I made many suggestions
of reorganisation to Chiang Kai-shek and he asked me to take on
the job of reorganisation in China, it sounded a marvellous opportunity, but then Madame Chiang and Donald both raised the
question—How are you going to get things done? And they advised
me after I got back not to attempt it as all my efforts would be defeated by the characteristic difficulties of the Chinese people. In
fact they must work out their own salvation in their own way. It is
the same with Russia, I feel, and I am certain that a whole host of
things have happened and will happen that I and others will regard
with horror and intense dislike. They are happening now. I dislike
the whole atmosphere—but if Stalin were to ask me tomorrow for
advice (which he won't do!!!) what should I say about it?

Cripps wrote this after some three months of his isolation:
an impressionistic narration resulting from the impact of

Moscow and the Russian leaders upon the man of Christian Socialist ideals, the trained lawyer of capitalist Britain, the experimental scientist, the expert administrator from a country that had begun its industrialization several hundred years earlier. His estimate of the cultural levels of the Russian people, their carelessness of time, their backwardness in organization, the collectivization of agriculture, had for its yardstick the high levels of industrial society and the ideals of Christian Socialism. The result, here, as in China, was a mixture of despair, hope, and faith. He concluded his letter,

I am more than ever convinced of the undesirability of dictatorship and totalitarian regimes, but also more than ever convinced that some better forms of democracy must be invented if we are to prove democracy the right form of government—not for some ruling class—but for the people as a whole. . . . They (the Russians) have taken on an immensely great and difficult task and each little forward step is something upon which they can congratulate themselves; their failures are the opportunity for our sympathy and help, which we cannot give if we insist an calling a pathless desert a broad and macadamed highway. Viewed in this objective light we can perhaps be a bit more charitable about the motes in their eyes and a little more conscious of the beams in our own political eyes.

In the middle of September he met a fellow lawyer, Vishinsky, who had just been appointed chief assistant to Molotov. For nearly two hours they argued about the English seizure of the Baltic gold. He said of this meeting,

I liked him both in looks and in conversation. He is a trained lawyer and has a good brain, I should think. We started by mutual compliments on each other's careers as lawyers!! It all went very smoothly and pleasantly though our expressed views were 100% divergent. I shall try and keep a close and continuous contact with him as, at present at any rate, he talks and discusses matters in a much freer way than Molotov and there is much more feeling of friendly contact with some realities.

But at the end of September, he still had to write,

There is no development of any sort in our relations with the Soviet Government and we are waiting to see how the new German-Japanese-Italian alliance will affect them. Not favourably to us, I feel, for the present at any rate.

His days became more lively in a variety of ways. One Sunday he went to the Stadium, with 90,000 others, to watch a Moscow football team play a Bulgarian team. He enjoyed it so much that he went again, to see the famous Dynamo footballers play the Bulgars. Here he met the Belgian and Yugoslav ministers.

In these days he did not go to the theaters. He was waiting until his wife arrived. Another week and she would be with him. He was greatly excited and all his private thoughts were occupied with her coming.

The day when his wife and two daughters, Peggy and Theresa, were to arrive was a great day indeed. Stafford fussed about the Embassy in the mood of a schoolboy at the end of the school term packing his bags for the holidays. The night before he had given Joe a "wash and brush-up." Today he dashed out to the botanical gardens to buy flowers. Dahlias and chrysanthemums were all he could get at this time of the year and he made a goodly display of them. Then he got the news that the train was five hours late, but at last, at 1:30 in the morning, it drew in. Everyone was too excited to notice the chill of the night. Joe was at the station, too, looking his best, but a bit alarmed by the female invasion. The staff waited up to greet them and they were still taking supper at three o'clock, a happy family united again.

The family changed the whole atmosphere of the Embassy. Stafford's "chief consultant" and partner in affection, Isobel, was there. Now he could get through his work more quickly and more easily.

The arrival of the family was indeed an augury of better days. It coincided with a stir in diplomatic activity. The very next day Sir Stafford saw Molotov and Lozovsky and got permission to evacuate all British subjects from the Baltic provinces by way of Vladivostock. The Foreign Office in London at last began to talk with the Russians about the situation in the Far East. There were important changes in the British Cabinet and, says Sir Stafford, "They have 'noticed' the changes with— I think—pleasure and some degree of hopefulness. I rubbed them in yesterday to Vishinsky!!"

In the middle of October, he wrote,

Yesterday I saw Mikoyan and we at last started "Trade Negotiations." . . . There is obviously a complete change in outlook due to Germany's occupation of Roumania which has upset these people very much following on the Japanese alliance. Everything for us is much easier and the Press is more sympathetic. May it last!

Contrary to expectations, Germany did not follow up her conquests and invade Britain. Mussolini attacked Greece and Hitler marched into Rumania, which brought the Nazi armies to the border of Bessarabia, now a part of the Soviet Union. The latter had never recognized the seizure of this province by Rumania. After the signing of the German-Soviet pact in 1939 the Soviet Union had forced Rumania to return Bessarabia to Russia, not only as a rightful restoration of stolen territory, but as part of a strategical plan of defense against the coming attack of the Nazis. The occupation of Rumania by the Nazi Army was therefore a reminder of the approaching hour when the war would roll over her frontiers. Hence the change of atmosphere in the Soviet Foreign Office, and the timeliness of the proposals which Sir Stafford made.

Hardly had he presented his proposals to the Soviet Government than the British seized thirteen more ships which had previously formed part of the Baltic merchant fleet. The Soviets claimed that these ships belonged to them. The view of the British Government was that they were Baltic ships and the question to be resolved was whether the Russian occupation deprived their owners of their rights in them. Another problem arose over Russian participation in a Danubian Conference called by the Nazis. The Nazis had no right to call such a conference of the "Danubian Powers," of which, under the treaty, Britain was one. The British Government objected to Russia's recognizing such an illegal conference.

It appeared to the Soviet Government that the voice of Cripps in Moscow was completely out of tune with that of his Government in London. Another cold spell set in around the Embassy in Moscow and Sir Stafford had more time on his hands again. He went with Isobel to see the Russian Ballet—"very lovely and a great enjoyment." At the end of October he wrote,

The diplomatic struggle is growing in intensity and is tending more and more to orient itself around Russia as she remains the great uncertain factor in the situation. There is no doubt her sympathies are with Greece and with Turkey—for very practical Russian reasons—but whether and what that will mean it is impossible to say.

Direct conversations had ceased. Cripps was dependent for his news on B.B.C. bulletins, whatever arrived in the mail, and what he could gather from what he called the "Club," an assembly of colleagues in the Embassy, and from the gatherings of the various foreign ambassadors whose news was derived from sources similar to his own. Describing this collective source of opinion in a letter he says,

We have of course a mass of gossip all of which is interesting—from various angles—and much of which is amusing—like all gossip, because it deals with personalities. By means of it, testing it out, evaluating and weighing you can get a "hunch" this way or that as to how things are going but there is a very strong natural tendency for one to adopt an attitude of one of the two extremes. You either wish-think yourself into an attitude by taking all the favourable bits of news and gossip or else you do precisely the opposite and everything looks inevitable blacker and blacker. And of course, as you only discuss these matters with known friends, that is discuss them freely and openly, you tend to react on one another and make each confirm the others pre-existing view—a sort of "mutual admiration club" effect! One has to try to be objective even quite outside one's own personal likes and dislikes and that is a very difficult thing, but naturally the value of one's judgment depends upon how far one succeeds.

He had to wait on events, and big events too. But no doubt these atmospherics had their influence upon him. In the midst of this waiting for a turn in the tide of affairs, there came the great anniversary of the Bolshevik Revolution. On November 6, Cripps attended the Revolutionary Anniversary meeting in the Bolshoi Theater. There were present the heads of the Government, party and Soviet leaders from various institutions, leaders of industry, the trade unions, the co-operatives. The meeting was followed by a magnificent concert which went on into the early hours of the morning and was the prelude to the great march-past and display in the Red Square on the "day of the Revolution." That, he wrote,

. . . . was an amazing day of brilliant sun and cloudless blue sky, and it was a most impressive review. I liked the march-past of the people which followed the military parade, when hundreds of thousands streamed past with every kind of banner and device on sticks. It really gave one an idea of masses. But we came to the conclusion that it wasn't as inspiring as the Durham Gala Day, because one felt it lacked the spontaneity and was too much a government-organized affair.

To the people of the West, the name "Red Square" has a political connotation, but it had that name long before there were any "Reds," for the Russian words for "Red Square," also mean "Beautiful Square." Flanked by the lovely Kremlin wall, with its towered gateways and turrets, its flower garden of graves where the revolutionaries of earlier years lie buried, with Lenin's tomb of varicolored marble standing in the middle—an admirable platform from which orators can address the hundreds of thousands who on such days fill its spaciousness— its beauty is unrivaled. At one end, through which the demonstrators flow, stands the Museum of the Revolution. At the other end, where the masses leave the square, stands the quaint many-colored Church of St. Basil, dating back to the Middle Ages. Once the Czars had a monopoly of this square, and their governments organized there only military parades and executions.

The celebration had just passed when a diplomatic bombshell dropped into the "Club." Molotov went to Berlin to confer with Hitler. Cripps made a note,

I have listened to a great deal of speculation as to Molotov's actions and intentions, but the truth is that no one knows at the moment what, if anything, it all means. I had nearly 2½ hours with Vishinsky on Monday evening and made a very strong protest to him against Molotov's un-neutral behaviour, and also pointed out that we must assume the visit amounted to rejection of our proposals unless I had the assurance to the contrary, which I only got in a very ridiculous form, i.e., that Molotov's visit had nothing to do with their relations to us, it was only a return of Ribbentrop's visit, etc. etc.

Still nothing happened. No one could get more than speculation about the conference at Berlin. The atmosphere was very unpleasant. As if to make things worse for Cripps, a few days later he was startled to indignation, but this time not by the Russians. His trade proposals to the Soviet Government had been made in secrecy, to keep the Germans from knowing anything about them. Suddenly, while at breakfast one morning, he heard them being broadcast by the B.B.C.! It seemed to him that every step he made in Moscow to create better relations with the Soviet Government was followed promptly by some stupid counteraction on the part of the Government at home. He wrote a long personal letter to Halifax telling him, "It isn't any good my remaining in the circumstances the announcement created." There was no doubt about his anger. He thought the British Government had played straight into the hands of the Germans. Irritated by isolation and the bungling of affairs at home, he was unhappy. "Perhaps after Christmas," he thought, "we shall wake up to another bout of political activity."

The Cripps family had a happy Christmas party at the Embassy. The embassies had their "seasons." The Russian winter had settled in. Deep snow was everywhere. The colored domes of the churches of Moscow and all its towers and minarets, its squares and great highways, were a glistening white. The Cripps went to the dacha in the woods and tried walking in the forest garden. Then, Sir Stafford says, "We went for a promenade round the village looking very miserable wading through deep snow." He kept up his routine of an early morning walk with Joe, although Joe "was a bit miserable too as his toes kept getting so cold that he limped on them and I had to keep stopping to give them a rub."

At the end of the second week in January it was evident that neither his protests about Molotov going to Berlin, nor his formal politeness, nor anything else in the diplomatic armory had induced the Russians to alter their course. In his diary he made a remarkable suggestion—whether it was a "hunch" derived from his conversations with the diplomatic club I cannot say. He wrote,

At the moment these people seem more sphinxlike than ever and I doubt if even the Germans know what they are thinking! There are indications of something being on the tapes with Japan, I think an attempt to encourage Japan to go to war with America and so get Japan defeated and that danger out of the way! . . .

They really are very realistic and intelligent politicians from the point of view of the national interests of Russia for the present. The supreme test will be if they can survive the whole war without coming into it or only come in when their victory is certain!

A week later, he wrote,

Things point in the direction of something being concluded in an attempt no doubt by the Russians to destroy the Japanese danger through the agency of the Anglo-American Far Eastern fleets! That is to say, to drive Japan towards the south and into war with America. That is sound policy for the Russians to protect themselves in the East!

If the subsequent decision of the Japanese to strike at America and Britain was really due to Russian inspiration, history will record it as a master stroke of Russian diplomacy.

At the beginning of April he saw signs that the Russo-German political clash was coming nearer:

Everyone is wondering what Hitler will do—whether he will turn against the Balkans or this country or try the invasion of England. The general opinion is that time is turning against him now and that he will have to decide by the beginning of June at the very latest—but probably he will do so long before then and we may find ourselves en route for the Urals or Siberia! ! ! !

Matsuoka came to Moscow, and Russia and Japan, on April 13, signed a non-aggression pact. The Russians deemed it of such importance that Stalin went personally to the station to bid farewell to Matsuoka. The pact was variously appraised. Goebbels declared that it signaled "to the world that four great powers were now in full and irresistible alignment." In Britain and America it was generally believed that Russia had thrown in her lot with the aggressor powers. Cripps did not accept this view. He said,

I regard the Japanese Pact as anti-German since its only object can be to protect the Russian Eastern frontiers in the event of an attack on the west by Germany. . . . The place is full of rumours of German attacks. . . . It is sufficiently serious to cause people to start discussing evacuation plans. . . .

I can't yet make up my mind except to the effect that there is a state of tension here which may have grave results—or may not in the end! . . . I have decided to try and see Molotov to ask him about the Russian attitude in an indirect way.

Molotov refused to see him. He therefore saw Vishinsky and put in a stiff written statement, which Molotov ignored. Whatever confidence the Soviet Government might have had in Sir Stafford personally, they did not believe in the British Government. He may have had the voice of Jacob, but they had no doubt about the hands of the British Government being the hands of Esau.

On the last day of April he wrote:

I still think there won't be any war now but there is no doubt a danger of it and everyone is talking about it, not only amongst the diplomats but amongst the Russians as well. I expect these people will be able to do enough appeasing to avoid it—if Hitler lets them.

The afterthought is appropriate, for there comes a time when diplomacy is of no avail in the affairs of the world. Powers can use diplomacy to negotiate concessions of territory, economic and political agreements, but they cannot negotiate one another out of existence. Hitler wanted more than "lebensraum." He wanted the destruction of the Soviet regime, and that could be settled only by the arbitrament of war. The die was already cast. Diplomacy had assumed the role of hiding that fact. Cripps was thinking in terms of diplomacy as the deciding factor, watching for the breakdown.

By May 6, something definite appeared among the rumors:

The political atmosphere is most confused here at the moment as Schulenberg (the German ambassador) says he hasn't seen and doesn't want to see the Kremlin people and that they can send for him if they want to talk to him—at the same time the Germans are denying any possibility of attacking Russia, while in Bucharest they are saying it is all arranged for mid-June! Then it is said (through chauffeurs' gossip!) that Schulenberg is packing to leave for good and is very depressed about things.

A few days later he thought the situation was clearer. Stalin, in addition to his other functions, had become Prime Minister in place of Molotov, and the Belgian, Norwegian, and Yugoslav missions had been told to close down and leave.

A day or two later Rudolf Hess dropped from the skies into Scotland. What did that mean?

Sir Stafford's complete inability at this stage to make contact with the Russian leaders was leading him into depression bordering on cynicism. At the end of May he was still of the opinion that the Germans and the Russians would make another agreement, but he was not so sure that they were going to get the opportunity. The attitude of the German ambassador did not appear to signify cordiality between the two governments.

Sir Stafford arranged for his wife and daughter Theresa to go to Sweden and began preparations for the evacuation of the Embassy. He was becoming convinced that zero hour was approaching and that undiplomatic deeds were very near. A telegram arrived asking him to fly home for consultation. Evidently the Government also felt, and possibly already knew, that the next great turning point in the Second World War was at hand. On June 11, 1941, he and his wife arrived "unexpectedly" in England by airplane. He was convinced that the break would come in the middle of that month.

On the fateful day of June 22, all uncertainty, even in the realm of diplomacy, was at an end. Molotov broadcast to the people of the Soviet Union,

Today, at four o'clock in the morning, without giving any reason to the Soviet Government and without a declaration of war, German forces attacked our country, invaded our frontiers in many places, and raided our towns of Zhitomir, Kiev, Sebastopol, and several others. . . . This unheard-of attack is without example in the history of civilised nations. The attack on our country has been made in spite of the fact that there is a non-aggression pact between Germany and the U.S.S.R. which has conscientiously been kept in every detail. . . . Now that the attack on the Soviet Union has taken place the Soviet Government has given our forces the following order: Beat back the enemy's invasion and do not allow the enemy forces to hold the territory of our country. . . .

The same day, before the nine o'clock news, the British Prime Minister made a broadcast. Never was he more clearly the spokesman of the most keenly felt of British emotions. British hearers thrilled with pride, even in the midst of their deep horror at this extension of the war, to hear their Prime

Minister associating the country closely with their new allies. Churchill said:

I have to make a declaration, but can you doubt what our policy will be? We have but one aim and one single irrevocable purpose. We are resolved to destroy Hitler and every vestige of the Nazi regime. From this nothing will turn us—nothing. Any man or State who fights against Nazism will have our aid. . . . We have offered to the Soviet Government any technical assistance which is in our power and which is likely to be of service to them. . . .

I will say, if Hitler imagines that his attack upon Soviet Russia will cause the slightest division of aim or slackening of effort in the great democracies, who are resolved on his doom, he is greatly mistaken.

Thus, at one stroke, massively tragic as it was, all the obstacles to an alliance of Britain and Soviet Russia were swept aside. Cripps was publicly acclaimed for the services he had rendered. When Churchill addressed the House of Commons, he said,

It was this assessment of impending events that caused me to ask His Majesty's Ambassador in Moscow to return to this country for consultation. I felt that his experience and his advice would be invaluable to us at such a time, and so it has proved. The House and the country are deeply indebted to my Hon. and learned friend, the Member for East Bristol—if I may give him for a moment his Parliamentary, rather than his diplomatic description—for work done under conditions of the utmost difficulty. For the reasons I have given, he was unable to conclude those pacts or agreements which are dear to the diplomatist's heart, although today they enjoy but a brief butterfly life. Yet it is clear that, by his influence, and by his example, my Hon. and learned friend has shown to the Soviet Union the fundamental desire of His Majesty's Government to maintain our relations upon a normal footing. When he returns to his post, he will be able, with his marked ability, to advise and direct the help which it is the declared intention of His Majesty's Government to give to the Soviet Union at the present time.

On June 24, 1941, Cripps was informed that "at the Prime Minister's request the King has been pleased to approve that you be sworn of His Majesty's most honorable Privy Council."

The Labour Party leaders were not quite sure what to say. The Communist Party decided that Cripps was not so bad after all and promptly acclaimed the war as a righteous war against Fascism. They did not say that it had been such from the beginning, for Stalin had not yet said that. One day he would, and did.

There was another man, lying seriously ill, whom at the earliest moment after his arrival in England Stafford rushed to see. His father was near the end of his journey. He also said "well done" to Stafford and was well pleased with his son. It was their last meeting. On June 28, 1941, Cripps was again on his way to Moscow to consummate the alliance for which he had striven so long, and which events had now thrust upon Britain and the Soviet Union, despite all efforts to keep them apart.

XV. Job Completed

A NEW stage of the world war had now begun. It should not be ignored that in this new phase not one power came into the war voluntarily to form an alliance against the Fascists because they loved their allies or had the same ideals. Had it been possible for the Soviet Union, after the betrayal of Czechoslovakia by Britain and France, to keep out of the war, she would have done so. Had the Japanese not attacked, the United States would have continued to look on from afar until the Fascists had jeopardized their interests and challenged their existence by some other attack. The disassembling of the old peace system had been carried to its completion with every state governed by its particular class interests and outlook, narrow, nationalistic, and conservative. The new alliances thrust upon the powers were marriages of convenience and not of love, the converging of the battle for existence and not a fundamental accord in aims. They would say the same things but not mean the same things. Stalin would not become a Churchill, nor Churchill a Roosevelt. Within the framework of the alliances all the old clash of interests would be still there. Old prejudices, suspicions, fears, distorted visions, conservative habits, pursuit of independent aims under cover of common interests, would continue to operate under the umbrella of idealistic charters, grand slogans, and cloudy dreams of a victorious peace. So profoundly would these forces be at work that there would be no common pooling of resources, only aid to one another within limits. With no common strategy, each would calculate what it could do at the minimum cost to itself, and speculate where each would be in relation to the other in the outcome.

Nevertheless, they would accommodate one another under the pressure of their enemies. Churchill would see to it that the diatribe he had written against Stalin in his book of portraits would be left out of the wartime edition. Stalin would toast his wartime friend and watch him carefully. Such was the character of the period that began when Stafford Cripps returned to Moscow to open a new chapter in his career as Ambassador.

Gone, at least for a while, were the isolation and frigidity which had marked his earlier period. Having flown by British plane, he was met at Archangel by the heads of the forces and the local soviet and a representative from the Foreign Office. Waiting to fly him to Moscow was Marshal Timoshenko's huge Douglas, luxuriously fitted out as a staff plane. Within a few hours he was met at Moscow by a great assemblage of distinguished persons. Twice that day he saw Molotov, who greeted him warmly. Then he saw Vishinsky and Mykoyan and made arrangements for the meeting of the Military Mission with the Russian military authorities. He wrote:

The atmosphere is so different here that it is difficult to realise it is the same place politically. I am very glad I came back; although I may not be able to do a great deal I think I can probably do more than anybody else. . . . There is a most terrific battle going on around the old Russian frontier north and south of Minsk about 400 miles off and it is as yet undecided. The Russians seem calm and confident as to the immediate result though they are fully conscious of the tremendous pressure that is being exerted upon them.

On July 8, he had his second meeting with Stalin. They met to talk over the terms of a treaty of alliance. Time and place were appropriate. The time was 1941, when London was being bombed from the skies and the Nazi armies were smashing their way toward Moscow. The place was Stalin's room in one of the Kremlin buildings—a large room simply furnished, a large desk at one end of the room, and on the wall behind it a large portrait of Lenin. A long table ran down one side of the room at which there were enough chairs for the members of the Political Bureau of the Communist Party. On this wall was another portrait, that of Karl Marx, the pioneer of "Scientific Socialism." The room was in a large house, part of a block of houses within the Kremlin walls which surround ancient palaces and churches built by various rulers of Russia in the course of seven centuries.

The Kremlin stands on a plateau at the center of Moscow and from it radiate great highways to the outskirts of the city. One side of the Kremlin faces the beautiful Moscow River, and from this river bank stretches another great wall, known as the old Chinese wall, reaching deep into the city and telling of the days of an ancient invasion when the Tartars overran Muscovy. All the centuries of a thousand years have left their marks upon the Moscow of today. Moscow stands at the center of the greatest land mass of the world and is the capital of a Union covering a sixth of the land surface of the earth and embracing some 180,000,000 people. At this time and in this place, the leader of this great people, son of a Georgian cobbler, who became a Marxist while a student in a religious seminary and dedicated his life while yet a youth to the Bolshevik Revolution, met with the Ambassador of the British Empire. The Ambassador was the son of a baron, reared and trained as a ruler in all the appropriate institutions, public school, university, and Church; scientist, lawyer, political leader, Christian socialist, Member of Parliament, Privy Councillor.

They were strikingly different in appearance. Sir Stafford, tall, slim, bespectacled, clean-shaven, ascetic-looking, the cultured gentleman. Stalin, comparatively short, rugged as one who has battled his way through storm and stress, swarthy, black-haired with black mustache, easy of bearing in his loose khaki jacket with its single red star. Both men look you straight in the eyes. Both have the habit of direct speech with a minimum of circumlocution. Both are quick thinkers and both like words to represent deeds. Each knew what the other wanted from this meeting; they quickly came to the points of agreement, and the draft was made.

I do not mean to give the impression that these two men thought alike, approached all questions alike, had the same philosophy of life and understanding of history, or had the same aims. In these matters they differed most profoundly. Both men were scientists. Stalin was a social scientist, convinced that human society had its own laws of motion and that while man made history, he made it with the materials which history gave him, changed society, and in the process changed himself. He believed that out of man's creative labor in the production of the means of life, mankind had created society.

This society is composed of classes, defined according to their relationship to the ownership of property, the means whereby the wealth of society is produced. These classes of property owners and nonproperty owners, which had been differentiated and developed by the labor process, had been in continuous conflict since the dawn of history. One form of property-owning class superseded another in the governing of society. He was convinced that until the nonproperty-owning industrial working class became the ruling class and abolished the old divisions of mankind according to property, and society as a whole socially owned all the means of wealth production, this social conflict would continue. The means to end this conflict lay in the leadership of the working class to the creation of a working-class state, in alliance with other oppressed classes. This alliance he believed would establish socialist society as the means of its transition to Communism. While this class conflict characterized society everywhere, he held the view that it did not develop uniformly in all countries and that, therefore, Socialism could be established in one country long before it could in others. This, he said, had been done in the Soviet Union, which could and would enter into friendly relations with states of differing kinds which were agreeable to such relations. Changes in other states, he argued, would be determined by the relationship of the classes within them, and not by changes imposed from the outside.

Sir Stafford did not accept this view of society and its development. He believed that there were laws of nature, such as biological laws, chemical laws, state laws, moral laws, but not laws of society's development. He recognized that there were classes in society and that they struggled against each other. But this for him was not a decisive feature of social life. He regarded society as local and national aggregations of individuals, each with a soul of his own. Every individual, of whatever social class, needed a good social environment in which to develop the spirit of human brotherhood and co-operation in social well-being. He was a Christian, believing in God the Father and Jesus his Son, as the divine example of what each man should aim to be. He believed that a socialist society would be for all men the most desirable form of society, the means to the fulfillment of human brotherhood and co-operation, the most efficient and necessary means of organizing economic and political life, if it could be achieved. He wished, however, to transcend the class struggle and achieve socialism by the consent of the people of property to surrender their private ownership to the community at fair compensation.

Both men were of high principle and great character; men whose integrity was unquestioned and whose sustained intensity of purpose had brought them into the forefront. They met to discuss neither their positions nor their political theories. They met to discuss a specific matter—the making of a treaty of alliance between the Soviet Union and Britain for the waging of a common war against the Fascist powers.

The outcome of the discussion was the Anglo-Soviet Agreement published to the world on July 12, 1941:

(1) The two Governments mutually undertake to render each other assistance and support of all kinds in the present war against Hitlerite Germany.

(2) They further undertake that during this war they will neither negotiate nor conclude an armistice or treaty of peace except by mutual agreement.

When the time for the short ceremony of signing the agreement arrived, fifteen people gathered in the Kremlin. There were Stalin, Molotov, Vishinsky and other officials of the Soviet Foreign Office, and heads of the Army and Navy. Molotov signed for the Soviet Union, Stafford Cripps for Great Britain. So at last Cripps could rejoice in seeing come to pass an agreement for which he, more than any other man among the leaders of the two countries, had striven.

Incidentally, the signing of this document was on an auspicious day in the life of Stafford and his wife, Isobel. It was the thirtieth anniversary of their wedding. If the new event of the union of the two countries should prove as successful as their marriage union, then it would be a success indeed and the two countries would travel through the years ahead in happy accord.

But would it be so? After all, was not the union of the two countries a marriage of convenience? Did it mean that when the knot was tied each endowed the other with all his worldly goods, and for better or worse they would travel together "un-

til death do us part"? Analogies usually fail to stand up to
analysis, and none more so than this. For here we have two
modern powers, one a Socialist State of workers and peasants,
and the other the oldest of the modern capitalist, imperialist
states, which only a few months earlier were almost at the point
of war with each other. When the blotter rolled over the marriage certificate on July 12, would the British leaders forget
the role of the Comintern in the internal affairs of the capitalist
nations? Would the Soviet leaders blot out of their minds the
memory of the twenty-three years of hate which Churchill and
his colleagues had inflicted on them? No. Both powers acknowledged that their paths had converged in a life and death struggle against powers that threatened their very existence, and
none but fools would deny the urgent necessity of each helping
the other against the common enemy. But each power brought
into the alliance all their yesterdays; neither Stalin nor Sir
Stafford had any illusions about that. Cripps realized that it
would not be easy to make the partnership into a real working
accord.

One of the first things he did on this day of the treaty-signing
was to introduce to Stalin the leaders of the British Military
Mission, who had returned to Moscow with him, for a frank
talk about exchange of military information and what aid they
could render. He was anxious to get the two groups quickly
working together. He could see at a glance that the test of the
soundness of the working agreement would be the amount and
kind of aid the British would render as the Nazi onslaught increased in fury. Hitler calculated that his forces could drive
the Red Army to the Urals within three months. The battle
for Smolensk was raging. In England the estimates among authorities varied. Some thought that Hitler would fulfill his
prediction. The optimists thought "the Russians could last out
six months." And there were those in high places who rejoiced
in the turn of events and hoped that the Germans and the
Russians would knock each other to the point of exhaustion,
and then Britain could settle accounts with both. There were
also those who thought that the British should regard this
period of Nazi concentration as a breathing space in which
they could play a defensive role along the far reaches of the
Empire, ready for the time when Hitler, having smashed the

"Bolshies," would turn again to attack Britain with full force. Only a few political outsiders at this time entertained the fantastic notion that the Russians could take the full impact of the Nazi onslaught, exhaust it, and turn loose a counter offensive that would "tear the guts out of the Nazi army," and could then smash their way to Berlin and beyond.

Cripps knew nothing of Russia's military might and said so; but of two things he was convinced: First, that now the blow had fallen, the Russian people would fight with a tenacity and a passion without measure. Second, that Britain should be a straight and honest partner in the alliance, willing to give sacrificial aid of every kind and compel Hitler to relax his attack in the east by forcing him to divert forces to the defense of the west. This he believed to be sound military and political strategy. It would hasten the end of the war and insure the unity of both peoples for the years of peace. When he had signed the Treaty of Alliance he had felt that his purpose in Moscow had been accomplished, and that the sooner he could be released in order to serve the purpose of winning the war in Britain itself, the better. All that he could do now was to break down the suspicions of the Russian leaders and facilitate effective co-operation between the British Military Mission and the Russian military authorities.

Meanwhile, he had to make arrangements for moving the Embassy staff eastward, should the expected bombing of Moscow make it necessary, and the staff had to receive instructions in fire-fighting and the like. A good shelter had been made in the basement of the Embassy. One of these days he would find himself living the life of many whom he had left behind in England. The first air raid on Moscow was on July 21, 1941. Fire bombs dropped on the Embassy roof. Writing home about it, he said:

It started about 10.30 and didn't stop until 4 o'clock this morning. With the first wave of bombers we got three fire bombs and then another with the next wave. We tackled three quite well but the fourth was in a part of the roof that we couldn't reach. It got hold thoroughly and had it not been for the magnificent work of all the personnel led by the three heads of the military mission the place would probably have been burnt out. As it was they managed just to hold it till, after about an hour, the Fire

Brigade were able to come. They were all splendid and there wasn't
a whimper even from a child. There was very little high explosive
near us and though there were some bad fires as far as one can see
they were all got under control fairly quickly. There are no signs
of any this morning except some smoke in one place where the
worst fire was. The Kremlin was unscathed. We are expecting a
succession of nights now that they have started.

The damage to the roof is quite bad and the whole place is in
a mess with the water which is dripping through the ceilings. There
was a regular cataract down the front stairs last night. The worst
of the fire was over my bedroom, but luckily it was all at the end
away from my bed so that I was able to sleep there to the accompaniment of water dripping into two buckets and the firemen
hammering away in the roof as well as the fighters flying over and
a few final bombers coming! . . . Joe was awfully good and didn't
seem to mind in the least so long as he was with me.

One day brought a surprise which, he said, "I wouldn't have
missed for anything." He had been to the Kremlin to see Molotov when, on an air-raid alarm, they ordered him down to the
basement in an adjoining building. Whom should he meet
there but Litvinov, a leading figure of the eventful years between the two wars. There was a time when this man had been
reputed to be the most able foreign secretary who had ever
appeared before the Assembly of the League of Nations. He
was now elderly and suffering from heart trouble. They talked
of old times and the eventful years since Sir Stafford had leaped
into the political arena and they had got to know each other.
Litvinov expressed the view that the men mainly responsible
for the present state of affairs were Simon, Chamberlain, and
Laval. He thought that the League of Nations could have
stopped all aggression if it had been properly used in the first
instance against Japan in 1931. He told Sir Stafford that he had
warned both Eden and Halifax that a situation was bound to
arise in which Germany would have overrun the whole of
Europe except Russia and England, and that then the only
question would be as to how the powers would arrange themselves for the final round. Any two might be against the other
one! Litvinov was relieved that things had turned out as they
had.

In these days Cripps met Stalin often. They got on well together because they were perfectly frank with each other and talked in "the language of arithmetic and not algebra." In one of these talks Sir Stafford persuaded Stalin to grant an immediate amnesty to every Polish citizen. There was later a story set going in London gossip circles that Stalin preferred to negotiate with men like Beaverbrook and the drinkers and diners, in preference to the "ascetic" Stafford Cripps. That of course is nonsense for the gullible who can swallow anything.

When Cripps thought his affairs were working satisfactorily, he began to raise the question of his return to England. There was a thing agitating his mind that he would have much liked to carry through, and one cannot help wondering whether, had he been able to do so, it might not have greatly changed the subsequent relations between the two countries after the war. He wanted, possibly more than anything else, to reach an understanding with Stalin concerning postwar Europe. But such a discussion he could not introduce without the prior agreement of His Majesty's Government, and at the same time the Government had no ideas concerning the shape of Europe after the war. So he thought he would like to get back to England to study this problem, discuss it fully with the Government, and return as a special emissary to Stalin. It was a good idea, but one that would come to nothing. History was being made at such a pace and on such a world-wide scale that Cripps would find himself caught up by the course of events and called upon to fulfill other missions of great importance.

August arrived, and Sir Stafford and the other ambassadors were still in Moscow, much to their surprise. Co-operation was not working as well as it should have worked. However great the frankness and directness of Stalin, it did not alter the fact that below him, and especially in the middle ranks of the bureaucrats, the old prejudices remained and the old suspicions were as rampant as ever. The military mission got neither the information nor the co-operation to which they thought they were entitled. British help seemed not to be forthcoming. There were hold-ups in the shipping of goods. Then a British journalist indiscreetly published some facts as to Russian air raids on Berlin, including the airdromes from which the Russian bombers flew.

By the middle of August, Cripps had become quite sensitive

to the military position on the Russian front and was feeling that

too many people at home are failing to realise that this is not another war in which we will help if we can but the same war and that now Russia is one of our fronts and must be regarded and treated as such. Just as we should undertake some relieving action if it were on a front of our own so we ought to take every risk to relieve the pressure before it is too late and we lose a great part of the benefit of this front as we shall do if there is any collapse which we might possibly help to avoid by more active help.

He was feeling, too, that the western governments did not share this point of view and were slow to react to the situation on the Russian front. Harry Hopkins had been in Moscow. President Roosevelt and Prime Minister Churchill had issued a proclamation about the aid that Britain and America would render, but it was not until September 10 that Sir Stafford received an intimation of the proposed conference with Beaverbrook and Harriman. This conference was to deal only with supplies, and there were no signs whatever of any relieving action on the West.

The German attacks were proceeding with terrific fury. The battle for Smolensk had ended, and two mighty efforts were being made against Leningrad and Kiev. According to the orders issued by the Nazi generals when the battle for Smolensk began, their armies should by that time have taken Moscow. One day it will be recognized that this battle was possibly the greatest in history, possibly even greater than the later battle of Stalingrad. Its significance in the history of the war is like that of the battle of the Marne in the war of 1914-1918. There, the allied armies held, and from that date the ultimate defeat of the Germans became assured. The battle of Smolensk destroyed the myth of the irresistibility of the blitzkrieg. It raged for thirty days and nights, and at the end of it the Germans bestrode a town of charred ruins after colossal carnage on both sides. But the Russians had called a halt to the blitzkrieg, had shaken the faith of the Nazi Army in its own invincibility and its fantastic conceptions of the time within which it could conquer the Soviet Union. The battle of Smolensk broke the back of the central attack and compelled the Nazis to spend another sixty days in reorganizing their forces before they could advance toward Moscow. The Russians had lost tremendously in casualties, but their army remained intact, ready to bend still further, until the full impact of the German offensive had been exhausted. Then would come the recoil and the unleashing of the mounting reserve armies that were building up in the rear of Moscow, which would sweep the German armies out of the Soviet Union like a mighty broom of destiny, scatter them across the battlefields of Europe, and dump the remnants on the ruins of Berlin.

As Cripps sat fretting in Moscow about the lack of relief action in the West and the slowness of even material aid, the Germans were attacking Leningrad in full fury. Not a few people now swallowed their criticisms of Russia's attack on Finland. It was now clear to all that had not the Russians shattered the power of the Finns to attack them from the outskirts of Leningrad in the rear, Leningrad could never have survived. The fall of Leningrad would have meant the collapse of the northern front and the certain encirclement of Moscow. Leningrad did not fall.

Kiev fell and the Russian line had to bend again. Throughout this tremendous drama, in which the Russians were being strained to the limit of endurance, and in which more of them were slaughtered than their allies lost in six years of war, no relief action came from the Allies. Herbert Morrison made a speech to the effect that Britain, *commensurate with her safety,* would do all she could to help! The Russians remembered Munich and the rapidity with which Britain and France had organized an expeditionary force to rush to the aid of Finland!

Sir Stafford was worried by the effect of all this on the Russians. But the Beaverbrook Mission was on the way. A great thrill came when the radio reported that British tank production had gone up fifty per cent after it had been promised that the tanks would be sent to Russia! At the end of September, the Beaverbrook-Harriman Mission arrived. Sir Stafford was not present at the meetings of the heads of the Mission with Stalin. Beaverbrook left the British Ambassador rather high and dry, with little information about the proceedings. And he would leave him with most difficult problems. For Beaverbrook was evidently making the maximum of promises, much in the spirit of Father Christmas, while revealing nothing of Britain's capacity to fulfill the promises.

When the mission left, the troubles began. It was soon demonstrated that while Sir Stafford thought the war should be waged as one war, it was not and would not be so. There was not a pooling of resources but conditional help between wartime "friends," each still suspicious of the other, and both carrying into their friendship glowing embers of their old enmity, all the prejudices and habits developed in their differing social and political histories.

On October 14 a trade-union delegation arrived, led by Sir Walter Citrine. The next day Molotov sent for the ambassadors to tell them that the Government had decided to evacuate Moscow and that the Diplomatic Corps would go with them. That was at one o'clock. They must start from Moscow that night at nine o'clock. Stafford wrote of this meeting in a letter home:

> I have never seen him looking so tired and ill. He had obviously been up all night and the decision hurt him terribly as one could see. He was deadly pale and his collar all awry whereas he is generally very neat and tidy. He looked completely exhausted and I think was. We said that we would like to send away the rest of our staff and stay with him until the last moment but he begged us not to, and on his direct request we said that we would go with the rest. He stated that they intended to defend Moscow at all cost and to continue fighting to the end. They are obviously very hard pressed and it makes my heart sore that our help should have been so long delayed as to mean a great victory to the Germans. We shall have to pay the price in years of suffering.

The German tanks and motorized infantry had broken through the Russian defenses and were on the high road to Moscow. They were advancing with immense forces. Eighty divisions were engaged in an all-out effort to seize the capital. Unprepared for winter warfare, they had to get Moscow before the winter set in, or lose all hope of victory. On October 15 they passed Majaisk and seemed in sight of their goal. The Russians flung into the battle some of their finest divisions, and in the following forty-eight hours the snow-covered battlefields and icy roads were the scenes of terrific fighting. The Soviet Army drove the Germans back almost to Majaisk.

Whatever the cost, Russia had to go through these months of carnage alone. All the world looked on and wondered how long now before the end. But the world did not yet see that behind the amazing defense lay a master strategy which had yet to show its full face.

Added to the theory of defense in depth which had governed the Soviet Government's political strategy since the signing of the German-Soviet pact, there was also the application of the "theory of reserves." In practice it meant that the Russians, after stubborn fighting, would retreat rather than allow the issue to be fought to a finish, would keep their army intact and tire the enemy. When the point had been reached where the Germans showed signs of exhaustion, the Soviet Army, which had been accumulating its reserves in the rear, would launch the counteroffensive with fresh troops equipped with massive material. Application of such a theory demanded foresight, infinite patience, tremendous fighting capacity, and sound judgment of the moment for the counteroffensive. The attack which drove the Germans back on Majaisk was not the decisive turn of the tide. It was still part of the defensive pattern. But it was the signal that the time was near.

In these anxious days, when there was fear that the Germans might break through to Moscow, Cripps and the other ambassadors and their staffs set out on an indescribable journey to Kuibishev. They had to suffer all the inconveniences of railway improvisation under most extraordinary circumstances. Masses of people, machinery, and factory equipment of all kinds were moving east, while thousands upon thousands of soldiers, guns, tanks, artillery, and every kind of military equipment were moving west. The congestion on the railways was tremendous. One wondered that anything moved at all. Military orders had to receive priority. About a hundred Britishers with Sir Stafford and mountains of baggage arrived at the railway station at eight o'clock to find it besieged by crowds of people also going east. The G. P. U. performed the policeman's service of guiding them through the crowds to a restaurant set aside for the diplomats. It was dark and it was snowing, and lights were not allowed. They were to have left at nine. They left at 1:00 A.M. Slowly they proceeded through the night, Sir Stafford and Joe sitting side by side in a wagon-lit. The train stopped, started, and stopped. Other trains, incredibly long, rolled past them loaded with machinery from Moscow factories.

The second day was much like the first. They averaged about ten miles an hour. They ate from the stocks of food they had brought with them. The Americans kept hot coffee on tap. On October 20 they arrived at Kuibishev, where they were dumped into a big barrack of a house that had been recently used by the Pioneers (Russian Boy Scouts). The next day, when they had got settled in and made the best of the accommodations, Sir Stafford went to see Vishinski and discovered that the General Staff and Molotov and company had not left Moscow. He demanded in vain that he and some of his staff and the heads of the Missions should be sent back to Moscow at once. The one thing in life which Cripps cannot tolerate is to be left isolated, with nothing to do or no means of doing the things he wants to do. Kuibishev was well associated in his mind with this kind of irritation. It was here that he and Geoffrey Wilson had had to wait with nothing to do on their way back to Chungking nearly two years earlier. Now he was here again and frustrated at every turn.

Sir Walter Citrine came along and he agreed that the British Government ought to send troops and equipment to the Russian front without delay, somewhere, somehow. The lack of aid had by now begun to impede talks with the Russian leaders on any subject. The Lease-Lend Agreement included a proposal that the Russians should supply free any British troops sent to Russia. Sir Stafford's attempt to settle the agreement came to nothing. He could not get further than the Russian point that "the question did not arise yet for there were no British forces in Russia." He was at a loose end. More than ever he felt that his work in Russia was completed and that he should make for London at the earliest possible moment. But he still had to hang on in irritation at Kuibishev.

The great hour of decision on the fate of the German advance was coming nearer and nearer. During October and November, the Germans managed to advance within thirty miles of Moscow. But it had become plain that the spirit was going out of the attack. By the first of December the Soviet High Command were convinced that decline had set in. The temperature fell sharply. By December 5, the Russian winter had really begun. The Russians knew that winter was their great ally and were prepared. At dawn, on December 6, the "greatest realist" of his time gave the order to counterattack. With dramatic suddenness and stupendous power, the huge reserve army, which had been accumulating and preparing for this day behind Moscow, splendidly equipped for winter warfare, struck irresistibly. The German armies were flung back. Moscow was set free from danger. So decisive was this defeat that the Germans would be unable to start any spring offensive, and midsummer of 1942 would pass before they could attempt a serious trial of strength. They failed at Leningrad too. Indeed, there would be but one more stupendous effort, culminating at Stalingrad.

Rivers of blood had flowed from the Red Army in those terrible months of savage fighting in the regions overrun by the Nazi armies. A great population had been decimated, hundreds of towns and thousands of villages had been utterly destroyed. The losses of men and material had been such as had been seen in no other war in all history. And still, little aid from the West had arrived.

On December 7, the day after the Germans were driven away from the gates of Moscow, the Japanese struck their treacherous blow at Pearl Harbor. Two more great powers were engulfed in World War II. The alignment of forces was complete. But once again, it was an alignment of powers, not a pooling of resources into a single war against a single enemy.

No sooner had the Germans been set back than permission was given for the ambassadors to return to Moscow. Sir Stafford returned, rejoicing, on December 11. The day after his return there was an air-raid alarm. The guard insisted that he should go to a deep shelter. On arriving at the shelter, in pitch dark, "I bashed my head," says Stafford, "against what I believe to have been the edge of a black marble pillar. I bled like a pig and then lots of people came to give first aid!"

The next day the doctor replaced the bandage the first-aiders had put on with "a neat little piece of gauze covered with collodion" and all was well.

Anthony Eden arrived to confer with Stalin and Molotov. Cripps felt depressed because he thought that more and more the Allies would be fighting two separate wars, and that the Russians would step up their claims as they became more certain of victory. He saw in that meeting that Stalin and his colleagues were now speaking and acting with confidence and without strain.

But Eden brought Stafford good news. The Government had agreed to his return to England! He could make arrangements to leave on January 6. The arrangements were not difficult. His greatest problem was Joe, whom he could not take with him. He hated to leave him behind, for they had been great friends. It was easier to say farewell to humans than to Joe. Cripps left him to be looked after by his successor.

After farewell meetings with staff and friends and the leaders of the Soviet Union, he gave a farewell message to the people of the Soviet Union. He said:

Hitler's pride has been broken by the impact of your resistance, and today his forces are rolling back.

The whole civilised world proclaims your victories, and we, your Allies, are proud to count ourselves as such, but the end is not yet.

Your successes, magnificent though they are, permit no slackening of effort on our part or yours.

The alliance between our two great countries must be made firmer and stronger yet, so that together we may accomplish the task so well begun.

When victory comes, of which we are so confident, our two nations will have the privilege of leading the peoples of Europe toward a civilisation of sanity and co-operation. Together we must march forward to that victory. Together we must work and plan to bring about the happier life which their suffering and their patience have earned for masses of humanity.

With these parting words, he left the Soviet Union for England. The world acclaimed his ambassadorship to Moscow as a triumph, a job well done, and most people agreed with him that what needed yet to be done there could be done by others. But what next? He was still a man without a party, a leader without an army, an independent M.P. whom the Labour Party had rejected and the other parties could not have.

XVI. What Next?

WHAT Stafford Cripps did immediately after he arrived in England in January, 1942, was characteristic of the man. It was a postscript to his work as ambassador and, in many ways, as important as anything he was able to achieve in Moscow. His first task was to convince the people at home that Russia could defeat the Germans, and his second, to see that she should not fail through lack of help from Britain.

He did not allow the emotional thrill of the Soviet victory to unbalance his judgment. He knew that the stemming of the tide did not mean that the Germans were yet defeated. He knew only too well that the savage drive into western Russia had destroyed great economic and industrial resources, besides inflicting human losses the magnitude of which Britain would never comprehend. The Russians had saved a vast amount of machinery and factory equipment from destruction, loaded it on hundreds of trains, and moved it far behind the scene of battle. He knew, however, that it would take months to get the factories into production once more and to replace the losses in war equipment which the Red Army had sustained.

Russia's toughness had been a tonic to the British people after the long series of defeats which they had grimly heard recounted since the beginning of the war. Against the background of unrelieved disaster, the tremendous defense of the Soviet Union lit the sky with splendor and hope of victories to come. Now they asked whether the Russians could hold out and win through. Cripps was convinced that they could if they received the right kind of help and if the British people put into the war the same spirit as the people of Soviet Russia. He gave a press interview on his arrival. "When I left," he said, "the Russians had their tails up." But he felt that few in Britain realized how much Russia needed help.

Writing in the *Tribune* of February 6, he said,

We speak with pleasure and with pride of the fact that the Russians applied the "scorched earth" policy in their efforts to stay the advancing Germans—that is, while the Germans are still advancing. But do we ever think what it has meant to the hundreds of thousands of peasants who have to be left behind in the scorched areas—left behind to meet, unarmed and unprotected, the German anger and hate? These countless thousands are as much the true heroes of war as any soldier on the front line. Faced by cold and starvation they hang grimly on.

As the German troops go forward they organise themselves into guerilla bands, ambushing and destroying in the forests and along the highways and risking and meeting the most terrible suffering and torture in case of capture. That has been the life of millions of the ordinary humble peasants in the occupied parts of Russia, and that heroism has played a vital part in the war. It is indeed a total war, total in its suffering and total in its effort. Has it been total in the same intense degree so far as we in England are concerned and the part that we have played?

To an enthusiastic audience of 3,000 in East Bristol, he said that he had returned with one main purpose—to urge the necessity of closer co-operation between Britain and the Soviet Union. He said that what impressed him most was the self-sacrifice of the ordinary people of Russia, who had a much better idea than Britain of the meaning of total war. He continued,

There seems to be a lack of urgency in the atmosphere of this country. It is almost as if we were spectators rather than participants. Perhaps I might compare it to the difference between a keen and enthusiastic supporter of a football team and one of the members of the team. After the match, the supporter goes home and thinks it all out, not as part of his own active effort, but as something he has seen and studied. . . .

This war is not a game to be played according to certain rules. It is a life and death struggle for survival and in that struggle there are, and must be, no particular interests.

We must get rid of the idea that there are two separate wars in Europe; that we are fighting one of them and the Russians another. It is a single war. We must treat the Soviet Union as our allies in a single war, with full consultation and full confidence. We must place our resources where they are most needed in the

views of the allies as a whole. If we do that; if here we work with
100% effort; if we give to Russia all the support we can, then, in
my view, there is every chance of Germany being defeated by this
time next year.

That speech was to his constituency. His most active supporters had organized a reception for him, followed by the
public meeting. But what a fluttering among the mandarins
of the Labour Party! The East Bristol Labour Party still looked
upon the man without a party as their spokesman and rushed
to give him welcome and to hear all he had to say. But some
were nervous lest they offend Transport House. What should
they do? One man had the bright idea, which all approved, that
he should telephone to Labour Party headquarters for instructions! So the question was put, "May we attend the reception to
Sir Stafford Cripps?" What a problem! Back to Bristol came the
reply, "You may attend a reception to the ex-Ambassador to the
Soviet Union, but you may not attend a reception to Sir Stafford Cripps, ex-member of our party." Bristol laughed long, and
thousands flocked to hear him, caring not at all about the
mighty problem thus resolved.

That evening he delivered a tremendous speech to the waiting millions of radio listeners. They were stirred, not merely
by the content of his message, but by the manner of the telling
of it. Calm, quietly spoken words, simple and direct, every
sentence ringing with deep feeling and passionate sincerity,
came steadily to every listener in the British Isles and to millions outside:

I hope that all of you who are listening-in are settled comfortably
by your radio, warm and well sheltered, with a feeling of gratitude,
even though some of you have been bombed out of your homes,
gratitude that you still have a roof over your heads, enough food
to eat and the means of keeping out the cold.

You have had snow and cold during this winter—but not the
cold of Russia, where 30 to 40 degrees below zero are no exceptional
experience.

You have known the tragic horrors of prolonged aerial bom-
bardments, many of you have lost members of your families or
friends, and still more of you will have had your homes and your
possessions destroyed—but you have not experienced the brutalities
and the savage violence and rapine of the Nazi invaders.

Many of you are members of the Home Guard and have to train and watch, but you have not yet had to turn yourselves into guerilla fighters behind the enemy lines, certain that you would die of torture if you were captured.

I know that you have worked and are working long hours and your food rations are not as ample as you have been accustomed to in times of peace—but you have not been starved, stripped of your clothing in the bitter cold open streets and forced to work day and night as slaves for a foreign enemy, building roads and fortifications to defeat your own countrymen.

I want you to realise the difference between the fortunes of war as you have experienced them and as they have been suffered by millions of our Russian allies. Those sufferings are going on at this very moment, while we sit in comparative comfort and safety— borne by the workers of all kinds, the co-operative farmers, doctors, actors, managers, mothers and children—all our counterparts in Soviet Russia.

This was not new to his hearers, but few men had had the courage to say it with such force and conviction. British workers had a guilty conscience as they listened to the news from Russia, but so far it had been inchoate, ineffective. Sir Stafford went on to another point which commanded even quicker agreement among the workers:

The Russians will tolerate nothing that decreases the war effort or the efficiency of the fighting forces. Hoarders of food, black-marketeers and other saboteurs who try to take advantage of the difficult conditions of the country are given short shrift when they are discovered. . . .

It would be difficult for the Russians to understand the tolerance which is shown in this country to these fifth-columnists.

Here was someone in authority who recognized that equality of sacrifice was a farce, and that many people were fighting a very comfortable war, meanwhile frustrating efforts to get to grips with the problems. He went on:

Had our efforts in production been greater we should not now be retreating in North Africa.

Each hour of work that is lost, each day that we do less than we might by way of productive effort, each needless article that we use, makes our total effort less effective and lets down someone, somewhere who is giving his life to save all that we hold dear—whether it be in Russia, Malaya, Africa or elsewhere.

Every hour by which we can shorten the war will mean the saving of hundreds of lives and of the suffering of millions. The cry goes up all over the world "How long?" Each one of us can give an answer through our unstinted sacrifice. That answer must be "Not a moment shall be lost through any failure of mine. I will not let you down by slackness or selfishness on my part."

Now he passed from the challenge direct and the moral appeal to the longings that were in every man's heart in greater or lesser degree. He lifted his talk from the level of the plane and the valley to the heights of everyone's dreams. He went on,

We are anxiously reaching out to that time when the new world for which the peoples are longing, and for which almost every man and woman is daily hoping, begins to show itself in clear outline on our horizon.

Not the new order of brutalised domination with which Hitler has sought to delude the people, but a world of new values, cleansed of the old evils and offering a full and free manhood to the people of every class, religion, nation and colour—that practical ideal for which equally as the people of Russia and of the occupied countries of Europe are in reality really fighting, that hope which makes all sacrifices seem worth while, that positive achievement which we are determined shall issue from this ghastly war, itself the negation of every teaching of our Christian civilisation.

His final appeal struck home to his listeners as nothing they had heard since the war began. Every man and woman felt it to be a personal message as from one inspired by a Messianic mission:

Today our needs and those of our Russian allies are as great and as pressing. Victory will continue to hang in the balance so long as men and women hesitate to play their full part. The future beckons to us across the bleak and agonising months of war that still lie between us and victory. Let us hasten forward, impelled by our own efforts to greet that more sane and happy future.

That speech swept Stafford Cripps to heights of popularity such as he had never before experienced. The feeling toward him was comparable only to that toward Churchill after Dunkirk. People talked of him as the "alternative to Churchill."

Certainly it determined for him an answer to his personal question "What next?" Overnight he had won the support of millions of his fellow men, belonging to all parties or to none. His future had long been a matter of public and private discussion. Immediately after he had signed the Treaty of Alliance with Russia in 1941, *Reynold's News,* the weekly paper of the Co-operative movement, had carried an article which said,

Some day, Sir Stafford will return from Moscow, a hero of victory, his public record unstained even by the suspicion of past failure. He will not return to the Bar. He will not return to the Labour Party unless that Party is wise and generous enough to invite him to join. He will have a great following. His sense of power, never modest, will be developed fully. He will be dressed up in the garb of leadership—and he will find somewhere to go!

The *Manchester Guardian* had no doubt that Churchill would welcome the opportunity of enlisting Cripps' services. The *News Chronicle* had said,

There will be general disappointment if Stafford Cripps is not offered a high position in the War Cabinet. He is one of the few leading figures in the Government or outside, who command popular confidence.

It was no surprise therefore when Churchill invited him to become Minister of Supply. It has been asserted that he refused to take on this job because it did not carry with it membership in the War Cabinet. This was not wholly the case. He declined the post because he was convinced that neither he nor anyone else could make a success of it with the existing relations between the Minister of Supply and the Minister of Production, who was Lord Beaverbrook. Subordinate to Beaverbrook, who would be responsible for allocations and priorities of materials, any Minister of Supply would be impeded in his job. Sir Stafford expressed his regret that under the circumstances he must decline the offer. At the same time he had expressed his willingness to undertake any special tasks "as for instance, with regard to India."

After his famous broadcast there was a reconstruction of the Government. Arthur Greenwood, Deputy Leader of the Labour Party was dropped from the Cabinet. Clement Attlee,

leader of the Labour Party, became Secretary of State for
Dominion Affairs. Oliver Lyttleton succeeded Beaverbrook as
Minister of Production. Cripps was appointed Lord Privy Seal
in place of Clement Attlee. Then, to the surprise of all,
Churchill resigned his position as Leader of the House of
Commons, and named Cripps to succeed him. Churchill said
to the Commons that he did not resign "without sorrow from
that post." Then he added,

I am sure, however, it is in the public interest, and I am sure
also that my right hon. Friend the Member for East Bristol, the
new Lord Privy Seal, will prove to the House that he is a respecter
of its authority and a leader capable of dealing with all the incidents, episodes and emergencies of House of Commons and Parliamentary life.

In his new position Sir Stafford was responsible for the management of the Government's business in the House. He was
a member of the War Cabinet, which was the supreme body
in control of the war effort in its military, civil, and economic
aspects, as well as in ultimate control over all other aspects of
Government policy. In the words of Mr. Churchill, the six
members of the War Cabinet were "collectively and individually responsible for the whole policy of the country; and they
are the ones who are alone held accountable for the conduct
of the war."

When the House of Commons opened on February 24,
Churchill sat on the Government Front Bench, with Stafford
Cripps on his left and Clement Attlee on his right—a remarkable transformation since that memorable day when Sir Stafford
had faced a packed house of angry Tories and demanded that
the Government show a common-sense attitude toward the
arrest of the British engineers in Russia. Now the "rejected of
the Labour Party" stood side by side with the leaders of the
two large parties, acclaimed by both for his services, and about
to lead the House of Commons itself. At no time in the history
of the British Parliament, in war or in peace, had a man without a party held so honored a position.

A two-day debate on the war situation began. The Government had been under severe criticism for its inefficient conduct
of the war. Did the changes in the personnel of the Govern-

ment mean a change in policy and offer hope of a new spirit
and direction? Cripps was to wind up the debate for the Government. For two days he sat taking notes. When he rose to
speak, the House was full to overflowing as on that other great
occasion, but this time he was received with cheers.

Let me start [he said in conversational tones] by saying to the
House in all sincerity that I am most anxious to make the criticism
and the co-operation of the members as fruitful as possible, from
the point of view of our joint effort to win the war. I shall regard
my position as Leader of the House as having for its object the
interpretation of the views of the House to the Cabinet and also
the views of the War Cabinet to the House.

In that opening he at once won the confidence of the House.
For so long it had felt completely frustrated, that what was
said by the House mattered little, that it had become a receiving chamber for what the Government cared to tell it. Cripps'
declaration that he was to be the voice of the Commons in the
Cabinet was of a new kind and meant new life for the House
itself. He continued,

I have in the past been a critic myself of many things and Governments, and I fully appreciate the fact that both critics and supporters alike are out to help to win the war and to make, each in
his own way, that contribution which he feels able to make to the
united war effort. . . .

If, however, we are determined to preserve and use to the full our
machinery of democracy, we must not be afraid to examine its working, with a view to creating from it a machine of the maximum
efficiency for our purpose, whether that purpose be victory in the
present or reconstruction in the future.

After paying tribute to those who had been pulling their
weight he spoke scathingly of those

who appear to regard their personal interests in a manner which
is not consonant with that totality of effort which is required if we
are to come through the present difficulties with success. The Government are determined that such an attitude cannot be permitted
to persist. . . . We are not engaged in a war effort in which we can
have as our motto, "Business as usual" or "Pleasure as usual." The
Government propose to take such measures as may be necessary to

prevent the abuse of the wishes of the majority of the people by any small or selfish group.

Quickly following this speech came new regulations. The use of petrol for any reason but that of work was prohibited. Sports were curtailed. Clothes were more severely rationed. And, as such things happen, the blame for these austerity measures was laid not on the necessity of winning the war, but on Cripps himself.

In his speech he had promised a debate on India: "The Government are much concerned about the situation there and the debate will take place upon the basis of a Government decision in this matter."

What did that mean? Those who remembered his continuous pressure upon the Government before he went to Moscow thought that this man had promptly used his new position to further his views concerning the future of India. They would not have long to wait for confirmation. Three weeks later Churchill made the statement in the House:

We propose to send a member of the War Cabinet to India, to satisfy himself on the spot, by personal consultation that the conclusions upon which we are agreed, and which we believe represent a just and final solution, will achieve their purpose. My right hon. and learned Friend the Lord Privy Seal and Leader of the House has volunteered to undertake this task. He carries with him the full confidence of His Majesty's Government.

So the unexpected had happened again. What was the meaning? Was Sir Stafford a scapegoat of the party politicians who had made this appointment, confident that he would fail, and that they could lay the blame for failure on him? The facts rule out such an interpretation. That there was a serious situation in India all knew. Affairs there were going from bad to worse and India was moving rapidly toward a great political explosion. Unless some agreement could be arrived at with the leaders of the Indian people, the British Government would be faced with a war of independence on the part of the four hundred and fifty millions of India.

Before he became a member of the Cabinet, Sir Stafford had indicated his willingness to be used on "the India question." Now that he was Leader of the House, he would have been well justified in turning down any suggestion that he should go to India on this mission, if the claims of personal ambition had ruled his mind. It should have been clear to those who were at all acquainted with his experiences in the Labour Party that personal ambition is not the leitmotiv of his career. If it were, he would never have pursued the course he had with the Socialist League, the Unity Campaign, and the Popular Front Campaign. The explanation of his appointment is simple. He was convinced that India should be free. He was convinced that an agreement could be made with the Indian leaders as to the ways and means and time that Indian freedom should be attained. He was convinced that he, of all men in Britain, had the best qualifications to win the co-operation of the Indian leaders and to ensure agreement. To accomplish that now, in this hour of crisis, was an urgent and necessary service to the winning of the war. Under such circumstances and with such views, calculations about his future career meant nothing to him.

XVII. The Mission to India

WHEN Stafford Cripps returned from India in 1940, he had said:

There is an immediate danger of an outbreak of non-co-operation by the Indian people, as a result of the British Government's refusal to grant self-government to the Indian people and the right to decide their own future.

Some of his friends now tried to dissuade him from going to India. Some members of trade-union branches and local Labour parties were suspicious of the motives of the Government.

Certainly there were grounds for suspicion. The terms he was to offer to the Indian leaders had not been announced.✓ The Prime Minister, Mr. Churchill, had never hidden his light under a bushel or failed to make it clear that he was against Indian independence. Had the entrance of Stafford Cripps into the War Cabinet produced some wondrous change in this old war horse of British Imperialism, or was Cripps yielding innocently to blandishments? The *Times* said of him and his mission,

He is certainly aware of the difficulties which lie before him. He is not a man to be daunted by those that are real, or to tolerate for a moment those that are merely the product of ill-will, misunderstanding, or red tape. Whether or not he achieves success, he will have deserved it. And he has deserved, and will receive, the gratitude both of India and of his own country.

The problem was far from simple. When Cripps left India on Christmas Day, 1939, the war seemed a long way from India. The Indian Congress leaders had denounced Britain for declaring India at war without consulting the Indian people. They were insisting that any joint defense of India against an external enemy must be preceded by India's independence. On that issue there was no difference between Hindu and Moslem. But on the issue of war there was a division between Gandhi and many of his supporters and the Congress leadership. Nehru and the majority of the Working Committee rejected Gandhi's pacifism.

In June, 1940, immediately after the collapse of France and Petain's armistice, Gandhi wrote in his paper, "I think French statesmen have shown rare courage in bowing to the inevitable and refusing to be a party to senseless mutual slaughter." When a German attack on Britain seemed imminent he sent a message to the British War Cabinet begging them and every Briton to adopt a "nobler and braver way" of fighting and let Hitler and Mussolini "take possession of your beautiful island if they wish."

The Working Committee of the Indian National Congress did not share this pacifist view. "The Committee," said its resolution of June 21, "are unable to go the full length with Gandhi, but they recognise that he should be free to pursue his great ideal in his own way and therefore, absolve him from responsibility for the program and activity which the Congress has to pursue."

The Congress program outlined an independent defense organization of public security throughout the country. But while thus denouncing co-operation with the Government, it went on to offer co-operation on terms. It demanded the full independence of India and the formation of a provisional National Government to give effect to it. This provisional Government should be so constituted as to command the confidence of all the elected elements in the Central Legislature and secure the closest co-operation of responsible governments in the provinces. On these conditions the Congress was prepared to "throw its full weight into organizing the defense of India."

The situation was not made less difficult when Winston Churchill bluntly stated that the Atlantic Charter was not intended to apply to India. Had matters remained as they were after that statement, then the Cripps Mission was utterly doomed before it set sail.

However, several things had happened in quick succession.

First, the Government had released unconditionally those who had been imprisoned in the course of the passive resistance movement. This led to the second event. One of the released was C. Rajagopalachari, known better and more affectionately to his friends and admirers as "Rajaji." He was Prime Minister of Madras, a lifelong colleague of Gandhi, and a man of keen intellect and strong character. On his release he took issue with Gandhi and declared that political issues should not be mixed up with non-violence ideology. He said that "if the party's political issues were conceded by the Government, then it should assume responsibility and wage war against the Axis powers."

The third event shocked not only India but the whole world. The Japanese struck at Pearl Harbor and set forth "on the road to Mandalay" and India.

"Rajaji" talked the Working Committee of Congress into a typically English compromise. His idea was to secure from the Government a broad recognition of India's right to independence, and the giving of effect to that recognition, *as much as possible,* during the war. At the Committee meeting where he made this proposal the official report said he secured an overwhelming majority. Actually he received 45 votes against 15, with 140 members not voting.

One other event of importance preceded the second visit of Cripps. Generalissimo and Madame Chiang Kai-shek arrived on the scene. T. A. Raman says:

Evidently the main purpose of the visit was to talk to India's political leaders, to urge the importance of a united front against Japan and to demonstrate friendly interest of the head of a powerful state in the cause of Indian self-government. After the official reception by the Viceroy, the review of the troops, and so on, China's Generalissimo had several meetings with leaders of all sections and parties, the longest ones with Pandit Nehru, who had visited him in 1939. Gandhi met him towards the end of the visit and they had a conversation of no less than four hours and a half at Calcutta. Judging from the account in the Harijan by Gandhi's secretary, the Mahatma dilated at length on passive resistance and asserted that it could not be used effectively against armed invasion. The Generalissimo said gently that non-violence may be useful in certain circumstances and against certain enemies, but not against the Japanese. They would not—he suggested—let Gandhi propagate his faith and would make short work of any attempt at organised opposition. Gandhi however maintained his ground.

It is not surprising that Madame Chiang Kai-shek praised Nehru as a great man with a world vision, but described Gandhi as too obsessed with the national struggle to possess a world outlook—and also as "a person of cloudy vision."

It had not been difficult up to now for the Indian Congress to subordinate its views on the world struggle against Fascism and Nazism to the issue of Indian independence. But when the Japanese approached India it was not so easy. The announcement that Cripps was to go to India created intense excitement and anticipation on all sides.

He arrived in Delhi on March 23, accompanied by Frank Turnbull of the India Office, David Owen, and Graham Spry, who were secretaries to the mission. The mission was giving to the world, and to India in particular, the impression that everything was cut and dried, and in true Crippsian style had been settled "the day before yesterday." Cripps announced on his arrival that he intended to complete his mission in fourteen days and said that he believed that in that time, with energy and good will, the essentials of success could be achieved.

He plunged into meetings and discussions from the moment of his arrival. His secretarial staff took over completely from the Viceregal staff which had made all the preliminary arrangements, and Cripps began talks with those in authority both in central and provincial Governments, as a prelude to meeting the party leaders.

He himself later told the House of Commons:

I was most anxious that there should be no suspicion whatever that His Majesty's Government were handpicking those whom I saw, and, consequently I asked the main organisations themselves to appoint those whom they wished to meet me. This they did, and they mostly expressed the wish that I should not interview any other members of their Working Committees. Certain individuals I saw such as Mr. Gandhi, Sir Taj Bahadar Sapru, Mr. Joshi and Mr. Kayakar, the present or past Prime Ministers of all the Provincial Governments, the Governors of the Provinces and lastly, but by no means least, the members of the Viceroy's Executive Council. It was to this latter body that I first disclosed the details of the draft Declaration, immediately on my arrival in India, and after seeing them each one individually, it was to the same body I first announced the failure of the agreement. As the House will know, I kept the draft Declaration from publication for the first week of my stay in Delhi, during which time I submitted it to all the principal Indian representative leaders personally. It then became clear that its contents were becoming generally known, and it was considered better that it should be published, and this was done.

So all the procedure was correct. No one could cast a stone at him on that score. The proposals were water tight. There was no room for maneuvering with the Indians. They had to say "yes" or "no" to the proposals as a whole. Sir Stafford himself spoke with conviction of the declaration.

The talks with the party leaders began on March 25, and he was in his element. First he saw Azad, the President of the Congress Party, and then Jinnah, President of the Moslem League. But he was quite sure that the key man was Gandhi. The next day he telegraphed to Gandhi saying that he would be glad to have an opportunity of a talk with him. He received the following reply,

Thanks for your wire. I was present at the meeting of the Working Committee when it was agreed that on behalf of the Congress only the President and Pandit Nehru should see you. You know my anti-all-war views. If despite that you would like to see me I shall be glad to see you.

Cripps replied that he expected to see him the following day. Thus it happened that Cripps and Gandhi met before the publication of the Cabinet plan for India.

That interview lasted two hours. Gandhi had traveled specially from his home in Wardha, and when he arrived at the house where Cripps was staying, Cripps went down the steps and opened the door of Gandhi's car. After the interview both were cheerful and Gandhi facetiously remarked that he had taken a vow of silence and could not indicate what they had discussed. One sensed, however, that the old lawyer-politician had enjoyed himself and had not given anything away to the younger man. Louis Fischer reports that later Gandhi told him:

When Cripps arrived he sent me a telegram asking me to come to see him in Delhi. I did not wish to go, but I went because I thought it would do some good. I had heard rumors about the contents of the British Government's offer he brought to India, but I had not seen the offer. He gave it to me and after a brief study, I said to him, "Why did you come if this is what you have to offer? If this is your entire proposal to India, I would advise you to take the next plane home." Cripps replied, "I will consider that."

What was the document which produced this complete and outspoken, and one might add, contemptuous dismissal of the mission and its message? Here it is in all its detail:

His Majesty's Government, having considered the anxieties expressed in this country and in India as to the fulfilment of the promises made in regard to the future of India, have decided to lay down in precise terms the steps which they propose shall be taken for the earliest possible realisation of self-government in India. The object is the creation of a new Indian Union which shall constitute a Dominion, associated with the United Kingdom and the other Dominions by a common allegiance to the Crown, but equal to them in every respect, in no way subordinate in any aspect of its domestic or external affairs.

His Majesty's Government therefore make the following declarations.

(a) Immediately on the cessation of hostilities steps shall be taken to set up in India, in the manner described hereafter, an elected body charged with the task of framing a new constitution for India.

(b) Provision shall be made, as set out below, for the participation of the Indian States in the constitution-making body.

(c) His Majesty's Government undertake to accept and implement forthwith the constitution so framed subject only to:

(i) The right of any province of British India that is not prepared to accept the new Constitution to retain its present constitutional position, provision being made for its subsequent accession if it so decides. With such non-acceding provinces, should they so desire, His Majesty's Government will be prepared to agree upon a new constitution, giving them the same full status as Indian Union, and arrived at by a procedure analogous to that here laid down.

(ii) The signing of a treaty which shall be negotiated between His Majesty's Government and the constitution-making body. This treaty will cover all necessary matters arising out of the complete transfer of responsibility from British to Indian hands; it will make provision, in accordance with the undertakings given by His Majesty's Government for the protection of racial and religious minorities; but will not impose any restriction on the power of the Indian Union to decide in the future its relationship to the other member states of the British Commonwealth.

Whether or not an Indian State elects to adhere to the constitution it will be necessary to negotiate a revision of its treaty arrangements, so far as this may be required in the new situation.

(d) The constitution-making body shall be composed as follows, unless the leaders of the Indian Union in the principal communities agree upon some other form before the end of hostilities:

Immediately upon the result being known of the provincial elections which will be necessary at the end of hostilities the entire membership of the lower Houses of the Provincial legislatures shall, as a single electoral college, proceed to the election of the constitution-making body by the system of proportional representation. This new body shall be in number about one tenth of the number of the electoral college.

Indian States shall be invited to appoint representatives in the same proportion to their total population as in the case of British India as a whole, and with the same powers as the British Indian members.

(e) During the critical period which now faces India, and until the new constitution can be framed, His Majesty's Government must inevitably bear the responsibility for and retain control and direction of the defense of India as part of their world war effort, but the task of organising to the full the military, moral and material resources of India must be the responsibility of the Government of India with the cooperation of the peoples of India. His Majesty's Government desire and invite the immediate and effective participation of the leaders of the principal sections of the Indian people in the counsels of their country, of the Commonwealth, and of the United Nations. Thus they will be enabled to give their active and constructive help in the discharge of a task which is vital and essential for the future freedom of India.

Gandhi is reported to have said of this document, when asked by Cripps for his reactions, "If the Congress President asks my advice, I will say that the British proposals form a post-dated cheque on a crashing bank." What Cripps said in reply to the downright statement of Gandhi we do not know.

The Working Committee of Congress held a meeting the day after the publication of the plan. So also did the Working Committee of the Moslem League. Not a single member of the Congress Committee was in favor of acceptance of the proposals as they stood. But Cripps was not in a position to maneuver, to accept suggestions or make modifications. He had come to persuade them to accept the plan as a whole. That was the instruction given to him. Nevertheless they went on talking. Gandhi was not present.

What is the inside story? Nehru saw Cripps twice that day. He dined with him in the evening, before Cripps' broadcast. He was the only person who could have offset the influence of Gandhi. This day, March 30, was the most important day of all, and Nehru was the focal point of what was happening. Nehru has himself written of his first reactions to the plan:

I remember that when I read those proposals for the first time I was profoundly depressed and that depression was largely due to the fact that I had expected something more substantial from Sir Stafford Cripps as well as from the critical situation that had arisen. When analysed there were so many limitations, and the very principle of self-determination was fettered and circumscribed in such a way as to imperil our future.

The plan of the British Government was obviously divided into two parts. The first dealt with the future constitution and its making. The second dealt with the immediate present. The first part was what Gandhi described as a "post-dated cheque," the date being the cessation of hostilities. That in itself was an advance on the nebulous dates that had beclouded the horizon of Indian independence hitherto. The nature of what was written on the cheque would decide whether it was a fraud or not. What Gandhi read on the cheque caused him to turn from it in contempt. What Nehru, the next key man in the situation, read on the cheque threw him into deep depression.

But there was the second part of the plan. This said that, because there was a war on, the Indians must continue in subjection and fight the battle of freedom, with the British but *under* the British, accepting their subordination as of yore. What the Indians had demanded was immediate freedom and the alliance of a free people, under their own National Government, with Britain and her allies against the Axis powers. Stafford Cripps and the British Government were emphatic that the Indian proposals were impossible of application, because they would mean an alteration in the constitutions of Britain and of India. A thing like that could not be done in wartime, although wartime appeared to many people to be just the time in history when such changes had been made. Indeed, the Indians and the rest of the world had, a few months previous to the coming of the Cripps Mission, seen Britain herself offer to collapsing France an entirely new constitution, involving the most profound alterations in the constitution of Britain.

What Nehru thought of the plan of "post-dated" freedom he wrote in a book while in prison some months later. An extract is given here because it sums up the mission as it appeared to one of the chief actors in the drama:

The proposals dealt essentially with the future, after the cessation of hostilities, though there was a final clause which vaguely invited co-operation in the present. That future, while asserting the principle of self-determination, gave the right to provinces not to join the Indian Union, and to form separate independent states. Further the same right of non-accession to the Indian Union was given to the Indian States and it should be remembered that there are nearly six hundred such states in India, some major ones and the great majority tiny enclaves. These states, as well as the Provinces would all join in the constitution-making, would influence that constitution and then could walk out of it. The elections in the provinces for the constitution-making body would take place under the existing system of separate religious electorates; that was unfortunate, as it would bring with it the old spirit of cleavage, and yet, in the circumstances that was inevitable. But in the states there was no provision for elections and their ninety million inhabitants were completely ignored. The semi-feudal rulers of the states could nominate their own representatives in proportion to the population. These nominees might contain some able ministers, but, as a whole, they would inevitably be representative of the feudal rulers. The constituent assembly or constitution-making body would be a curious mixture of elected and non-elected elements, the former chosen by separate religious electorates as well as by certain vested interests, the latter nominated by the rulers of the states. To this had to be added the fact that there would be no pressure to accept joint decisions, and the sense of reality which comes from evolving integrated and final decisions would be lacking. The tendency for many of its members would be to act in a wholly irresponsible manner, for they would feel that they could always withdraw and refuse to accept the responsibility for carrying out those decisions.

Stafford Cripps had obviously run up against minds as acute as his own. Neither Gandhi nor Nehru could be won over with a "post-dated cheque" or with emotional appeals for unity against the Fascist powers. Once that fundamental difference became clear, and it was clear from the moment the Indian leaders read the document, all subsequent discussion could only take the form of elucidating details and a mutual searching for points of vantage.

On the evening of March 30, Cripps stepped from the conference room to broadcast to the Indian people. Froom Tyler, writing of this event, said,

The earnest persuasive voice which had pleasantly surprised British fireside listeners one Sunday night in the previous winter was now heard through India explaining the British offer. Cripps made full use of the radio. He realised that, although only five million of India's 390,000,000 could read newspapers, they could all listen to loud-speakers, although almost 90% of the entire population were country dwellers, his voice, or the voice of the interpreter, could go out to them and they could be acquainted with the mighty issues which were being decided for them by their leaders in Delhi. So immediately after the proposals had been made public Cripps broadcast to the Indian people, and his voice was heard in the bazaars, in remotest villages, in the houses of the rich Anglo-Indians, and in the clubs and hotel lounges where Indian Civil Service officials and British businessmen, whose personal future was involved with the political future of India, sat sweltering over their chota-pegs. It was the voice of the Motherland offering freedom to four-fifths of her subjects. It was the voice of the new world "of organised and co-operative freedom" in which Cripps passionately believed.

That was the effect on a British journalist; but it did not have the effect suggested on the Indian people. It would require much more than the charm of Sir Stafford's voice to work the miracle of transformation involved in making England into the "motherland" of the Indians. Nevertheless he did deliver a powerful speech, in keeping with his mission, full of "promise" and "responsibility" and challenge. He said,

The British Government want to make it beyond doubt that we and the British people desire the Indian people to have full self-government. We desire the Indian Constitution to be as free in every respect as that of Great Britain or as that of any of the Dominions.

The principle on which the proposals are based is that the new constitution should be formed by the elected representatives of the Indian people. The British people are determined to do their utmost for the defence of India in which they are confident the Indian peoples are eager to play their full part. . . .

Britain hopes and expects to see an Indian Union strong and united because it is founded on the free consent of all its peoples. It is in the hands of the Indians only whether they accept the lead which Britain is giving them. If the Indians fail to accept this opportunity the responsibility for that failure must rest with them. If the British proposals are rejected there would be neither the time nor opportunity to reconsider the matter until after the war.

The next day the arduous discussions continued. Gandhi and Nehru were drafting the conclusions of the Congress Party for consideration by the Working Committee. The Working Committee of the Moslem League again adjourned without finishing its discussions.

The emphasis shifted from the future to the present. How much share in the responsibility for defense was contained in the proposals for immediate co-operation? The Indians wanted full responsibility. The British document said partial responsibility. Cripps was reported to have told Indian leaders that the Viceroy was willing to have a Defense Minister, with restricted functions, on the executive council. Such a member would have no control over strategy, which would be the concern of the Commander-in-Chief under the direction of the War Cabinet in London. Azad, on behalf of Congress, expressed the opinion that Congress could not appeal to the Indian masses to treat the war as their own problem if the National Government had no voice in the management of defense. Unless defense matters were in the hands of an Indian member he could not support the British proposals. "Rajaji" told a correspondent that distrust on this question of defense was likely to wreck the entire scheme as well as to endanger the safety of India.

Cripps asked Nehru and Azad to meet him again on April 2. He was expected to place before them a formula which he had already discussed with Moderate leaders. This was understood to envisage an Indian Defense Minister to preside over a Defense Council of which General Wavell would also be a member. The portfolio would also cover civil defense and air-raid precautions. It was said too that Cripps had been in touch with London by telephone, and to have made it clear that all parties were demanding a greater share in defense.

Then came Thursday evening, April 2, when the Congress Party reply was handed to Cripps by Nehru and Azad. The party objected to the proposals on three main grounds: refusal to transfer the Defense portfolio to Indian hands; the impairment of national unity implied in the proposal which gave each province the right to secede from the Indian Union; and the fact that the Indian States would be represented in the Constituent Assembly by "palace nominees" and not by representatives elected by the people. It was believed that the reply did not close the door to negotiations.

The next day Cripps met General Wavell and announced the postponement of his departure from India. He had suddenly become optimistic:

I think I can possibly do something useful next week. I think one may generally say that the points of difficulty are coming down to fairly narrow limits, and with common goodwill we may be able to solve the difficulties. I want to try to do that.

On April 4 Cripps introduced Nehru and Azad to General Wavell and left them to talk over the question of the Defense portfolio. Gandhi left for his home in Wardha, having nothing more to say. During the week end Cripps saw members of the Government and Air Marshal Collyer. It was understood that on Tuesday he would announce the result of the Mission. This was postponed until Wednesday. On Tuesday Cripps handed to Azad and Nehru the British War Cabinet's reply to the party's counter proposals. That interview lasted only eight minutes. It was clear that the climax of the drama was at hand. Into the picture stepped Colonel Louis Johnson, personal representative of President Roosevelt, to see if he could render any service. He saw Nehru and Azad. Then Cripps saw Jinnah and afterward Jinnah made the statement that it was clearly understood that the Defense portfolio would be administered by an Indian. Excitement was mounting. Was there agreement after all?

The Congress Working Committee considered the British Government's reply at a four-hour meeting in the afternoon. Azad told the press that the Congress reply would be communicated to Cripps the following morning. But discussions continued throughout the following day. A new formula appeared to have emerged, based upon the position in Australia, where General MacArthur was Supreme Commander while Mr. Forde was Commonwealth Army Minister with powers and responsibility over distant and clearly defined fields. This was being discussed by the Congress and Moslem League Working Committees. Colonel Johnson appeared to be taking a large part in keeping the negotiations going.

April 9 was still another day of negotiations of which the world knew nothing. Cripps saw Azad and Nehru at a lengthy meeting in the evening. Clearly, final issues were under discussion.

What was obvious from the moment the document was handed to the Indian leaders and published to the world was that the British Government were not prepared to yield one inch of power to the Indians *now,* and wanted their willing co-operation as complete subordinates on the strength of a "post-dated cheque" of a questionable character. Neither the earnest advocacy of Sir Stafford, nor his drive, nor his eloquence could persuade the Indian leaders that there was more than this in the proposal he had brought. Indeed, the more Nehru and Azad drew out the details, the more hollow appeared the proposal and the deeper Indian suspicions became. Congress agreed without hesitation that the responsibility for strategy and control of operations should be in the hands of General Wavell, but what could be expected from them when they discovered the functions which would fall to the Indian Defense member? He was to attend to canteens, stationery, supply of petroleum, amenities of the troops, schools, demobilization after the war, the entertainment of foreign missions, relations with the press, the evacuation of threatened areas, and the co-ordination of signals!

The Working Committee delivered its final letter which closed on the old note of bitterness and distrust which had been sounded so often before the mission came, but for nearly three hopeful weeks had been hushed. It said,

Unhappily even in this grave hour of peril, the British Government is unable to give up its wrecking policy. We are driven to the conclusion that it attaches more importance to holding on to its rule in India as long as it can and promoting discord and disruption here with that end in view than to an effective defence of India against the aggression and invasion that overhang it.

To this attack Sir Stafford made no rejoinder. The breach was obviously past mending. He held his last press conference on the morning of April 11. He explained that as the Congress and the League and other bodies had rejected the draft declaration, it would now be withdrawn. On that day too he made over the radio a farewell address to the people of India, which was relayed around the world:

You will have heard that the draft declaration which I brought to India on behalf of the War Cabinet and which I explained to you the last time I spoke over the wireless has been rejected by your leaders. I am sad that this great opportunity of rallying India for her defence and her freedom has been missed. . . .

In the past the British Governments have been accused of using vague terms to cloak a lack of purpose; and when they stated that it must be left to the Indian communities to agree among themselves it has been said that this was only a device by which Great Britain might indefinitely retain its control over India. But Congress since the outbreak of war has repeatedly demanded two essentials as a basis for its support of the allied effort in the war, first, a declaration of Indian independence and second, a constituent assembly to frame a new constitution for India. Both of these demands find their place in the draft declaration. . . .

He expressed his profound regret that the British offer had been turned down and then appealed to India to join willingly in the struggle against the common enemy. He continued:

. . . Now is the time for India and her people to join their courage, their strength and their endurance in this great heroic and world-wide army of the common people, and to take her part in those smashing blows for victory against brutality and aggression which shall for ever free the masses from the age-long fear and tragedy of war.

He left for England the next day.

There is an epilogue to this chapter which cannot be ignored. A few days later he rose in the House of Commons to report. He said in a masterly survey that the difficulties which arose in his negotiations "fell under three heads. First were those relating to the method of determining the new constitution; second were those relating to defense; third were those relating to the general form of the interim government."

"First," he said, "was the use of the word 'Dominion.' . . . This was not a matter of prime importance." It is difficult for the outsider to understand why, if there is no difference between "dominion status" and "independence," the British Government and Sir Stafford were so reluctant to use the word "independence."

The second objection, he said, "was a most substantial one. That was the right of non-accession of the Provinces after the new constitution had been decided upon by a constitution-making Assembly."

In this relation he asked the members of the House to study the resolutions of Congress and the Moslem League and then to look at the draft declaration. They would "come to the conclusion that the draft declaration did no more than Mr. Gandhi and other Congress leaders had constantly stated they were prepared to do, that was, to keep open the issue of Pakistan, and they would also realize that the scheme for the draft declaration was as fair a compromise as possible between the two extreme views."

The third and last objection was in regard to the position of the Indian States. Congress had protested not against the Indian States coming into the constitution-making authority, but against their representatives being nominated by the rulers and not elected by the people. After expressing how desirable such a change was, Sir Stafford said,

But for the moment, we can only deal with the situation as it exists historically. . . .

However, none of these three differences with the Congress Working Committee would have been decisive of a negative result. . . . The final question which was raised at my last and long meeting with the President of the Congress and Pandit Nehru was as to the form of the temporary Government that should be in power until the end of the war and the coming into operation of the new constitution. I had from the outset made it clear to all those whom I saw that it was not possible to make any constitutional changes— except of the most insignificant kind—prior to the new constitution which would come into operation as a result of the labours of the constitution-making assembly. . . .

The question as to the formation of a new Government and how the members of the Viceroy's Executive should be treated and how the business therein should be conducted were, of course, essential matters for the Viceroy who had to carry on the Government of India, and not for me as a member of the War Cabinet on a visit to India. . . .

So the delegate completed his report and handed in his mandate. No one in England laid at his door the blame for the failure of the Mission. Tributes were paid to him on every side. While this time as he stood before the Commons there was no glory of a well-won triumph, there was universal appreciation of the fact that where he had failed, no one in their midst could have succeeded.

XVIII. The Minister of Aircraft Production

STAFFORD CRIPPS had not long returned from his mission to India when Mr. Churchill made some Cabinet changes which involved switching Cripps to two extremely important jobs. He became Minister of Aircraft Production and chairman of the scientific research committees concerned with radio and methods of defeating the submarine. These new jobs meant demotion from the War Cabinet, although he would remain a member of the Government. The Prime Minister himself described the change as solely due to "a most serious war need." Others read into it that there had been some clash between Churchill and Cripps.

It is true that there had been differences of opinion between Cripps and the Prime Minister. Cripps had asked to be relieved of his membership of the War Cabinet, but at Churchill's request had refrained from pressing his point. The year 1942 was one of continuing reverses for the Allies, and Churchill desired that their differences should not be made public at a time when major military operations were pending. After the launching of the North African offensive and the victory of El Alamein, Churchill's prestige and public morale were so high that changes could be made without any untoward reflections on the Government or the Prime Minister.

Churchill has a high opinion of Stafford Cripps. He regards him "as a great loyal gentleman of high intellectual ability," indeed as the one man of outstanding intellect in the Labour Party, and a most loyal colleague in Government. He thought it a magnificent act of patriotism and loyalty when at his request Sir Stafford agreed not to press their divergence of views. As Churchill remarked to the author, "everyone knows what political capital can be made out of such an occasion." He thought Sir Stafford most suitable for the post of Minister of

Aircraft Production, having remembered his great experience at Queensferry during the First World War and his remarkable capacity for handling facts. "And the more facts he has to deal with the better," said Churchill puckishly, "since everybody knows Cripps' capacity for work."

Cripps had all the necessary qualifications but one for the post of Minister of Aircraft Production—he had no previous experience as a minister in charge of a government department. He welcomed the appointment although it created a sensation within the ministry and the industry. Many employers hated him. The permanent staff were curious and not a little alarmed, knowing him only by reputation. One new colleague exclaimed, "We're all right now, because we have briefed the best counsel in the Cabinet." Churchill had no doubts about the wisdom of his choice.

The Ministry of Aircraft Production was born because of an acute crisis in 1940. The *Aircraft Builders* says:

> The M.A.P. like all other big wartime Ministries, was a very different thing and very much bigger and more complicated than an ordinary peace-time Ministry. It was, in fact, a peace-time Ministry to which had been added the task of planning for and controlling in considerable detail a huge industry. The people who formed its staff naturally reflected this dual function. On the one hand they might be professional Civil Servants; on the other, they might be business men or technical specialists.

> In addition to the central organization in London, there were twelve regional organizations. Resident representatives were also appointed in most of the larger factories. Throughout the war aircraft production was by far the biggest industry in the country. Its requirements were ever changing, improvements and new types of aircraft were continually being introduced, and the whole industry was subject to the ceaseless demands of changes in the strategy of the war.

Sir Stafford's predecessors had not reigned long in his new post. Beaverbrook had been the first to hold it—for less than one year. There was an element of challenge in the appointment. No one in the ministry felt that they had come under the control of a novice. With characteristic speed, Cripps swiftly made himself thoroughly acquainted with the ministry, its structure, staff, and problems. Nor was he content to have all the data on paper. Good management meant for him personal contact with staff, managements, and men and effective co-operation with all of them. Sir Wilfred Freeman, the permanent secretary under him, says he was "the most punctual man I have met in my life." Sir Edwin Plowden thought him "the best Minister I ever knew." He worked all under him to the limit of their capacity, but his own capacity seemed unlimited. Freeman says, "He was the only Minister I know who, if you gave him papers to read, no matter how long or how difficult, first thing in the morning, I'd have them back."

George Blaker, who worked with him as Private Secretary later at the Board of Trade, has said,

I remember very well my first day working for Stafford Cripps. It was a busy day, not much connected with ordinary administrative work, and at the end of it there was a pile of urgent papers to a depth of several inches requiring his attention. He said "If we don't finish our work during the day, let me take it home, and it will be done by the morning." It always was done by the morning. I have never met anyone with such a capacity for quick, thorough work. When I discovered that he habitually worked until 2 or 3 o'clock in the morning to achieve this result, and still got up early, the papers had to be strictly rationed, in the hope he would get more sleep.

Another says of him, "Cripps is an extraordinarily clever man and has a tremendous capacity for work. He is busy every moment and amazes us with all the subjects he tackles. Yet he never fusses. If you are going to a meeting you don't have to worry, 'Has he got his papers?' and he doesn't turn round saying 'Where's this and where's that?' When he goes onto the platform he is the master of the subject."

Yet another says, "Stafford is essentially a research student, scientist and experimentalist. He is a great believer in using the expert, the technician. But the picture of 'Austerity Cripps' is a press 'phoney.' In the small circle of people with whom he works he is warm, human, friendly and understanding and has a great sense of humour and a gift for pulling with the team. In big meetings his brain takes over and he can't give the time for a little joke because the momentum is on. He is intellectually so far superior to others and is impatient of obstacles."

There are criticisms of him for not conceding enough to the stupidity of people. One says that he makes the mistake of thinking that when he has defeated a person in argument he has convinced him. But all bear testimony to the fact that in an exceedingly short time the man who had become the Minister of Aircraft Production without previous ministerial responsibility had become an outstanding administrator, leading the largest wartime industry of two million workers with great skill and wisdom.

It is one thing to get to grips with the personnel of a government department. It is another to establish similar good relations with the managements of private industry and the workers in it.

It is fair to say [reads an extract from the *Aircraft Builders*] that by and large, management in the aircraft industry consisted of highly capable, energetic industrialists of considerable individuality, who had strong views on most subjects, and naturally particularly strong views on all things connected with the production of aircraft. These firms between them virtually represented the sum of the country's knowledge and experience in this field. They knew it, and were rightly proud of it.

The demands made on these firms with the outbreak of war were enormous. The entirely new factor in the situation was that these highly capable and individualistic managements were called upon to accept direction and control from a central ministry. Much of the technical staff of the ministry was necessarily drawn from the industry itself, but the partnership which in the end developed between the ministry and the many firms of varying sizes was not only a remarkable achievement in itself but a tribute to Cripps' capacity. The experience gave him considerable insight into possible methods which could be used after the war for controlling an industry without nationalizing it. His "planning mind" seized upon this experience with enthusiasm and it would soon color his views about Socialism.

In 1943 he convened a national conference of representatives from the management and workers in the aircraft industry. Here he revealed his mastery of his job. He first sought to make everyone conscious of the industry's place in the strategy of war. Then he passed on to the place of the ministry itself in relation to the industry. The department, he said, "was not to set up as a producing body, its purpose being to co-ordinate the whole activity of the aircraft industry and to facilitate by planning and the creation and allocation of capacity, the maximum program." He dealt with phasing, planning, the different types of aircraft under production, materials, changes in the program, the incorporation of modifications, spares, the repair organization, sub-contracting, and then some of the difficulties. Here he spoke like an expert.

He had to meet some criticism concerning his action in taking over a firm and putting in his own management. His reply to this had no ambiguity about it:

> Our regional officers are constantly in touch with firms within their districts with a view to intervening where necessary. The Production Efficiency Board, which I set up when I joined the Ministry, has a general power to enquire into the efficiency of firms and to give them every assistance in coming up to standard, if they are not efficiently managed.
>
> The extreme case of putting in a Controller, or even taking over a firm, is only resorted to where other measures have proved ineffective. I shall not of course hesitate to take appropriate action wherever it is necessary.

From the heights of his department he came down to the man on the job in the factory. He said,

> I have no doubt that Joint Production Committees afford a new and most valuable opportunity for the exchange of views on all production matters between the management and the workers in a factory. I think that my interest in the Committees is probably well-known to you, and I shall certainly never be backward in showing my gratitude to them for the very excellent work they are doing in helping to secure increased efficiency and production. I have now had a very considerable experience of them, having attended between one hundred and fifty and two hundred in my visits round the country, and although they vary somewhat in personnel they are, by and large, working very successfully for a new institution. . . .
>
> This new weapon of industrial democracy is now part of our democratic way of life. It is of the greatest importance that we should develop the Production Committees on right lines as a permanent part of our industrial structure.

From the moment he became Minister of Aircraft Production to the end of the war he preached these themes unceas-
ingly and helped to put them into practice on a scale such as
obtained in no other industry.

In this direct contact with those employed in the aircraft
industry the Cripps "partnership" worked industriously. Isobel
Cripps went with Stafford on hundreds of visits to factories.
His secretary Allan Jarvis recalls this in a letter:

I remember the part she played in the many factory tours he
went on. While Stafford was discussing engineering and production
with the management and technicians (showing a technical grasp
which astonished the professionals) Isobel could usually be found
in some remote quiet corner with the women workers or some
group of young people. She was very sure in her grasp of the importance of the human factor in industry; quick to assess the
"morale" of any shop and to sense the mood of the work people,
and she could therefore accurately report to the Minister on this
aspect of their work. They were both of them agreed on its importance and it was of inestimable value to Stafford to have this
help from Isobel for the pressure of time kept his attention focussed
on the technical side. . . . Isobel has been of immense assistance.
She somehow finds time to see and talk to, sometimes at very great
length, an incredibly large number of people, always with a view
to creating or sustaining their feeling that they are working as part
of a common cause. Always she shows infinite patience and understanding in smoothing out relationships between the frequently
highly charged and temperamental people involved. It is through
this extension of his influence through her activity and her very
effective projection of both their personalities that Stafford has been
able to exercise his power of leadership and inspiration over such
a diverse range of interests—religion, education, health and housing,
the arts, music, films and the theatre. It is an incredible achievement and it is the partnership as such which deserves the credit.

Two years after Cripps had taken on the job he was able
to report:

The manpower employed by the aircraft industry, and all the
subsidiary industries which go to making aircraft accessories has
increased about twenty times. . . . The proportion of women employed in the industry has risen 40%. In the last twelve months
the industry has turned out 27,273 aeroplanes. The weight of air-
frames produced from March 1943 to March 1944, was fifty times

greater than in 1936, seven times the weight of 1939, and not far short of four times that in 1940.

In these eventful years he was also chairman of the Radio Board. It was not until the war was over that its work was revealed to the public. One day in September, 1945, he told to a press conference the story of the evolution of radar, which had reached its highest point of development during the war, and of the wonderful team of scientists who had concentrated on the problems of radio location and produced the mechanisms which enabled the pilots of every kind of craft to find their objectives in the dark, through the fogs, and in the sea.

Once he had got into his stride with his departmental duties and felt he was the master of them, and those under his direction were "going his way," he began to express himself on other matters.

He continued to develop his approach to Christianity and politics. His theme was always the same—he wanted practical Christianity which worked seven days a week and was not merely a Sunday soporific. But 1943 was the year when political leaders, sensing that the tide of war had turned and Britain would be on the winning side, began to feel their way toward the postwar situation and to take stock of the trends of public opinion. Churchill made a famous speech that set the fashion in kite-flying. Morrison followed with a speech in which he would be on safe ground—a coalition if the Labour Party thought so, and no coalition if it didn't.

Stafford Cripps followed these two leaders of parties and spoke as the man without a party. Speaking to his constituents in Bristol he said,

My views are still those for which you elected me, I belong to no party. It was on that basis I joined this Government and while I remain in the Government I shall join no party, old or new. . . .

How are we to pass from this National Government, this wartime coalition of parties to a Progressive active Government, which will be prepared to carry through a program after the war, that will not give us all we want, but that will give us a sufficiency to make certain that we are on the right road to progress and that will enable us to solve the problems with which we shall be faced?

He took note of what Churchill and Morrison had said, but

he did not throw any light on his future course and was content to say, "When the time comes I shall do what I have throughout sought to do and that is to take the action which I believe best serves the interests of my constituents and my country."

Many were the discussions he had with his friends of those coalition days and with those who had been associated with him in the Popular Front campaign. Two things which had emerged clearly were that to continue as a leader in politics he must have a party behind him and that there was no basis upon which he could found a new party. One close friend had written to him, about the time of his return from Moscow, a letter of great frankness and courage in which he had said,

The only mass political organisations at the moment are the Conservative and the Labour Parties, and I do not believe that there is the slightest hope of achieving anything in the near future except through one of these two organisations. . . . The political line-up after the war *must* be broadly the Conservative party standing for reaction and the vested interests, and the progressives who want to see done the things that you and I want done, organised— where? If a new organisation is impossible, as I believe it is, they *can only* be organised in the Labour Party. . . . If I am right about that, and if it is true that the party is generally right minded you have an organisation in which you can do something . . . after the war. If on the other hand you either antagonise the rank and file of the Labour Party or do not carry them with you, no amount of support from the intelligentsia or unattached people with the right ideas or disgruntled Tories will be of the slightest importance in getting big things done.

His friend was brutally frank about his previous record in the Labour Party.

Unfortunately you don't start with a clean slate! There is the history of your eight years association with the Labour Party. I've thought about it a lot and talked to a lot of people about it, and I think I know the attitude of the average party member about it. It may be a misguided attitude, but whether it is misguided or not, it is a fact that has to be taken into consideration. The Socialist League, the United Front, the Popular Front may all have been dead right in theory—I think they were and so does a large section of the Party—but all of them, to put it bluntly, were flops, and re-

sulted in your being turned out of the Party by a democratic vote
(even though we know how democracy works inside the party).
The very deep and rather cow-like loyalty of the party member
expects a man either to submit to such a democratic vote or else
washes its hands of him—e.g., Mosley and the 1931 people. I'm
pretty certain that that is what it did to you in 1939, but now,
thanks to your work in Russia and the patent incompetence of the
present leaders, it is prepared to give you another chance. But that
means that you have to be on your best behaviour!

What the party member objects to is your forming groups within
the party. Because you are the outstanding figure in these groups,
they always come to be identified with your name. . . . I'm convinced that another case of that will finish you with the rank and
file of the party and therefore with any kind of mass support in this
country.

There were those who sought to persuade him to form some
new combination of the disillusioned in the old parties. He
listened to them all but continued along his way, waiting until
the war should end.

The war thundered on. After the last great Nazi drive eastward, culminating in the epoch-making defense of Stalingrad,
the Red Army moved to the West until the Nazi Army was
driven back upon the ruins of Berlin. The U-boat menace had
been shattered by the British fleet and air forces. "D Day" was
followed by the Allied Second Front marching also toward
Berlin. The year 1945 opened with the triumph of the Allied
armies clearly in sight.

In February, 1945, the Executive Council of the Labour
Party, after some complicated negotiations concerning a local
dispute in his constituency of East Bristol, formally readmitted
Stafford Cripps to the Labour Party. He was the last of the
prominent United Front leaders to return, as Aneuran Bevan
and George Strauss had returned in October, 1939.

Thus once more he stepped into the main stream of Labour
politics with the tide flowing toward a general election. The
nearer the end of the war came, the less tenable became the
coalition of the parties. There had been some discontent with
the truce, but there were no major developments until 1944,
when the Prime Minister himself spoke of the "odor" of dissolution in the air.

The country was ready for an election. The Government had outlived its popularity. There had been a great swing to the left in public opinion. The influence of Russia, the many profound changes that had taken place in the course of the war, and the success attending the state organization of economy, had convinced vast numbers that what could be done by the state for the organization of war could be done by it for the organization of the peace. The end of the Coalition was at hand.

On May 6, Cripps entered the fray on the issue of a party election. Speaking at Widnes, he said that there was no democratic alternative to a party fight:

I am convinced that there is really only one fundamental issue, but that issue is absolutely basic to all our politics.

The Conservatives profess their willingness to encourage private enterprise, which benefits and suits more influential supporters as the means to secure the best job in production. The only drawback from the point of view of the advocacy is that never yet in the history of the world has an unplanned and uncontrolled private economy succeeded in getting rid of unemployment or avoiding vast wastage of materials and labour.

The Labour Party takes the diametrically opposite view.

We say that all industry and all great services like transport and coal and power supply must be so organised as to give to the people as a whole the maximum that is possible. In fact the production of the country must be considered as a great public service, as in fact it is, and that we must not only see to it that we get produced those things that we want. In other words the necessaries for the country and the people must take priority over the luxuries and semiluxuries.

In order to achieve that end we must be prepared to use whatever method of organising our industry proves to be best. We have no interest in preserving or destroying private enterprise except to create efficiency in our production.

The new theme of a planned mixture of state ownership and controlled capitalism emerges here completely.

Two weeks later he received a great and cordial welcome at the annual conference of the Labour Party held at Blackpool, amid all the excitement of a near-election atmosphere and under the chairmanship of Cripps' old colleague and supporter, Ellen Wilkinson. He made one short intervention in

the debate on the statement of policy, "Let us face the Future."
He could not know at the time how great would be the responsibility that would fall on his shoulders for the implementing
of this program, but those who heard him commented on the
difference of emphasis in this speech compared with his challenging speech after the fall of the Labour Government in
1931. Then he had talked much about the breakdown of
capitalism and how "capitalism must go." Now his theme of
"planned economy" was uppermost:

We should not underestimate the difficulties of a national plan
for our industries. Those of us who have been concerned with the
planning of war industries—in my particular department we have
had fifteen thousand firms to control and to plan—realise that when
we come to the broader national plan that will be required, with
its degrees of nationalisation and control in different industries, we
shall be faced with a very difficult technical task, a task made the
more difficult because no due preparations have been made for its
accomplishment.

The second point I want to stress is the need there will be for
expediting our Parliamentary arrangements. If you look at the
volume of legislation that will have to flow from this programme,
even over a period of five years, you will realise that in a peace-time
Parliament, with all the tricks of the Opposition that are open to
those who wish to delay legislation, it is not going to be by any
means an easy task to get the job done. Our possibility of seeing
this program through to the end will depend largely upon what
we can show the people we can accomplish in the early months of
our power. That is the time when we shall have the chance and we
have got to see to it that machinery of Parliament and of Government is such that we can make an effective contribution to the
carrying out of this program in those early months.

On May 7, 1945 the war in Europe came to an end.

Fifteen days after the bugles had sounded "cease fire" in
Europe, Churchill tendered his resignation and the Coalition
Government was dissolved. Polling day was fixed for July 5.
Meanwhile a "caretaker government" carried on.

Stafford Cripps at once came to the front of the Labour
Party's election campaign. He spent little time in his own constituency. It was a safe Labour seat and he was returned with
28,000 votes out of 58,000. His election address was of a more
domestic type than were those of the other Labour ministers.

In front there was a photograph of himself with his wife. He told the electors that it was with their backing that he went to Moscow and joined the War Cabinet upon his return. It was with their good wishes that he went to India as representative of the British people. As all Europe had moved to the Left, the Labour Party would be best suited to keep friendship with the new governments, and would be a government in broad sympathy with the views of the Russian people.

Speaking in Wembley on June 4, he gave warning, should a Tory Government be returned, of a coming clash of interests between Great Britain and the Soviet Union. Of course he was speaking on the assumption that his Labour colleagues meant what they said when they assured the electorate that there would not be a "continuity of foreign policy." He said:

Any suspicion on either side, any lack of understanding, will tend to drive both Russia and our country to resort to private schemes of security which will bring us into an inevitable clash of interests.

At all costs we must avoid being drawn into the position of rival spheres of interest, one in the west and another in the east. But the cost is a genuine honest desire to understand and co-operate with the Soviet Union.

The question of Anglo-Soviet relations, he was convinced, was the most important and critical in British foreign policy, and he was also convinced that the Labour Party could handle the matter better than any other party.

Ringing the changes on these themes, he toured the country for the Labour Party to help the candidates in other constituencies. He traveled three thousand miles in thirty days, breaking his trip to entrain for a B.B.C. broadcast in London. He gave as many as six talks a night. The speeches were never written in advance. He carried a little set of notes typed on cards. Often his sole manuscript was the pasting up of an opposition speech reported in the day's press. His only written speech was given in Edinburgh on the subject of India. A few days earlier, while in Dundee, he had learned of Nehru's release from prison.

To conserve his energy during this grueling period, he worked according to a plan. Every morning he would meet his chauffeur, secretary and companion, Allan Jarvis, for an

8:30 breakfast in the hotel where they had spent the night. They would wade through all the morning newspapers. He would then retire to the hotel's reading room where he would go through a fantastic amount of correspondence, writing scores of letters in his precise, clear handwriting. Then to the road. Sometimes Stafford drove. When Jarvis drove, Stafford enjoyed brief cat-naps. When the travelers arrived at their destination, they would deposit their bags at a hotel, enjoy a luxurious tea, and spend a free hour, during which time Stafford would relax. With the day's travel behind him and speeches ahead, he would talk of legal and political battles in which he had been a participant, in which the litigants were usually world-famed figures or organizations, highlighting his narration with anecdotes and equally amusing word portraits of the disputants.

They finished their tour by spending three campaigning days in East Bristol, where Isobel had meanwhile been working. There, as everywhere, his speeches were in the nature of lectures that were both political and religious in tone and substance.

Broadcasting played an important part in the election and Cripps naturally was in the list of broadcasters. The two most famous broadcasts were the first two, given by Churchill and Attlee respectively. Churchill made every conceivable blunder, and the contrast the following night when Attlee spoke was overwhelming. The day of the results was quite fantastic too. None expected them to reveal so complete a change-over in terms of party power. There were in the House of Commons 640 seats. Before the election there were 359 Conservative members. After the election there were 189. Before the election Labour had 164. After the election Labour had 393.

Cripps, with an eighteen thousand majority, addressed a triumphant meeting of Labour supporters in Bristol. By his side were his wife and three other Labour M.P.'s for Bristol divisions. He was no longer a "man without a party"—but a leader of the Labour Party, certain to be among the chosen members of the Government now to be formed.

The next day the newspapers announced that the new President of the Board of Trade was the Right Honorable Sir Stafford Cripps, P.C., K.C., M.P.

XIX. Britain's Economic Controller

STAFFORD CRIPPS' appointment as president of the Board of Trade was welcomed. The *Economist* said:

Sir Stafford Cripps is the best President of the Board of Trade in the upper ranks of the Labour Party; he combines Socialist orthodoxy with an understanding of how industry functions—a rare and happy combination.

What the *Economist* understands by "Socialist orthodoxy" is not clear, but the praise from this quarter may have been due to Cripps' election broadcast, in which he stressed the importance of efficiency, and particularly managerial efficiency, in industry. Within a few weeks he showed that he was in earnest on this point. But before that he had to make an important broadcast to the United States on behalf of the Labour Government. He did this only five days after the election results and the resignation of Prime Minister Churchill. Once more he made it clear that his socialism and that of the Labour Government had a new emphasis, that of "planned economy" without emphasis on change of ownership. He said:

Labour put forward a limited program to be carried out in the next five years.

We sought power to plan the orderly development of the country's resources, bringing some few of the more important industries and services under national ownership, while retaining a system of planned and controlled private enterprise for the rest.

In this way the Labour Party believes it can make our democracy more effective and more all embracing in its scope, and hopes to be able by these means to raise the general standard of living throughout the country.

But the Labour Government was not yet free to give undivided attention to the fulfillment of its election program. Although the war in Europe was over, Japan had yet to be reduced to unconditional surrender.

During the war British, American, and Canadian scientists, without intimating their activities to their Russian allies, had produced the atom bomb. Without warning to the world, American airmen dropped an atom bomb on Hiroshima. On August 14, the war with Japan also came to an end. From this date the British Labour Government began to implement its election program.

The circumstances facing it were extraordinary. Britain had emerged from the war with her Empire disintegrating, her economy exhausted, and completely dominated by America. The latter had forced her to sell £1,000,000,000 of her securities to pay ready cash for supplies at the beginning of the war. To carry on the war she had become a debtor to every one of her Dominions and to India. Her debit balance to the United States on Lend-Lease Account was £4,200,000,000. Her internal debt had reached dimensions undreamed of in her history. She began the First World War with a national debt of £800,000,-000. She came out of the Second World War with a debt of £26,000,000,000, after the United States had wiped out her debt on Lend-Lease account. She had paid half the cost of the war by stepping up taxation, and half of it by borrowing. She began the war with 21,000,000 tons of merchant shipping which earned her £150,000,000 a year to set against her imports. Almost half of her merchant ships were sent to the bottom of the sea in the U-boat warfare. Her export trade had shrunk to approximately 29 per cent of what it was in 1939.

No country in the world is so dependent upon foreign trade. Importing 50 per cent of her foodstuffs and raw material she needs a great export trade in order to pay for her imports. But the uneven development of the world's economy had left Britain in the perilous position that the country from which she secured the greatest proportion of her imports could not take payment in goods. Her main sources of supply were the United States and the countries dominated by United States economy. These, however, exported not only the goods which Britain sorely needed but also the goods which Britain exported. Only a fraction of the goods Britain imported from America were paid for by exports from Britain. Hence, Britain had to pay the balance either in dollars or in gold. The economy of Europe was in ruins and every country outside Russia and the countries associated with her stood in the same relationship to American countries as Britain. All countries needed imports from America. None was in a position to pay cash for them, nor were they in a position to pay by the export of goods. In any case, America was not in a position to accept such payments on the scale which would balance the goods received.

Millions of British soldiers, sailors, and airmen were spread across the earth, impatient to return home. The economy of the country was still geared to the demands of wartime and not of peace. The state machine for the control of the economy in wartime was in the hands of the Labour Government, with the heritage of a disintegrating Empire and the responsibilities thrust upon a victorious power to make the peace of the world. Such was the situation when the British Labour Government was formed in 1945 and Stafford Cripps became president of the Board of Trade.

He was not, by virtue of his post, in charge of the whole economy of the country. His department had to deal only with a sector of the economy that was not state-owned, and with imports and exports. Though a big department and important, it would have to fit into the general plan which the Government would pursue under the higher direction of Herbert Morrison and Hugh Dalton, the Chancellor of the Exchequer. The plan as a whole would have to include the switch-over from war production to peace production.

The government plan included the nationalization of the Bank of England, the coal industry, railway and road transport, gas, electricity and steel industries; State direction of industry and economy by a licensing and permit system for the use of scarce raw materials; the continuance of the wartime technique of high taxation, borrowing and saving; the direction of both State and private capital investment, new raw material and trade developments within the British Empire; bulk purchases and bilateral trade agreements with foreign countries; re-distribution of labor forces to the export industries, and large capital development of British agriculture.

Cripps had started off by assuring America that the Labour Government was not about to inaugurate Socialism in Britain, but was attempting nothing worse than to prove that the Labour Government could run State capitalism far better and more efficiently than the Conservatives. Now he had to pick up the threads of his department and to prove that he, at any rate, had on him the hallmark of efficiency. One of the defects of the British Parliamentary system is the necessary combination under each responsible minister of a vast amount of pure routine work with policy formulation. Cripps, therefore, had to get down at once to working out his policy for half-and-half control of industry while performing day-to-day detailed work. For example, on the first day, he answered questions on the shortages of boots, shoes, clothing, the delay in the delivery of textile machinery, how many square feet of industrial floor space were still under requisition by Government departments, the surrender of clothing coupons for surgical belts, applications by ex-servicemen in Cardiff for licenses to set up in business on their own, the publication of an international trade directory, requirements of Brazil for agricultural machinery, rehabilitation of British trade in Yugoslavia and the Baltic countries, clearance regulations in Peru and Ecuador, the supply of bedding for students, the monthly production of cotton goods, and work in ordnance factories.

Of the big jobs waiting to be tackled, the first was cotton. An efficient and highly productive cotton industry was vital both for the export drive and for the demands of home consumers. More fundamentally, it was to provide a test case in the application of efficiency techniques to industry remaining in private hands.

Cripps began with a nationwide warning that clothes were going to remain in short supply. Speaking to an audience of employers and operatives, in Oldham, a Lancashire cotton town, on August 11, he said that a point had been reached in the supply of cotton cloth where it was doubtful whether the ration could be continued at its present rate.

That was a pretty grim beginning for the general public, and again many people began to hold Cripps responsible for the austerity, instead of the condition of British economy. But he did not let matters rest there. Turning to the cotton industry itself he said:

It is not part of the present Government's policy to nationalise the cotton industry provided that the industry upon which more than two million of our people depend directly or indirectly for their living carries through with expedition the measures necessary for its reorganisation.

To find the measures necessary for reorganization, he announced that a "working party" was to be appointed, consisting of four representatives of the employers, four of the trade unions, and four independent members and a chairman appointed by the Board of Trade. This group was to review all the many existing plans for the industry and produce the final plan by Christmas. Other such groups were to be set up for other industries; all of them were to be tripartite; in each case the employers' and the workers' representatives were to be selected from panels nominated by the associations of the employers and of the unions.

This plan for reorganizing industries was Cripps' distinct contribution to industrial administration. It was a bold experiment which went much further than the trade-union movement had hitherto gone in its demands for the application of the principle of "sharing in the control of industry." It meant the assumption by trade unions of a share in general responsibility for the organization of industry at a higher level than the Joint Production Committees of wartime. After years of discussion in the trade-union movement the leaders had rejected the principle of trade-union representation on the Boards of Control of socialized industries. They were quite prepared for trade unionists to be members of these Boards of Control but not as representatives of the unions. The unions were not prepared to take any responsibility for the running of industry.

When reports of the "working parties" had been received and studied, the department would have to lay down the minimum requirements to be placed upon the industry in the national interest. Then it would be for the partnership to see that those requirements were carried into effect. Cripps said,

This was only a general picture of the way in which the Board of Trade proposed to proceed. A very great and important part would have to be played by the Trade Unionists, and so far as the trade union representatives are concerned the whole reputation of the trade union movement will be at stake as well as our own industrial future. It was a time for concentrated teamwork. There was no short cut—hard work and hard work alone could win us the prize of success and with that success continued power to progress to further heights.

There was no aspect of production to which he did not give attention. He spoke on the need for good designing in industry. He said at a meeting of the Council of Industrial Design:

Design is a factor of crucial importance to British industry today, whether we think of what is due from our own producers to our own people, or of how best to meet the very live competition we shall have to meet in foreign markets. At home, our common objective is a higher standard of living. And we must not think of that desirable aim merely in quantitative terms, regardless of its character, that is regardless of the quality of what our income can buy. You can have squalor and ugliness even amid riches.

Suddenly, however, he was called upon to leave his department in the hands of a deputy for some months. The Labour Government had on its hands the problem of the future of India, which the Coalition Government had been unable to solve.

After the failure of the Cripps' Mission in 1942, many leaders, including Nehru and Gandhi, had been sent to prison. When the war ended and they were released, Stafford Cripps and his wife, then in the midst of general election campaigning, sent Nehru their greetings. Nehru replied:

Dear Stafford,

It was good of you and your wife to send me a message of greeting on my discharge from prison. I appreciated it very much. I am ashamed that I should have delayed in thanking you for it. I was overwhelmed with messages from friends and at the same time had no rest anywhere. Except for a day or two at home I have had to be on the move and I have only now come back for a few days stay at home. After a long period in prison, both the body and the mind require adjustment to the new environment, especially the mind. So, as soon as I could manage it I fled to the mountains in Kashmir and lived or rather dwelt for many days far from newspaper and post telegraph offices. I feel better for the change. But so much adjustment and adaptation are necessary. I suppose that will happen gradually. The difficulty is that one does not get much chance of doing so in a rapidly changing world, with new problems, or old problems in new shape, cropping up from day to day.

> I hope both of you are well,
>> Yours very sincerely,
>>> Jawaharlal Nehru.

Yes, that was it. "Old problems in new shape" were thrusting themselves forward. Half the human race, dwelling in the lands of the East, all the peoples of the prewar colonial and semicolonial lands of the Empires, were giving notice to the western powers to "get out." Released from the threat of a Japanese invasion, the Indian people were again able to give undivided attention to their claim for freedom. The western powers had talked freedom and democracy; now let Britain put to the proof their declarations.

Fortunately for India, and for England, the impact of the war had so changed the minds of the British people that they had elected a Labour Government committed to give India her freedom at the earliest possible date. Above all, the Labour Government did not want an Indian revolution on its hands. It had appointed Lord Pethick Lawrence to the India Office and instructed the Viceroy of India to begin new negotiations with the Indian leaders. Convinced that time was short, the Labour Government decided to send three Cabinet Ministers, Lord Pethick Lawrence, Mr. Alexander, the first Lord of the Admiralty, and Sir Stafford, to see if it were possible to do what the Mission of 1942 had failed to do. The real force within the Mission would once more be Stafford Cripps.

Mr. Attlee made the Independence question clearer than it had ever been made by any British Prime Minister. He said,

India herself must choose what will be her future constitution; what will be her position in the world. I hope that the Indian people may elect to remain within the British Commonwealth. . . . But if she does so elect, it must be by her own free will. . . . If, on the other hand, she elects for independence, in our view she has a right to do so. It will be for us to help to make the transition as smooth and as easy as possible.

Even that declaration could not at once wipe out the deep, century-old suspicion that Britain was up to her tricks again, finding a new way of keeping her grip on India under the

banner of freedom. After all, it was difficult for Nehru and
Gandhi and a host of others to forget that the same people
who were now talking so pleasantly had been members of
governments that had forced them to spend a quarter of their
lives in prison. Nor was the record of the previous Labour
Government one to inspire confidence. Attlee and Cripps,
Pethick Lawrence and Alexander had been members of it, and
it had filled the jails of India to overflowing and was responsible for thousands of Indians being killed—in short, it had
governed exactly as a Tory Government had done. The only
difference the Indians had been able to discern was that the
Labour Government was more self-righteous about its deeds
of repression and its members wore choir-boy's surplices to hide
their imperialist souls. As Nehru put it, "They forget that
today they are addressing a sensitive, proud and virile people
who will not put up with any patronage or anything smacking
of superiority."

So the Labour Cabinet Mission set forth to give back to the
Indians the "brightest gem in the British Crown." Sir Stafford
and his companions, arriving at New Delhi airfield on March
24, 1946, were met by the Viceroy, Field Marshal Viscount
Wavell, a great soldier and a liberal-minded politician, representatives of the Government of India, the Service Com-
manders, and about a hundred correspondents from newspapers
of all shades of opinion. Cripps was at once surrounded by the
pressmen, but he resolutely refused to talk. "I am not going
to say anything to the press," he is reported to have said, "only
that we had a very good trip and I shall meet you all
tomorrow."

"You are looking fatter than you were last time," a voice
called from the pressmen.

"That's cauliflowers and carrots," replied Cripps, and there
was a round of laughter.

Characteristically, Cripps had added to the party certain
advisers of his own choosing from outside the official circles
of the India Office. Only one of these, Major Billy Short, was
knowledgeable about India, through having lived and worked
there for many years. Woodrow Wyatt was a young Labour
Member of Parliament. George Blaker was Sir Stafford's private secretary. One of the functions of this little group was to

assist in the realm of personal relationships. Sir Stafford wished
to feel in his own personal way the pulse of Indian affairs and
the thoughts and emotions of the people of India, both through
the filter of official channels and outside it. In this way he
could augment his close personal contacts with Indian leaders.
This method of keeping in touch was powerfully reinforced
during June. Isobel flew to India when Stafford fell ill. She
began to make her own contacts and friendships, especially
among Indian women.

Through all the day-to-day changes, Cripps kept always in
mind a goal that lay beyond the immediate future. He thought
forward to the possibility of a true friendship between India
and Great Britain, which would endure no matter what formal
links might be broken in the grinding processes of history.

The conditions and the atmosphere favored extremism.
Nationalist election propaganda had left the country simmer-
ing. The authority of the Government was at a low ebb. Patel,
on behalf of Congress, demanded the immediate transfer of
power. Congress, he said, would not accept Jinnah's solution
of Pakistan. Jinnah, however, expressed the determination of
the Moslems to achieve Pakistan "by negotiation if possible,
by bloodshed if necessary."

In this situation the Mission began the same kind of procedure as on the occasion of Cripps' previous visit in 1942.
First, meetings with the Viceroy's Council, and then a whole
series of talks with Gandhi, talks with Nehru, talks with Azad,
talks with Jinnah, with Provincial Ministers, ex-Ministers,
leaders of organizations of all kinds, leaders of the "Untouchables," the trade unions, the parties, the Congress Committee,
representatives of the Chamber of Princes, press conferences,
and so on.

After three or four weeks of intensive discussions, the Mission decided to rest for a few days and on April 11 issued a
statement as to their position. It said,

The Cabinet Mission came out with a view that a speedy settlement of the outstanding questions was essential. They have, since
their arrival, heard the opinions of the most important political
elements in India. . . .

The Mission are confident that at this great moment in the history of India it will be possible, with mutual goodwill, to reach that

decision which the people of India so anxiously await and which will be welcomed throughout the world. . . .

When the Mission return they hope to find sufficient elements of agreement on which a settlement will be based.

The next important stage was the publication of the Mission's plan. The best summary comes from the *News Chronicle* of May 17:

The new plan for India consists of three main parts. One lays down the broad lines on which a future constitution should be based.

The second lays down the procedure for electing an Indian Constituent Assembly to meet as soon as possible in New Delhi and draft a constitution.

The third states that the Viceroy will proceed immediately with the formation of an interim Government to rule India while the new constitution is being drawn up.

The new India can be completely independent or can choose to be a member of the British Commonwealth. It should be formed on these lines:

1. There should be a Union of India, embracing both British and the native States which would deal with foreign affairs, defence and communications and have powers to raise money for these purposes.

2. The Union should have an Executive and a Legislature constituted from British Indian and States representatives. But—and this is the most important clause of all—any question raising a major communal issue in the legislature should require for its decision a majority of the representatives present and voting of each of the two major communities as well as a majority of all the members present and voting.

This clause, which bears all the stamps of Sir Stafford Cripps' mind, is the mission's plan for settling disputes between Hindus and Moslems. Pakistan they have ruled out as impracticable. So that anything affecting Hindus or Moslems, would have to be approved by a majority of both Hindus and Moslems, as well as a majority of all the members.

3. All subjects other than Union subjects and all residuary powers should be in the hands of the provinces.

4. The States will retain all subjects and powers other than those ceded by the Union. In short it will be a Federal State, like the United States, with the individual Indian States, such as Madras or the Central Provinces, having all powers except those specifically handed over to the Central Government.

5. The Individual States would, however, be free to form groups among themselves, with executives and legislatures and each group could determine the provincial subjects to be taken in common. This amounts to there being other small sub-Federations, for specific purposes, within the Main Union of India.

6. The constitutions of the Union and of the groups should contain a provision whereby any province could by a majority vote of its legislative assembly call for a re-consideration of the terms of the constitution after an initial period of ten years, and at ten-yearly intervals afterwards.

This Union constitution is to be worked out by Indians themselves—if they are willing. This is to be done by a new body, a constituent assembly.

Members of this would be elected by the present Hindu, Moslem or Sikh M.P.'s of the Provincial Legislative Assemblies. They would have, in the Constituent Assembly, seats in proportion to their populations.

These seats are to be divided up between the three main communities—Sikh, Moslem and General—and elected by their respective M.P.'s. The "General" community would include Hindus, Untouchables, and all other groups than Sikhs or Moslems. This, it is estimated, would give a total of 385 members, of which 93 would come from Indian native States and 292 from British India.

The native States would select their own representatives. 78 of these would represent Moslems.

Pakistan is, in the Mission's view, impracticable. Such a Pakistan would comprise two main areas, one in the north-west and one in the north-east. Yet the north-west areas would have a non-Moslem minority of 37.93% and the north-east a non-Moslem minority of 48.31%.

New minority problems would therefore be created. The individual Provinces could not be sub-divided to cut out these inner minorities. . . . But short of Pakistan, very full recognition is made of Moslem claims. The cultural, religious, economic and other interests of non-Hindu communities are fully protected.

The statement was received well by some, cautiously by others, and there was no out-and-out rejection. In Britain the reception was varied. Churchill regarded it as an able but "melancholy" document. He said:

There remains the discharge of our obligations to the Indian Minorities and to the Indian States. We must study the document with prolonged and searching attention in order to see that these duties have been faithfully safeguarded. It would seem at first sight that attention should be particularly directed to the position of the Muslim community of nearly eighty million, who are the most war-like and formidable of all the races and creeds in the Indian sub-continent and whose interests and culture are a matter of great consequence to India as a whole, and vital to the peace of India. Secondly, we must examine the provisions made for the depressed classes, or untouchables, who number nearly sixty millions, and for whose status and future, repeated assurances have been given and pledges made by many British Governments, in ancient and more recent times.

Finally, there are the relations which the Indian States, which comprise a quarter of the population and a third of the territory of the Indian sub-continent, are to have to the Crown and the New Government. . . .

Suddenly Cripps had to be taken to hospital suffering from strain due to overwork and the heat of Delhi. He was away from the Mission for ten days.

While the members of the Cabinet Mission and the various Indian leaders moved temporarily to mountainous Simla, to escape the oppressive heat of Delhi, an occasion for poetic reflection was offered to Cripps, who wrote

SIMLA

Rimming the distant circle of the pale blue sky
In never-changing whiteness stand the Himalayan heights.
The lesser hills fill the foreground, range on range,
Folding their tree-clad slopes into the deep valleys.
High above weaving in endless circles soar the kits,
In the cool and silent evening as Iqaza, the Psalmist's words
Lingering in my memory, rise to my lips:—
"I will turn mine eyes unto the Hills
  From whence cometh my strength."

The snow-capped mountains stand unchangeable
Rooted in timeless grandeur, their unsullied peaks
Flood the frail human mind with majesty eternal,
Symbol of that strength which comes from God alone.
That purity of purpose, divine and everlasting patience
And endless courage which are the very hall-mark of His love
Surrounding all who seek His help and guidance.

So it was the Psalmist saw those other hills
To which he turned his eyes and from them drew
His courage and his strength.

How relevant these words to his own hours of travail!

On June 3 he was able to resume his work. After he and the Viceroy had had conferences with Jinnah, the Moslem League Council gave a positive lead to the country by unanimously passing a resolution agreeing to work for the making of the future constitution and for an interim government. Cripps later paid tribute to Jinnah, when he said in the House of Commons: "It must have required no little courage and determination on Mr. Jinnah's part, in the light of the strong views held and very forcibly expressed by his followers, to support and carry this Resolution through the Moslem League."

At the same time, the Moslem League made it clear that it abated not one jot of its demand for the future division of India into two sovereign states—Pakistan and Hindustan—and it contradicted statements contained in the preamble to the Mission's proposals regarding the impracticability of Pakistan. The Congress was also prepared to accept the long-term plan as a basis on which a constituent assembly could be formed and a constitution agreed upon. Hopes were now rising for a complete agreement. The rock upon which this optimism foundered was the composition of the interim government.

On June 14 Congress definitely rejected the Mission's plan for an interim government. The Viceroy stepped into the forefront again with another effort. He proposed that the basis of representation should be for Congress Party 5, Moslem League 5, Depressed Classes (Congress wing) 1, Sikh 1, Parsee 1, Christian 1. But agreement was not to be had that way either. Gandhi insisted, rightly, that Congress was a nationalist and not a communal organization and therefore was entitled to nominate a nationalist non-League Moslem to the Viceroy's proposed cabinet. That "put the cat amongst the pigeons." Jinnah would not accept for the Cabinet a Moslem who was not a member of the Moslem League.

On June 26, the Cabinet Mission and the Viceroy issued a

statement. It welcomed the acceptance of the long-term plan, and went on:

The Cabinet mission and the Viceroy regret that it has not so far proved possible to form an interim coalition Government, but they are determined that the effort should be renewed in accordance with the terms of their statement of June 16th. . . .

As the Government of India must be carried on until a new interim Government can be formed, it is the intention of the Viceroy to set up a temporary caretaker Government of officials.

It is not possible for the Cabinet Mission to remain longer in India, as they must return to report to the British Cabinet and Parliament and also resume their work, from which they have been absent for over three months. They therefore propose to leave India on Saturday next, June 29th. In leaving India, the members of the Cabinet Mission express their cordial thanks for all the courtesy and consideration which they have received as guests in the country, and they most sincerely trust that the steps which have been initiated will lead to the speedy realisation of the hopes and wishes of the Indian people.

So near and yet so far. The British were finding it very difficult to get out of the tangle of communalism which they had fostered so long. Their concessions to the Moslem League had gone too far and thrust them into challenging the Congress Party's integrity as a national organization, by playing straight into the hands of Jinnah on the communal issue, although they knew that the Congress Party represented twice as much population as the Moslem League.

Cripps and his colleagues left India. By July 17, the final returns of the Indian elections to the Constituent Assembly were to hand, showing that the Congress Party had won 201 seats of 210 seats allotted to the general constituencies. The Assembly would be composed of 385 members. Of the 78 allotted to the Moslems the Moslem League won 73.

The quarrel between the Congress and the Moslem League became fiercer and communal disturbances began on a large scale. On August 12, the Viceroy turned to the Congress Party and invited Nehru to form an interim government. He invited Jinnah to nominate 5 names for a government of 15. Jinnah refused. He declared that the Viceroy had betrayed the Moslems and had struck a severe blow at Moslem India. Vio-

lence spread. Nehru continued to hope for the co-operation of
the Moslem League. On October 15, the League at last agreed
to enter the interim government. Still the violence grew. It
was reported on October 18 that nearly six thousand people
had been killed and fifteen thousand injured, mainly in
Bengal. Although the Moslems had entered the Government,
there was no real co-operation. In December the Indian leaders,
Nehru and Jinnah, went to London for discussions with the
British Government, but no satisfactory agreement was arrived
at. On February 20, 1947, the British Prime Minister, Attlee,
announced in Parliament that the Government intended to
transfer power into "responsible Indian hands" not later than
June, 1948. This represented an abandonment of the position
taken up by the Cabinet Mission document, which laid it down
that the British Government would hand over power to the
Indians only when the Constituent Assembly had produced an
agreed-upon constitution. Now Britain fixed a date to hand
power to an interim government and leave the Indians with
complete responsibility for settling their differences by agreement or by fighting them out to a finish. This was precisely
what Gandhi had asked for always.

It was hoped that fixing the date for the surrender of power
would drive the Congress Party and the Moslem League to
find a basis of agreement. At the same time, Attlee announced
that Lord Wavell, who had been appointed Viceroy in 1943,
would be recalled: "The King has approved his successor, . . .
Viscount Mountbatten, who will be entrusted with the task
of transferring to Indian hands the responsibility for the
Government of British India in a manner that will best ensure
the future happiness and prosperity of India."

Nehru described the British decision as a "wise and courageous one." Jinnah said, "The Moslem League will not yield an
inch in its demand for Pakistan." Disturbances continued.

The new Viceroy began the familiar job of interviewing the
leaders. At first Mountbatten urged the political leaders to
accept unreservedly the Cabinet Mission's plan of May, 1946.
But he made no progress along that line and later suggested,
and the British Government approved, that Britain should
transfer power at once to one or two governments, each having
Dominion status as soon as the necessary arrangements could

be made. This was, of course, a clear concession to the Moslems. So there were to be two Dominions, one in the hands of the Indian Congress, the other in the hands of the Moslem League, with the future of the hundreds of feudal princely states unsettled.

Nehru said, "It is with no joy in my heart that I commend these proposals though I have no doubt in my mind that this is the right course." His heart was sad because India was not being united as a nation in the moment that it became independent. Power was being handed over to two governments organized as communal powers, with a conglomeration of feudal states yet to be sorted out.

On August 15, 1947, the flag of independent India was raised at Delhi. Nehru, friend of Stafford Cripps, said at midnight that India would "wake up to life and freedom. We end today a period of ill fortune, and India discovers herself again."

So one more of the great aims which Stafford Cripps had set before him, and to which he had given unremitting energy, at last was realized. His was not the hand that finally sealed the pact, nor was it completed as he would have had it. But no man could deny that of all Englishmen none had rendered a greater service in the liberation than he. A new chapter of Indian history had begun to be written by the Indians alone.

Meanwhile, Cripps resumed his labors in the postwar economic battle of Britain. With that easy facility which had marked his career as lawyer and politician, he returned to his job at the Board of Trade and plunged into it as if there had been no gap of months of concentration on an entirely different task some six thousand miles away. He again stepped into the spotlight of publicity with a speech at Bristol, on October 27, 1946. In this he upset trade-union leaders of the Left and the Right and many others besides them. His speech was on industry, and he happened to say:

From my experience there is not as yet a very large number of workers in Britain capable of taking over large enterprises.

I have on many occasions tried to get representatives of the workers on all sorts of bodies and working parties. It has always been extremely difficult to get enough people qualified to do that sort of job.

Until there has been more experience by the workers of the managerial side of industry, I think it would be impossible to have worker-controlled industry in Britain, even if it were on the whole, desirable.

Every newspaper unsympathetic to Cripps and the Labour Government made the fullest use of this statement. One editorial read:

The astonishing declaration that few workers are capable of managing large scale enterprises was made last night by Sir Stafford Cripps, President of the Board of Trade, in Bristol.

Sir Stafford not only declared that "worker controlled industry" was almost impossible, but used a phrase clearly implying his doubt as to the desirability of the workers controlling industry at all.

It did not end there. A meeting of the Bristol Trades Council refused to accept a letter from him in which he dealt in further detail with the question of workers' control of industry. His letter read:

The Labour Party's policy is not syndicalist. It does not believe in "workers' control" as such. It is a fact that there are not enough trade unionists with experience of managerial functions, and I have pressed the trade unions to increase the educational facilities for their members on these problems.

I know from my experience in getting—out of a whole industry—enough trade unionists to man a single Working Party, how difficult it is and how difficult the T. U. C. and the Unions find it to get enough suitable men. Those who are qualified are already, most of them, hopelessly overworked on their own trade-union affairs and just cannot be spared.

Surely every member of the A. E. U. [Amalgamated Engineering Union] has to serve a proper apprenticeship before he is appointed to do his job; so must a person who is to take over management functions be properly qualified.

The Trades Council was annoyed. A member named Miss Jessie Stevens stole the headlines. She said,

The majority of us in this room have had experience of administrative work and in a managerial capacity. It is an absolute insult to the workers of the country that a philosophic and theoretical Socialist such as Stafford Cripps should make such a statement. It implies that the workers are so silly and incompetent that they would fall down on the job.

It was quite clear that class emotions had been stirred. Nevertheless into the lions' den went Sir Stafford to fight the matter out. The Bristol Trades Council organized a conference of five hundred delegates from trade unions, divisional Labour parties and Co-operative guilds to discuss the matter with him. On this occasion he said,

It so happens by the unhappy accident of history, that there are very few trade unionists who have hitherto had the opportunity to get the training necessary for management. It is quite wrong to imagine that, because a person is an intelligent worker or foreman, therefore he can, without training, become a good manager. There are in fact, at present, very few workers who could take on the job of management, not because they are workers, but because they have not had the opportunity of training for the job.

What I have stressed is the need to associate the workers with managerial functions to give them the chance which they have hitherto been denied. That is why I have advocated the extension of joint production councils and works councils, in which managerial functions can be fully discussed. That is why, too, I insisted upon the association of workers in working parties and in every other activity for which my department is responsible.

In this period Britain was hit by the hardest winter she had experienced for nearly a century. Deep snow, hard frosts, and terrific blizzards held sway for months and strained the economic apparatus of the country severely. Then followed heavy rains and great floods, bursting river banks. The opposition to the Labour Government gleefully rubbed their hands and laid the slowing-up of production and the dislocations at the door of the ministers and their "pet schemes." Newspapers capitalized the crisis, talked of the Government "falling" and of the need for a Coalition. The Government did not fall, but important changes did take place.

Herbert Morrison, the minister in charge of the economy in general, fell ill shortly before the crisis and Stafford Cripps was called upon to deputize for him in matters of economy and planning. This gave Cripps greater scope. He was now acting far beyond the range of the Board of Trade. He still needed to get his grip upon the financial apparatus to function freely as the complete economic co-ordinator of the Government and "planner in chief." Theoretically the economic policy and the financial policy should be geared to each other and under a single control. Actually, however, the Chancellor of the Exchequer had control of financial policy. Until the institutions of economic planning and co-operation merged with the apparatus of the treasury, the two departments could easily get at cross purposes. In practice it meant that Stafford Cripps as President of the Board of Trade and Deputy Minister of Economy was not the highest authority with regard to economic policy. Extraordinary circumstances were soon to make it possible to solve that problem, which was becoming increasingly apparent day by day.

Cripps was convinced that he had got the measure of Britain's economic problem. His great anxiety was not the mechanism or the human material of British industry, difficult as it might prove to reorganize and reinspire it. His greatest anxiety was the international economic situation, over which he could exercise no control and from which he could not insulate Great Britain. The crux of the immediate situation can be stated very simply. Lend-lease, upon which Britain had so much depended during the war, ended in August, 1945. At that time, Britain was getting 25 per cent of her imports from America and 20 per cent from Canada. But she was selling less than 5 per cent of her exports to America and less even than that to Canada. How then to pay for her imports? The total gold and dollar resources would not go very far. The only possibility was to ask for loans from these two countries. Agreements were made in the summer of 1946, with Canada for a loan of £273,000,000 and with the United States for a loan of £938,000,000. It was hoped that these would almost cover the estimated gap between the cost of imports and the proceeds of exports in the period of 1946-1948. But the plain fact is that instead of bridging the uncomfortable gap, the loans were spent at such a rate that very little was left at the end of a year.

Things were moving to a climax. Dalton had to announce the suspension of convertibility of the pound and Morrison, who was now in charge of the economic program again, with Cripps back at the Board of Trade, had to face the House of

Commons with a program of cuts in imports and a hint of a new loan. Cripps summed up the position:

> The time for the realisation of our aims and hopes has been set back by the inescapable economic facts of world development. . . . The battle of the balance of payments is as tough a proposition as this country has ever had to face. . . . Our failure or success will depend in the last resort on the spirit of the people. The quality of the effort that is needed is not such that it can be evoked by material considerations or by the intensification of self-interest or competitive self-seeking. There must be no sense of injustice and no favouritism or privilege except as the reward for an honest contribution to the needs of the people.

In September, what became known as the Cripps Plan was launched. He explained that its object was to raise exports to 140 per cent of the 1938 level as soon as possible, and certainly by not later than July, 1948. This involved raising monthly exports by £31,000,000, although this amount would only pay for imports at the current level. Any improvements in the standard of living could only come from a further increase in exports to the second target of 160 per cent set for the end of 1948. Other measures were a new coal target, a stepping-up of steel production, increase in the amount of home-produced food, tighter control over both public and private capital investment, and the introduction of a new "Control of Engagement Order" to assist in guiding those unemployed or becoming so into essential industries and services.

For some time Cripps held public attention with a campaign for his plan. There was no doubt that he was more and more looked upon as the key man of the Government with regard to economic matters—the master planner. On October 8, 1947, he was promoted to be Minister for Economic Affairs. This meant that he would be responsible in the whole field of production and exports and would be responsible jointly with the Chancellor of the Exchequer for all matters affecting the balance of payments.

Hardly had he assumed the new responsibilities than circumstances conspired to complete the centralizing of economic and financial control. Dalton, on his way to deliver his speech in the House of Commons, was indiscreet and disclosed the contents of his budget speech to an eager newspaper reporter. The next day he resigned, and Stafford Cripps became Chancellor of the Exchequer a few days later. The *Economist* of November 22 remarked:

Sir Stafford Cripps was the only possible choice to fill the vacancy. . . . One great gain from his appointment to the Exchequer, is that it has put to an end the pretence that financial policy can contract out of general economic policy. The central position of the Treasury in the British machinery of Government has long been a stumbling block to those who want to achieve a properly coherent policy in economic affairs. The arrival at the Treasury of Sir Stafford Cripps with his economic, non-financial outlook, is from one point of view, a satisfactory solution of the dilemma.

Now he had reached the highest point of his career. No man in the country, other than the Prime Minister, had so much power concentrated in his hands. From the point of view of orthodox economics and politics he was the master of his subject. His opponents in the House of Commons could only snipe at incidentals and could do nothing but praise the main lines of his recovery plan. His mastery of administrative machinery, and the apparently inexhaustible energy with which he translated his program into action, commanded the admiration even of his most severe critics. Newspapers freely called him the next Prime Minister.

His first review of the whole British economic situation from the vantage ground of the Chancellor of the Exchequer was made during a debate initiated by the opposition. There was a full house, as there usually was on such great occasions. All members were in their places. The public gallery was filled and in the Ladies' Gallery sat Isobel Cripps, as so often she had when Stafford was called upon to play an important role in any debate. Sharing as she does in his successes as well as his difficulties, she felt happy for him on this day. Eden was leading for the Conservatives. Everyone knew he was asking the most of a weak case and would really be a "chopping block" for Sir Stafford. Eden moved that:

This House views with grave concern the present state of the Nation and would welcome any well-chosen measures designed to check inflation and to restore the economic prosperity of the country.

Speaking immediately after Eden, Cripps agreed that it was necessary to arrest inflationary tendencies. How? He then told what the Government had done. He explained that high taxation on companies and high surtax on individuals diminished the amount that could be spent by the higher income groups. "Pay as you earn" income tax diminished the spending power of the lower income groups. Indirect taxation, principally on tobacco, beer, wine and spirits, together with purchase tax, bore upon all incomes, but proportionately more onerously —as indirect taxation was bound to do—upon the lower income groups. The rationing of food and clothing removed the danger that those with higher incomes would buy more than their share. Allocation of materials prevented, to a large extent, the use of those materials for less necessary production. In both cases the regulations worked properly only when the inflationary condition of the market was not so strong as to counter the controls. The control of prices prevented exorbitant profits on controlled articles, though the difficulties and imperfections of any price-control system rendered it difficult to apply. There was added difficulty owing to the inequality of efficiency between the differing producing units. Subsidies were granted to reduce the price of the most essential foodstuffs so as to hold the level of wages and salaries more stable.

On the financial side, the large budget surplus which was accumulating was a factor which tended to remove inflationary pressure. The autumn budget had increased the surplus. What part of the field, therefore, Cripps went on to ask, remained uncovered in order to prevent the present inflationary tendency from developing further?

The way we should all wish to overcome the danger [he continued] was by making more goods available on the home market. That was what we were aiming at. That depended however upon what we could do to increase our production over and above what we must send abroad to pay for our primary necessities of imported foodstuffs and raw materials. We had not yet achieved our export task, so that there could be no question, either of devoting more of our production to the home market, or of expanding our imports in any degree. We had not yet nearly enough exports to pay for our present level of imports. If we were to achieve, even with Marshall aid, a balance of payments, we must greatly increase exports, and if we could not increase them sufficiently we should be driven to reduce our imports still further.

He went on to stress the importance of regulating personal income, but that could be done only by free negotiation between the parties concerned. This led him to the question of the relation of wages to prices, and to the importance of stablizing wages and prices by voluntary co-operation between wage earners and wage payers. He wanted the employers to limit profits, the workers to limit wages, the sellers of goods to limit prices. This was hedg'ed around by a number of qualifications. There might be some adjustments within a general stable level of wages. There might be reasons for granting particular increases, but not general increases. The essence of his case was this:

> While we are in this struggle none of us can afford to improve our standard of living, because we cannot make more goods available for the home market, for some time to come. Unless we now exercise democratic restraint, the sheer facts of the situation will demand compulsions which certainly this Government is anxious to avoid.

So he continued his battle of the "gap"—centralizing, controlling, streamlining, moralizing, restricting, urging. Budget Day came, and standing where many famous chancellors had stood, he presented his first budget review of the economic and financial situation of the country, the progress it had made toward recovery, and the all-important test question of bridging the gap. Some incidental relief was given to the taxpayers, but the main line of his policy remained. He sounded the same somber, austere message and warning of the wrath to come unless the target of exports was achieved and Britain's competitive position in the world market was re-established. Considerable headway was being made, but it was too soon to say that Britain was within measurable distance of turning the corner.

His campaign for freezing wages met with some resistance in the trade unions, and that led one day to his greatest triumph within the Labour movement. He was invited to address the Trades Union Congress at Margate in September, 1948. He had frequently addressed Labour Party Conferences, and many times had been opposed by the trade union delegates within it. This was the first time he had met the trade unionists in their own Congress. With his usual facility he did what his colleagues rarely thought of doing. He prepared an analysis of the data upon which he would justify his case and had it sent to the council of the trade union congress, which printed and distributed copies to the delegates in ample time for them to study before he spoke. He not only succeeded in getting endorsement of his policy, but scored a personal triumph by his address and the way he dealt with the discussion.

At the end of September, prior to a journey to America, he told the British people with cautious optimism that, with continued aid from America in the form of loans and grants, Britain would close the gap between imports and exports by 1952. The gap was now closing. The rate of production was increasing. It could be even faster if industry accepted planning, his current major objective. Exports were growing. But world prices were rising and stepping up the cost of imports. Great difficulties still had to be overcome.

When he arrived in the United States he met American journalists, as on the occasion of 1940 when he returned from Moscow, China, and India. Then he was the man without a party returning from a personal mission. This time he appeared as the man in charge of British economy, and he amazed the questioners not only by his understanding of specifically British economic problems but his intellectual grasp of the world economic picture. At a press conference in New York City he was subjected to a long running fire of questions of every conceivable kind relating to economic affairs. His answers came back with rapidity, packed with facts and logic. Cosmopolitan journalists, accustomed by experience to distinguish between a "briefed" official and an official who writes his own brief, applauded Cripps for his range and mastery of so complicated a subject.

While in Washington, on September 30, 1948, he made another important speech to the members of the Federal Bar Association. This speech was important because it revealed, at the apex of his career, his whole outlook on human affairs.

He surveyed the drama of society's evolution to democratic forms of government and summed up his own thinking in relation thereto. This speech reveals more than any other where he has arrived since his first identification with Socialism and association with Communism. He said:

We are living to-day in a world of dynamic growth of ideas, of inventions, and of material development of every kind than civilisation has ever before witnessed. . . .

There can be no doubt that the whole relationship of man, as a social and political being, to material power has changed fundamentally in the last century of world history. . . . Time and space are being obliterated and the good or harm that one man can do by his influence and control over others has become terrifyingly great. The accident of bad judgment or lack of control arising from physical or mental sickness may condemn hundreds of thousands or millions of people to intense suffering. We have witnessed this very phenomenon in recent years. . . .

Democracy as we understand it denotes control by a freely ascertained majority of the people over what would otherwise become the irresponsible acts of their leaders. And as a principle of Government and of political organisation it is a thousand times more important today than ever it was before, because the power of those leaders in terms of life and death for millions of people has been so vastly magnified.

. . . But here we again come up against the complexities and difficulties of modern civilisation. Any community today must concern itself with a wide range of subjects, economic, technical, scientific, medical and so on which are really far too complex for even the most highly intelligent democratic electorate fully to comprehend.

The dynamic power of democracy is not in numbers or material strength or education or intelligence—though all these things have their place and some of them, like education, an important place— its power to operate is in the spirit of man and the free spirit of the people.

Our inspiration stems from the common tradition and a common reading of history. . . .

Of one thing we can be quite sure: that methods of Government cannot become the subject matter of international commerce. Ideas can and must flow freely round the world, but systems of Government must develop in their own native soil and according to the native genius of the people.

Our only safety for the future lies in the positive and conscious exertion of spiritual control over the material actions in all world communities. Freedom without spirit is a contradiction in terms and spirit without religion loses its substance and strength.

The world crisis is thus in my view basically a moral rather than a political or economic crisis. It cannot be solved by a formula however recondite or ingenious because it is in the ultimate result the willingness of the peoples through their governments to follow the concepts of their spiritual common sense that will determine the success or failure of our efforts. We must still do our best to devise plans and schemes which make a solution possible, but once we have decided what it is we ought to do we must put behind it all our spiritual and moral power.

Here is no iconoclast of revolution, but the superb Christian planner, steeped in his country's traditions and the traditions of his kind, wrestling with the crisis of modern society, seeking an organic development of the institutions in which he has lived and risen to power.

Cripps is as convinced today as he was in 1931 that the "gradualism" of the MacDonalds is as futile as it was when he penned his first letter on "socialist policy" after the collapse of the second Labour Government. But he has left behind the crudities of that eventful year when one and all within the Labour movement talked of the "breakdown of capitalism" and the need for a fundamental socialist change in the economic foundations of society. The crisis appears to him no longer exclusively as an economic problem but a moral problem, the control of material things by the spirit, through nationalist governments elected by the operation of political democracy.

Political democracy has become to him synonymous with the Christian way of life. It is to him what pacifism was to Gandhi, a means which is an end in itself. The nationalization of this industry or that he regards as a matter of expediency to be applied according to what is deemed to be in the national interest in the ordered development of the national life. He regards the planned development of the national economy as a whole, whether it be privately owned or state owned, as more important than the question of ownership. The interests of the nation are paramount in deciding what should be state owned and what privately owned, and political democracy is the Christian means whereby the spirit controls the material things of life.

A few weeks after his return to England, in a great clash with Winston Churchill on the question of the nationalization of the British steel industry, he made these points clear in practice for all the world to see. Standing in the House of Commons face to face with Churchill he advanced three reasons in favor of the nationalization of the steel industry:

Let me sum them up shortly. If as is admitted to be necessary there must be a large element of monopoly control in this vital element of our industrial economy, that control must be public and not private. No live and effective democracy can, in the circumstances, decide otherwise. Secondly, so far as foreseeing the future is concerned, we cannot take the risk of our steel supplies being inadequate because the industry may not consider it economic from its point of view to risk enlarging its capacity. The State must therefore accept the responsibility which can only be exercised in conjunction with ownership. Thirdly, from a strategic point of view, we cannot risk our defence position.

Churchill intervened:

The right honourable and learned gentleman is assuming that the House believes that the Government have adopted proper measures to safeguard our defence position, and he has no right to bring arrangements about the steel industry into the forefront of his argument when so much else has been neglected.

Cripps was not to be gainsaid. Sweeping Churchill's interruption aside he went on:

With the growing appreciation of the inter-relation of the great industries and services in the economic life of the country and of the need for foresight and planning, we have abandoned the conception that unlimited internal competition is always for the best. . . . Is it right or wrong if the nation believes that for economic reasons the steel industry should be nationalised, that that nationalisation should take place; or is there some peculiar right in the owner of this class of property to have his property preserved?

Churchill answered: "Yes." The argument became more exciting as Sir Stafford continued:

. . . and with it the power of control over the industrial life of the whole country?

I answer those questions without any hesitation by saying that, this challenge having been put forward by private interest, it is essential that democracy should assert its rights, as otherwise it must acknowledge for all time that it cannot touch those citadels of power, and that it is not the electorate but the owners of industrial property who shall determine the economic policies of the country. And the ugly alternative would then be that any such change which is to occur must be brought about by other and more violent means. . . .

A member interjected "By gunpowder?"

Cripps answered, "It is because we are preventing that, that Socialist Democracy is the true barrier against Communism."

Interruptions checked him. Churchill rose. Members called "Order. Order!"

Still Churchill sought to intervene and there were more cries of "Order." Cripps tried to continue and began: "I should be interested to hear . . ."

Churchill indignantly interrupted, anxious to claim that he had been a better fighter against Communism than any of them. But he was cried down with shouts of "Order" "Order." Cripps got in again: "I shall be interested to hear of any case in which Conservatism has proved a barrier to Communism in the same way that Socialist Democracy has been."

The clock struck ten. The debate was ended. But it would be renewed again and again. For here Stafford Cripps had revealed in all its completeness the consummation of the change in his outlook since he became a British statesman with power and the responsibility which goes with power.

The moment of the great change stands out clearly like a signpost in his career. When Chamberlain signed the Munich Pact he stirred Cripps' deep nationalism as nothing else had done. Cripps felt that England had been betrayed and that Chamberlain was guilty not merely of shortsightedness but of the most cynical immorality in the conduct of international affairs, and, instead of ensuring peace, had made war inevitable. From that moment Cripps began to shake himself free from the class-struggle politics which he had pursued since 1931. At that time he talked much of the "collapse of capitalism" and was so disgusted with the manner in which the capitalists handled the situation that he turned to the "working class" and bid them fight for power to reorganize the broken-down economy and build a new social life for the country. Although this aim was revolutionary he rejected outright any other than constitutional methods of action. He had grown up as a monarchist, a parliamentarian, a legalist, and was opposed to social violence. Empirical and pragmatic by nature and training, and above all a Christian moralist, he expounded his drastic program of socialization with vigor and conviction. But he was ever a consistent nationalist even in the exposition of his program of class struggle.

It was Munich that had changed everything for him. From the signing of that pact until the end of the war Britain's fate in world affairs concerned him more than the relation of the classes in Britain. He had desired the unity of the British people in a popular front to save Britain from Fascism and war. His Popular Front was not conceived as an alliance of classes, as propounded by the Communists, but as an alliance of people of all classes. His expulsion from the Labour Party deprived him of the means of further mass campaigns to this end. The war transformed the circumstances and produced the "government of concentration" or "the national Popular Front Government" at war with Fascism. He no longer relied wholly on the working class but on the nation. His national patriotism came into its own as the dominating influence. His experiences as ambassador, unofficial and official, strengthened his nationalism. His experience as an administrator controlling "private capitalism" gave him great confidence in the possibility of planning private enterprise. By the *practice* of statesmanship and acceptance of responsibilities he had become the planner of the new order of social democracy.

So the impatient Christian, who in 1931 morally condemned capitalism and challenged its supporters to make way for the social and economic regeneration of Britain by the working class, had become the mature Christian British statesman who believed that capitalism had not to be immediately replaced by socialism and that society could be more efficiently subordinated to the interests of the nation if human relations were made better. "The world crisis," he said in September, 1948, to the Federal Bar Association of America, "is thus basically a moral rather than a political or economic crisis." Hence, the problems of the world can be dealt with by Christianity transforming people in their relations one with another, irrespective of class and contradictory interests. He does not regard "private property in the means of production" as immoral, but does feel that, at times, it is inexpedient in the national interests that some parts of the national economy should remain privately owned. His differences with the Tories, as in the clash with Churchill on the nationalization of the steel industry, arose not from a difference of moral attitude toward nationalization as a principle, but out of the question of the expediency of its application at the present time. His challenge to the Tories today is not the challenge he made in 1931 of "Socialism versus Capitalism." His challenge is that it is necessary to control capitalism in the nation's interest; also that it is the most patriotic way of blocking the road to Communism and capitalist reaction.

Viewing his career in perspective, the crisis years of 1931 to 1939 constitute a violent deviation from gradualism, and it was the Second World War which drew him back to his traditional course. Intellectually, he had been capable of becoming a great revolutionary leader. But he is more than an intellectually brilliant man. He is today's supreme English expression of the Parmoor-Potter tradition of the practicing Christian, the patriotic English reformers to whom Communism was anathema, and ordered, planned progress, "without violent interruptions of the organic process," was the obvious mode of development for the Christian way of life. This tradition today governs all aspects of his policy and its tenets are established in his mind as a logical all-embracing philosophy.

Just as he emerged from class-struggle politics in home affairs onto the high ground of controlled national economy, so, too, was his outlook on international affairs transformed. His friendship for the Russian Revolution, upon which he won great fame, grew out of his class-struggle politics and lingered the longest because of his concentration on domestic industrial and economic affairs. But as the reorientation of the nations followed the defeat of the Fascist powers and took shape with nations aligning themselves according to the loyalties of their own political and economic system, the attitude of Stafford Cripps and other leaders of the Labour Party to Russia and its revolution changed. His role as the "master planner of Britain's mixed economy" now had its international complement. He figured, increasingly, as Britain's spokesman in the great attempt to plan the recovery of the Western nations of Europe and the Commonwealth into free, multilateral trading communities. In all his striving for Britain's recovery he had had to gear his plans to the larger Marshall Plan which aimed by means of capital assistance from America to enable each of its recipients to become independent competitive nations, without further assistance from the U.S.A. after 1952.

In the first year of the plan's operation Britain, under Sir Stafford's direction, made great headway. So much was this the case that he cautiously held before the people the prospect that by the appointed year Britain would be able to close the gap between imports from the U.S.A. and exports to the U.S.A. and thereby overcome Britain's dollar shortage. But 1949 saw "unforeseen" trends developing, crisis conditions which thrust Sir Stafford into the foreground of international economic and financial affairs. The gap had begun to widen again. Gold drained away from Britain's reserves at an alarming rate. A recession of trade had started in the U.S.A. World prices were falling. The sellers' market was replaced by the buyers' market. Britain's prices remained high and her sales to America contracted. The U.S.A., with lowered economic activity, bought less from the sterling area. The situation was exacerbated by the operation of the Intra-European Payments Agreement of the Marshall Plan. This had led to Belgium and Switzerland drawing heavily on Britain's gold. By June, 1949, the drawings of gold from Britain had reached disturbing proportions; her gold and dollar reserves had shrunk to nearly four hundred million pounds.

There were two aspects to the crisis. The main one was the gap in trade between Britain and the Western European countries and the U.S.A. The other was not so fundamental and was susceptible to immediate solution. That was the question of Intra-European payments. The first year's agreement ended on June 30, 1949. Could Sir Stafford persuade his colleagues on the European Recovery Committee to alter the payment arrangements? The Conference met early in July. From the beginning he literally dominated the scene. He succeeded in persuading the Committee to agree to changes in the arrangements covered by the Intra-European Payments Agreement for the second year of Marshall aid. These changes would stop the excessive flow of gold from European countries. That was announced as a "Cripps victory" and again, at home and abroad, he stood high in the esteem of men. But the major problem of the "dollar gap" remained, against which he had pitted his whole recovery plan, to be achieved without devaluing the pound as a means of combatting the falling prices in America. Standing before the House of Commons on July 7, 1949, he boldly justified his stand against the devaluation of the pound and made it clear that he would continue to stand by this and by his planned recovery program.

Thus he proclaimed to all the world that what he believes to ✓ be the Christian "middle of the road" way of life, the answer to Britain's and the world's economic problems, is Democratic Socialism, as against political democracy alone in the U.S.A., dominated by monopoly capitalism or the economic power of the few, and on the other side as against the dictatorship of the proletariat in the Soviet Union, dominated by the Communist Party.

Epilogue

AS I BREAK off this story of Sir Stafford Cripps, he has passed his sixtieth birthday. He is on the heights of power. Men speak of him as the Economic Dictator of Britain, and say that he has still other heights to climb and that he will surmount them. Becoming director of the British economy in the midst of extraordinary crisis conditions at home and abroad, he has so grappled with the problem which this high position has imposed upon him that even political opponents pay tribute to his masterly grasp of the tasks he has set himself. Already he is renowned as the man who put his country on the high road to postwar recovery. At no time, with the possible exception of the days immediately following his famous broadcast on returning from the Soviet Union, has he been held in higher esteem by the people of Britain.

And how different are the circumstances. Then, he was a leader without a party, dependent for the fulfillment of his role upon the support of the great parties which were functioning in a coalition he had striven to bring about. Now he has become a foremost leader of the Labour Party, which in 1939 had thrown him out, a veritable generalissimo of the army of Labour, holding the key position governing British economy and recognized as but one step removed from the premiership. These are not the only striking differences between the days before the war and after. Then he was in constant conflict with his fellow leaders of the Labour Party. Today he proceeds in happy harmony with colleagues he repeatedly combatted when the party was fighting for power. Their differences have been resolved in a common purpose and common responsibility. How far this is due to changes in the political outlook of Stafford Cripps or to changes in circumstances, the political theorist must seek out. But one thing is certain among all the changes. The application of the Christian ethic in his relationship with his fellow men, and the task of changing the world that all men could better live the Christian life, has been and continues to be the leitmotiv.

Indeed, it may justly be said that Stafford Cripps is a twentieth-century fulfillment of the Cripps-Potter family traditions. Through him speak Lord Parmoor, the Reverend Henry Cripps, John H. Cripps, Theresa Potter, Richard Potter, all of whom form part of that great humanistic trend of English social and political life so well exemplified by Shaftsbury, Kingsley, Toynbee, Farrar, and Archbishop Temple. His emergence into political life was through the church when, shocked by the First World War, he stepped into the leadership of the English section of the world alliance for promoting international friendship through the churches with its campaign for peace. The spirit of his emergence can well be expressed in his own poetic words:

THERE WAS A BABY BORN IN BETHLEHEM—
I know they say
That this and that's in doubt, and for the rest
that learned men—who surely should know best
Explain how Myths crept in, and followers' tales
Confused the truth.

I KNOW; but anyway
there *was* a baby born in BETHLEHEM,
Who lived and grew, and loved, and healed and taught,
And died:—but not to me—
When Christmas comes, I see HIM still arise,
The gentle, the compassionate, the wise,
Wiping earth's tears away, stilling the strife
Calling—my path is PEACE, my way is LIFE.

His decision to join the Labour Party and the acceptance of its program of action and its socialist aims was not an abandonment of the church in favor of this mode of application of the Christian ethic to social life. It was only a recognition of the fact that the church could not function as a political party. Instead of leaving the church, he devoted much time and energy to it with a view to rousing the Christian conscience to a realization of its social function. So much has he contributed

in this direction that he is recognized as the leading lay churchman of his day. The Reverend Mervyn Stockwood says:

I would hazard a prophecy—Sir Stafford is now regarded first and
foremost, as the politician who may save the country. In a century
hence he may be regarded first and foremost as the Churchman who,
following in the footsteps of William Temple, made Christianity a
vital and practical force in the life of the nation.

In this, as in every other activity, he has run true to form.
From boyhood to manhood, he must ride the fastest, work the
hardest, top the class, captain the team, capture the prizes. He
concentrated on the science of chemistry and eclipsed his con-
temporaries, becoming the youngest man of his generation to
stand before the Royal Society and deliver his findings in
original research to the leading scientists of his day. From the
youngest lawyer to become a K.C. he forged ahead until his
services were in greater demand than those of any other lawyer
and he was the highest paid lawyer in the kingdom. From the
law he advanced with speed into the foremost positions of administration and statesmanship. No one questions his status as
a leader of the British Cabinet or his brilliance as economic
director and chancellor.

But to Cripps himself, science, law, administration, and
statesmanship were not ends in themselves, nor were they
dominant in his life. They were incidental to the larger purpose, the tools, as it were, of his equipment for the fulfillment
of his mission of applied Christianity which has grown with the
passing of years. He is not a political theorist and has never laid
claim to be such. He is the missioner of the deed, the planner
of action. "By their deeds ye shall know them" is his challenging theme in Church and politics, and he deems in the words
of his poem that:

> Now is the urgent hour
> The world rocks in uncertain fate
> In Christ we have the power
> to lift the burden of our fear.
>
> Grant us the courage Lord
> To face the vision of Thy Cross
> And in the flame of Thy accord
> to win the prize of love.

Deep in our hearts there lies
the knowledge of Thy love and strength.
Give us the will that ties
our daily action to our faith.

Jesus Christ provides him with the moral concepts and conscience which he brings to bear upon every problem. His range
of subjects is extraordinary and his mind works with exceptional speed. His method of analysis is the characteristically
empirical one of the lawyer and the experimental scientist.
Analysis without action, however, is incomprehensible to him,
for he is pragmatic by nature and his mind demands that he
proceed quickly from words to deeds and results.

Of all his colleagues in leadership in church and state there
is none more self-controlled and composed. It is this which
gives to so many people the impression that he is cold, de-
tached, and unfeeling, lacking in emotion, a man of light
without heat, of austerity with no prospect of abundance. It is a
wrong impression, of course. As a British trade union leader has
said, "Cripps talks cold but acts warm." He is a man of deep
convictions, passionate feeling, and enduring attachments. In
no aspect of his life is this better exemplified than in his home.

Stafford Cripps married Isobel Swithinbank when he was
twenty-two years old and she was twenty. They have been married nearly forty years. To this day, and all through the years,
they have exchanged letters if separated from each other for
a single day. They have three daughters and a son, now grown
to womanhood and manhood, and six grandchildren. The
home and family have been the center from which Stafford
has drawn his strength and determined his course. Isobel has
been more than a wife and a mother to his children. She has
grown with Stafford out of the same social stratum, with the
same religious upbringing and social values and culture. She
has merged completely into the Crippsian tradition and has
fostered his ambitions, cherished his ideals, and "managed"
him as maternal women know by instinct how to manage their
men folk and the people who gather round them. So his home
has been more than a place of rest and relaxation. It has been
a powerhouse of affectionate inspiration and superb companionship and fellowship in a common way of life. I do not

mean to suggest that Isobel Cripps always stayed at home while Stafford went into the larger world; that would leave a false impression. When he went to Moscow as ambassador she joined him there. When he fought an election she would be in the constituency rallying the women to vote for her husband. When he visited factories she went with him. She went to hear him speak in the House of Commons. After his trip to China she and their daughter Peggy followed in his tracks independently on an unofficial goodwill mission, as a guest of the Chinese government, to see the results of the financial aid to China that had been raised in England over her name. Wherever she went, whether with him or to him, she carried with her the atmosphere of their home, which to both was the microcosm of the world of their dreams: the cultured, happy, well-to-do Christian home of the English countryside, the sheet anchor of their social life, and the spiritual source whence they drew their inspiration to launch forth into the wider world of the affairs of men.

Beatrice and Sidney Webb, aunt and uncle of Cripps, formed of their lives a great partnership in social research. Isobel and Stafford Cripps have formed a great partnership of Christian family fellowship in the professionalism of law, science, and politics.

Today Sir Stafford Cripps, P.C., K.C., M.P., F.R.S., Chancellor of the Exchequer, and Isobel his wife, live at 11 Downing Street, next door to the Prime Minister of Britain, who resides at No. 10. There he is grappling with the problems of British economy at home and abroad. With superb energy and serenity of mind he forges ahead, with patience, persistence, politeness, self-confident, self-controlled, knowing full well that the surest guarantee for tomorrow lies in the mastery of the job he is doing today.

He is physically and spiritually young. His mind is quick. He stands and sits upright; his eyes are bright and he looks at you fair, square, and pleasantly. He stands well poised and at ease, assured and confident. He has traveled far and wide. He has established himself in the front rank of the leaders of men.

Arosa—Nottingham—London
July 21, 1949

Index